Managing and Maintaining a Windows® Server™ 2003 Environment for an MCSA Certified on Windows 2000

Kalani Kirk Hausman

Bruce Parrish

CERTIFICATION

Managing and Maintaining a Windows Server 2003 Environment for an MCSA Certified on Windows 2000 Exam Cram 2 (Exam 70-292)

Copyright © 2004 by Que Publishing

International Standard Book Number: 0-7897-3011-1

Library of Congress Catalog Card Number: 2003103924

Printed in the United States of America

First Printing: November 2003

06   05   04   4   3   2

Trademarks

All terms mentioned in this book that are known to be trademarks or service marks have been appropriately capitalized. Que Publishing cannot attest to the accuracy of this information. Use of a term in this book should not be regarded as affecting the validity of any trademark or service mark.

Warning and Disclaimer

Every effort has been made to make this book as complete and as accurate as possible, but no warranty or fitness is implied. The information provided is on an "as is" basis. The authors and the publisher shall have neither liability nor responsibility to any person or entity with respect to any loss or damages arising from the information contained in this book or from the use of the CD or programs accompanying it.

Bulk Sales

Que Publishing offers excellent discounts on this book when ordered in quantity for bulk purchases or special sales. For more information, please contact

U.S. Corporate and Government Sales
1-800-382-3419
corpsales@pearsontechgroup.com

For sales outside of the U.S., please contact

International Sales
1-317-428-3341
international@pearsontechgroup.com

Publisher
Paul Boger

Executive Editor
Jeff Riley

Development Editor
Susan Brown Zahn

Managing Editor
Charlotte Clapp

Project Editor
Elizabeth Finney

Copy Editor
Mike Henry

Indexer
Tom Dinse

Proofreader
Linda Seifert

Technical Editors
Bill Ferguson
Ken Peterson

Team Coordinator
Pamalee Nelson

Multimedia Developer
Dan Scherf

Interior Designer
Gary Adair

Cover Designer
Anne Jones

CERTIFICATION

Que Certification • 800 East 96th Street • Indianapolis, Indiana 46240

A Note from Series Editor Ed Tittel

You know better than to trust your certification preparation to just anybody. That's why you, and more than two million others, have purchased an Exam Cram book. As Series Editor for the new and improved Exam Cram 2 series, I have worked with the staff at Que Certification to ensure you won't be disappointed. That's why we've taken the world's best-selling certification product—a finalist for "Best Study Guide" in a CertCities reader poll in 2002—and made it even better.

As a "Favorite Study Guide Author" finalist in a 2002 poll of CertCities readers, I know the value of good books. You'll be impressed with Que Certification's stringent review process, which ensures the books are high-quality, relevant, and technically accurate. Rest assured that at least a dozen industry experts—including the panel of certification experts at CramSession—have reviewed this material, helping us deliver an excellent solution to your exam preparation needs.

Best Study Guides

We've also added a preview edition of PrepLogic's powerful, full-featured test engine, which is trusted by certification students throughout the world.

As a 20-year-plus veteran of the computing industry and the original creator and editor of the Exam Cram series, I've brought my IT experience to bear on these books. During my tenure at Novell from 1989 to 1994, I worked with and around its excellent education and certification department. This experience helped push my writing and teaching activities heavily in the certification direction. Since then, I've worked on more than 70 certification-related books, and I write about certification topics for numerous Web sites and for *Certification* magazine.

In 1996, while studying for various MCP exams, I became frustrated with the huge, unwieldy study guides that were the only preparation tools available. As an experienced IT professional and former instructor, I wanted "nothing but the facts" necessary to prepare for the exams. From this impetus, Exam Cram emerged in 1997. It quickly became the best-selling computer book series since "…*For Dummies*," and the best-selling certification book series ever. By maintaining an intense focus on subject matter, tracking errata and updates quickly, and following the certification market closely, Exam Cram was able to establish the dominant position in cert prep books.

You will not be disappointed in your decision to purchase this book. If you are, please contact me at etittel@jump.net. All suggestions, ideas, input, or constructive criticism are welcome!

Ed Tittel

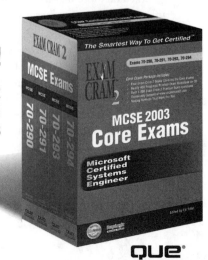

For Susan and Jonathan

About the Author

Kirk Hausman (MCSE+I, MCSD, MCDBA, MCSA, MCT, CCNA, CIW-A, A+, Network+, I-Net+, Security+) has been an IT professional for more than 25 years in the roles of consultant, trainer, programmer, security administrator, database administrator, IT manager, and network administrator. He is currently working as an Information Technology Manager and Lead Security Analyst for Texas A&M University, where he provides network architecture planning and support.

Mr. Hausman's studies include security, computer science, electronics technology, electrical engineering, mechanical engineering, and philosophy, as well as consulting in the IT field. His hobbies include designs in high-speed transportation, submersible propulsion, cosmology, interactive telepresence, technology in education, and virtual reality for use by those with disabling conditions.

One of his current projects includes the development of a shared interactive telepresence system that is designed to enable remote experience of widely varying environments by students, regardless of geographic location or disabling conditions. He is also working on implementing a zoological wireless telepresence system that is capable of allowing remote observation of animals in both natural and human-created environments, along with many other ongoing projects. Kirk can be reached at kkhausman@hotmail.com.

Bruce Parrish is an accomplished Computer Instructor and Consultant with 20 years computer experience. Bruce is MCSE certified on Windows 2000 and Windows NT 4.0. He also holds MCT, MCSA, MCP, CTT, A+, Server+ and Network+ certifications. Bruce provides networking services and support solutions for small businesses, specializing in Microsoft Small Business Server networks. Additionally, he has authored the *Server+ Instructor Training Manual*, co-authored *Designing Windows 2000 Directory Services Lab Manual*, and is a technical editor and reviewer for LANWrights, Inc. and Course Technology.

About the Technical Editors

Bill Ferguson, MCT, MCSE, MCP+I, CCSI, CCNA, A+, Network+, Server+ has been in the computer industry for over 15 years. Originally in technical sales and sales management with Sprint, Bill made his transition to Certified Technical Trainer in 1997 with ExecuTrain. Bill now runs his own company as an independent contractor in Birmingham, Alabama, teaching classes for most of the national training companies and some regional training companies. In addition, Bill writes and produces technical training videos for Virtual Training Company, Inc. and Specialized Solutions, Inc. He currently has titles including *A+ Certification, CCNA / ICND, Network+ Certification, Managing a Microsoft Windows 2000 Network Environment, Managing Microsoft Windows 2000 Security, Microsoft Windows XP Administration*, and *Server+ Certification*. Bill keeps his skills sharp by being a technical reviewer for books and sample tests for Que Certification. He is currently co-authoring the 70-297 Exam Cram 2 title for Que Publishing. Bill says, "My job is to understand the material so well that I can make it easier for my students to learn than it was for me to learn."

Ken Peterson, MCSA, MCSE + I, MCT is an independent technical consultant and technical editor. A resident of Las Vegas, NV for the past 20 years with his wife, Carol, and daughter, Emily, Ken has been an active member of the IT community since 1987, as a technical consultant for IT companies specializing in enterprise network design and support. His professional time is spent tech editing books, planning and implementing Active Directory and Exchange 2000, and teaching Microsoft Certified classes throughout North America, and his "off-time" is spent perfecting his golf game.

Acknowledgments

Kirk Hausman: As always, thanks to the editorial staff at Que for working with me to create this book. Without their careful checking of my work, you'd find this volume a whole lot less useful. Thanks to Jeff Riley, Dawn Rader, and Jawahara Saidullah for getting me involved in this project, as well as to Susan Brown Zahn, Elizabeth Finney, and Mike Henry for turning it into a book—any remaining errors are my fault, not theirs. Thanks also go to Tammy Graham, Kelly Maish, and Laura Robbins who somehow manage the translation from my rough efforts into a final product ready to print.

My family has always been a great source of energy, and this book like all other works, carries their signature as well as my own—from my parents who started me on this track long, long ago, to Susan who provided constant encouragement and support, to our 4-year-old son who provided the impetus to get me involved in writing again, and to friends close enough to be counted as family—without all of them, this work might not have come about as it did.

Bruce Parrish: I would like to thank Dawn Rader, Managing Editor of LANWrights, Inc., for her timely responses to my questions and her diligence in responding to my needs in a timely manner. I also extend my gratefulness to my loving wife, Karen, and my daughter Brooke, whose support and patience made this text a reality.

We Want to Hear from You!

As the reader of this book, *you* are our most important critic and commentator. We value your opinion and want to know what we're doing right, what we could do better, what areas you'd like to see us publish in, and any other words of wisdom you're willing to pass our way.

As an executive editor for Que Publishing, I welcome your comments. You can email or write me directly to let me know what you did or didn't like about this book—as well as what we can do to make our books better.

Please note that I cannot help you with technical problems related to the topic of this book. We do have a User Services group, however, where I will forward specific technical questions related to the book.

When you write, please be sure to include this book's title and author as well as your name, email address, and phone number. I will carefully review your comments and share them with the author and editors who worked on the book.

Email: feedback@quepublishing.com

Mail: Jeff Riley
          Executive Editor
          Que Publishing
          800 East 96th Street
          Indianapolis, IN 46240 USA

For more information about this book or another Que Certification title, visit our Web site at www.examcram2.com. Type the ISBN (excluding hyphens) or the title of a book in the Search field to find the page you're looking for.

Contents at a Glance

Table of Contents

. . . .

Introduction

Welcome to the *70-292 Exam Cram 2!* This book covers the Managing and Maintaining a Microsoft Windows Server 2003 Environment for an MCSA Certified on Windows 2000 exam. Whether this is your first or your tenth *Exam Cram 2* series book, you'll find information here that will help ensure your success as you pursue knowledge, experience, and certification.

This introduction explains Microsoft's certification programs in general and talks about how the *Exam Cram 2* series can help you prepare for Microsoft's Certified Systems Administrator (MCSA) and Certified Systems Engineer (MCSE) exams. Chapter 1 discusses the basics of Microsoft certification exams, including a description of the testing environment, and a discussion of test-taking strategies. Chapters 2 through 7 are designed to remind you of everything you'll need to know to take and pass the 70-292 Microsoft MCSA/MCSE certification exam. The two sample tests at the end of the book should give you a reasonably accurate assessment of your knowledge— and, yes, we've provided the answers and their explanations to the sample tests. Read the book and understand the material, and you'll stand a very good chance of passing the test.

Exam Cram 2 books help you understand and appreciate the subjects and materials you need to pass Microsoft certification exams. *Exam Cram 2* books are aimed strictly at test preparation and review. They do not teach you everything you need to know about a topic. Instead, we present and dissect the questions and problems that you're likely to encounter on a test. We've worked to bring together as much information as possible about Microsoft certification exams and the 70-292 exam, in particular.

Nevertheless, to completely prepare yourself for any Microsoft test, we recommend that you begin by taking the self-assessment that is included in this book, immediately following this introduction. The self-assessment tool will help you evaluate your knowledge base against the requirements for a Microsoft Certified Systems Administrator (MCSA) or Microsoft Certified Systems Engineer (MCSE) under both ideal and real circumstances.

Based on what you learn from the self-assessment, you might decide to begin your studies with some classroom training, some practice with Microsoft

Server 2003, or some background reading. On the other hand, you might decide to pick up and read one of the many study guides available from Microsoft or third-party vendors on certain topics, including the award-winning *MCSE Training Guide* series from Que Publishing. We also recommend that you supplement your study program with visits to www.examcram2.com to receive additional practice questions, get advice, and track the MCSA and MCSE programs.

I also strongly recommend that you install, configure, and play around with the software that you'll be tested on, because nothing beats hands-on experience and familiarity when it comes to understanding the questions you're likely to encounter on a certification test. Book learning is essential, but without a doubt, hands-on experience is the best teacher of all!

The included CD also contains the *PrepLogic Practice Tests, Preview Edition* exam simulation software for this exam. The preview edition exhibits most of the full functionality of the Premium Edition, but offers sufficient questions for only one practice exam. To get the complete set of practice questions and exam functionality, visit www.preplogic.com.

Taking a Certification Exam

After you've prepared for your exam, you need to register with a testing center. Each computer-based MCP exam costs $125, and if you don't pass, you can retest for an additional $125 for each additional try. In the United States and Canada, tests are administered by Prometric and by VUE. Here's how you can contact them:

➤ **VUE**—You can sign up for a test or get the phone numbers for local testing centers through the Web at www.vue.com/ms.

➤ **Prometric**—You can sign up for a test through the company's Web site, at www.prometric.com. Within the United States and Canada, you can register by phone at 800-755-3926. If you live outside this region, you should check the Prometric Web site for the appropriate phone number.

 To sign up for a test, you must possess a valid credit card or contact either VUE or Prometric for mailing instructions to send a check (in the United States). Only after payment is verified or your check has cleared can you actually register for the test.

To schedule an exam, you need to call the number or visit either of the Web pages at least one day in advance. To cancel or reschedule an exam, you must call before 7 p.m. Pacific standard time the day before the scheduled test time (or you might be charged, even if you don't show up to take the test). When you want to schedule a test, you should have the following information ready:

➤ Your name, organization, and mailing address.

➤ Your Microsoft test ID. Inside the United States, this usually means your Social Security number; citizens of other nations should call ahead to find out what type of identification number is required to register for a test.

➤ The name and number of the exam you want to take.

➤ A method of payment. As mentioned previously, a credit card is the most convenient method, but alternate means can be arranged in advance, if necessary.

 NOTE Microsoft Certified Trainers (holders of an active current MCT certification) should remember to ask for the MCT discount during registration, and be prepared to provide their MCP ID number.

After you sign up for a test, you're told when and where the test is scheduled. You should try to arrive at least 15 minutes early. You must supply two forms of identification—one of which must be a photo ID—and sign a nondisclosure agreement to be admitted into the testing room.

All Microsoft exams are completely closed book. In fact, you are not permitted to take anything with you into the testing area, including pagers, cell phones, notes, calculators, or any other objects that the testing center deems necessary to exclude from the testing room. You'll be given a blank sheet of paper and a pen (or in some cases an erasable plastic sheet and an erasable pen) for personal notes during the exam. This note page must be left with the testing center after completing the Microsoft exam.

We suggest that you immediately write down, on the provided paper, any specific details that you might have memorized before starting your exam. In *Exam Cram 2* books, this information appears on a tear-out sheet inside the front cover of each book. You are given some time to compose yourself, record this information, and take a sample orientation exam before you begin the real thing. I suggest that you take the orientation test before taking your first Microsoft exam, but because all the certification exams are more or less identical in layout, behavior, and controls, you probably don't need to do this more than once.

When you complete a Microsoft certification exam, the software will tell you immediately whether you've passed or failed, but does not provide a detailed scoring of your exam. If you need to retake an exam, you have to schedule a new test with Prometric or VUE and pay another $125.

> The first time you fail a test, you can retake the test as soon as you can schedule the next exam. If you fail the exam a second time, you must wait 14 days before re-taking that test again. This waiting period between re-takes remains in effect for all future re-takes of the same exam.

Tracking MCP Status

As soon as you pass any Microsoft exam, you attain Microsoft Certified Professional (MCP) status. Microsoft provides access to your transcript to enable you to track which exams you've passed and which certifications you've obtained. You can view a copy of your transcript at any time by going to the MCP secured site and selecting Transcript Tool. This tool enables you to print a copy of your current transcript to confirm your certification status.

> The MCP and MCT secured sites can be accessed by using your MCP ID through the MCP community site, found at **http://www.microsoft.com/traincert/community/**.

After you pass the necessary set of exams, you're granted the appropriate Microsoft certification. Official notice of the certification is usually processed after three to six weeks, so you shouldn't expect to get your credentials overnight. The package for official certification that arrives includes a Welcome Kit that contains a number of elements (see Microsoft's Web site for other benefits of specific certifications):

➤ A certificate suitable for framing, along with a wallet card and lapel pin, enabling you to proudly display your certifications for your peers.

➤ A license and guidelines for use of the applicable certification logo, which means you can use the logo in advertisements, promotions, and documents, as well as on letterhead, business cards, and so on. Along with the license comes a logo sheet, which includes camera-ready artwork. (Note that before you use any of the artwork, you must sign and return a licensing agreement that indicates you'll abide by its terms and conditions.) The logo graphics can also be downloaded from the MCP secured site.

➤ A subscription to *Microsoft Certified Professional Magazine*, which provides ongoing data about new testing and certification activities, requirements, and changes to the program.

Many people believe that the benefits of MCP certification go well beyond the perks that Microsoft provides to new members of this elite group. We're starting to see more job listings that request or require applicants to have MCP, MCSA, MCSE, and other certifications. Many individuals who complete Microsoft certification programs can also qualify for increases in pay and/or responsibility. As an official recognition of hard work and broad knowledge, the MCP credential is a badge of honor in many IT organizations.

How to Prepare for an Exam

Preparing for any MCSA- or MCSE-related test (including Exam 70-292) requires that you obtain and study materials designed to provide comprehensive information about the product and its capabilities that will appear on the specific exam for which you're preparing. The following list of materials can help you study and prepare:

➤ The Microsoft 70-292 Preparation Guide, which details the expected areas of focus for this exam, available from `http://www.microsoft.com/traincert/exams/70-292.asp`.

➤ The Microsoft Windows Server 2003 technical resources and documentation, which are available from `http://www.microsoft.com/windowsserver2003/`.

➤ The exam preparation materials, practice tests, and self-assessment exams on the Microsoft Training & Certification page at `www.microsoft.com/traincert`. The Exam Resources link offers examples of the new question types found on the MCSA and MCSE exams, along with new certification concentrations. You should find the materials, download them, and use them!

➤ The exam-preparation advice, practice tests, questions of the day, and discussion group conversations on the `www.examcram2.com` e-learning and certification destination Web site.

In addition, you might find any or all the following materials useful in your quest for Windows Server 2003 expertise:

➤ **Microsoft training kits**—Microsoft Press offers a training kit that specifically targets Exam 70-292. For more information, visit http://www.microsoft.com/mspress/certification/mcsa2003.asp. This training kit contains information that you will find useful in preparing for the test.

➤ **Microsoft Developer Network Library CD**—This quarterly CD- or DVD-based publication delivers numerous electronic titles that include coverage of .NET Framework, Visual Basic .NET, and related topics. Its offerings include product facts, technical notes, tools and utilities, sample code, and much more. A subscription to the MSDN Library costs $199 per year, but it is well worth the price. Visit http://msdn.microsoft.com/subscriptions/prodinfo/overview.asp for more details.

➤ **Study guides**—Several publishers, including Que Publishing, offer certification titles. Que Publishing offers the following:

  ➤ The *Exam Cram 2* **series**—These books give you information about the material you need to know to pass the tests.

  ➤ The *Training Guide* **series**—These books provide a greater level of detail than the *Exam Cram 2* books and are designed to teach you everything you need to know about the subject covered by an exam within the MCSA/MCSE track. Each book comes with a CD-ROM that contains interactive practice exams in a variety of testing formats.

➤ **Classroom training**—Microsoft Certified Technical Education Centers (CTECs), online partners, and third-party training companies (such as Wave Technologies, Learning Tree, and Data-Tech) all offer classroom training for Microsoft certification exams. These companies aim to help you prepare to pass Exam 70-292 (or other exams). Although such training might cost more than $350 per day in class, most of the individuals lucky enough to partake find this training to be quite worthwhile.

➤ **Other publications**—There's no shortage of materials available about Microsoft Windows Server 2003 and the Active Directory environment. The "Need to Know More?" resource sections at the end of each chapter in this book will give you an idea of where we think you should look for further discussion and research on each chapter's focus.

This set of required and recommended materials represents an unparalleled collection of sources and resources for Microsoft Windows Server 2003 and related topics covered in your certification track. We hope that you will find that this book belongs in this company.

What This Book Will Not Do

This book will *not* teach you everything you need to know about computers or even about a given topic. Nor is this book an introduction to computer technology. The Microsoft 70-292 exam is primarily focused towards MCSAs and MCSEs already certified on earlier Microsoft technologies, who want to demonstrate their skills with the new Windows Server 2003 product line.

If you are new to Microsoft network administration and are looking for an initial preparation guide, check out www.quepublishing.com, where you'll find a whole section dedicated to the MCSE/MCSA certifications. This book will review what you need to know before you take the test, with the fundamental purpose dedicated to reviewing the information needed on the Microsoft 70-292 certification exam in particular.

This book uses a variety of teaching and memorization techniques to analyze the exam-related topics and to provide you with ways to input, index, and retrieve everything you'll need to know to pass the test. Once again, it is *not* an introduction to Windows Server 2003.

What This Book Is Designed to Do

This book is designed to be read as a pointer to the areas of knowledge you'll be tested on. In other words, you might want to read the book the first time in order to develop an idea about your current knowledge of the subject material, and to identify areas where additional review is needed.

The book is also designed to be read shortly before you sit the actual test and to give you a last-minute review distillation of the entire subject matter in as few pages as possible. We think you can use this book to get a sense of the underlying context of any topic in the chapters—or to skim-read for Exam Alerts, bulleted points, summaries, and topic headings. Make sure to review the pull-out sheet just before you walk into your exam so that all the details will be fresh on your mind.

We have drawn on material from Microsoft's own listing of knowledge requirements, from other preparation guides, and from the exams themselves, in addition to a battery of third-party test-preparation tools and technical Web sites, as well as from our own experience with Microsoft Windows technologies and the exam. Our aim is to walk you through the knowledge you will need—looking over your shoulder, so to speak—and point out those things that are important for the exam through Exam Alerts, notes, practice questions, and so on.

The 70-292 exam makes a basic assumption that you already have a strong background of experience with the Windows Server platform and its terminology. On the other hand, because the 2003 version of this technology is so new, no one can be a complete expert. We've tried to demystify the jargon, acronyms, terms, and concepts and to provide clear details on where you can find additional information. Also, wherever we think you might flip past an important concept, we've defined the assumptions and premises behind that concept.

About This Book

If you're preparing for the 70-292 certification exam for the first time, we've structured the topics in this book to build on one another. Therefore, the topics covered in later chapters might refer to previous discussions in earlier chapters. It's probably best to completely read this book from front to back before returning to specific focus areas for review.

After you've read the book, you can review a particular focus area by using the index or the table of contents to go straight to the topics and questions you want to re-examine. We've tried to use the headings and subheadings to provide outline information about each given topic, making navigation easier for you during review.

After you have received your Microsoft certification, this book will also serve as an excellent review of the subject material as you use these skills within your personal or professional life.

Chapter Formats

Each *Exam Cram 2* chapter follows a regular structure, along with graphical cues about especially important or useful material. The structure of a typical chapter is as follows:

➤ **Opening hotlists**—Each chapter begins with lists of the terms we feel you should understand and the concepts you'll need to master before you can feel fully conversant with the subject focus of the chapter. The hotlists are followed by a few introductory paragraphs, setting the stage for the rest of the chapter.

➤ **Topical coverage**—After the opening hotlists, each chapter covers the topics related to the chapter's subject, building from general to more specific areas of concentration where appropriate.

➤ **Alerts**—Throughout the topical coverage section, we've highlighted material that is very likely to appear on the exam by using a special Exam Alert layout that looks like this:

 This is what an Exam Alert looks like. An Exam Alert stresses concepts, terms, software, or activities that will most likely appear in one or more certification exam questions. For that reason, any information found offset in Exam Alert format is something we consider worthy of unusual attentiveness on your part.

Even if material isn't flagged as an Exam Alert, *all* the content in this book is associated in some way with exam-related material. What appears in the chapter content is critical knowledge.

➤ **Notes**—This book includes an overall examination of networking and the Microsoft Server technologies to provide a framework for your understanding. As such, we'll delve into many aspects of Windows Server 2003 technology. Where a body of knowledge is deeper than the scope of the book, we'll use notes to indicate areas of concern or specialty training.

 Cramming for an exam will get you through a test, but it won't make you a competent IT professional. Although you can memorize just the facts you need in order to become certified, your daily work in the field will rapidly put you in water over your head if you don't know the underlying technologies involved.

➤ **Tips**—We'll also provide tips that will help you to build a better foundation of knowledge or to focus your attention on an important concept that will reappear later in the book. Tips provide a helpful way to remind you of the context surrounding a particular area of a topic under discussion.

 You should also read Chapter 1, "Microsoft Certification Exams," for helpful strategies used in taking a test. The introduction to the sample tests also contains additional tips on how to figure out the correct response to a question and what to do if you draw a complete blank.

➤ **Exam prep questions**—This section presents a short list of test questions related to the specific chapter topic, presented in a similar format to what you're likely to encounter on the real exam. Each question has a following explanation of both correct and incorrect answers. The practice questions highlight the areas we found to be most important on the exam and will help you become more comfortable with Microsoft's testing style.

➤ **Need to Know More?**—Every chapter ends with a section titled "Need to Know More?" This section provides pointers to resources that we found to be helpful in offering further details on the chapter's subject focus. If you find a resource you like in this collection, use it; but don't feel compelled to try to acquire all of these resources. We use this section to recommend resources that we have used on a regular basis, so none of the recommendations will be a waste of your time or money—many are even freely available on the Web. These resources might go out of print or be taken down (in the case of Web sites), so we've tried to reference several widely accepted resources for each topic.

The bulk of the book follows this chapter structure, but there are a few other elements that we would like to point out:

➤ **Sample tests**—The sample tests, which appear in Chapters 8 and 10 (with answer keys in Chapters 9 and 11), are very close approximations of the types of questions you are likely to see on the current 70-292 exam.

➤ **Answer keys**—These provide the answers to the sample tests, complete with explanations of both the correct and incorrect responses to help you clarify any subject areas needing review.

➤ **Glossary**—This is an extensive glossary of important terms used throughout in this book.

➤ **The Cram Sheet**—This appears as a tear-away sheet, inside the front cover of this *Exam Cram 2* book. It is a valuable tool that represents a collection of the most difficult-to-remember facts we think you should review immediately before taking the exam. You should note this information on the provided paper as soon as you enter the testing room, before starting your exam. These are usually facts that we've found require brute-force memorization. You need to remember this information only long enough to write it down when you walk into the test room.

You might want to look at the cram sheet in your car or in the lobby of the testing center just before you walk into the testing center. The cram sheet is divided under headings, so you can review the appropriate parts just before your exam.

➤ **The CD**—The CD contains the *PrepLogic Practice Tests, Preview Edition* exam simulation software. The preview edition exhibits most of the full functionality of the Premium Edition, but offers only sufficient questions for one practice exam. To get the complete set of practice questions and exam functionality, visit `www.preplogic.com`.

Contacting the Author

I've tried to create a real-world tool that you can use to prepare for and pass the 70-292 MCSA/MCSE certification exam. I'm interested in any feedback you would care to share about the book, especially if you have ideas about how I can improve it for future test-takers. I'll consider everything you say carefully and will respond to all reasonable suggestions and comments. You can reach me via email at kkhausman@hotmail.com.

Let me know if you found this book to be helpful in your preparation efforts. I'd also like to know how you felt about your chances of passing the exam *before* you read the book and then *after* you read the book. Of course, I'd love to hear that you passed the exam—and even if you just want to share your triumph, I'd be happy to hear from you.

Thanks for choosing me as your personal trainer, and enjoy the book. I would wish you good fortune on the exam, but I know that if you read through all the chapters and work with the product, you won't need luck—you'll pass the test on the strength of real knowledge and understanding!

Self-Assessment

The reason we included a self-assessment in this *Exam Cram 2* book is to help you evaluate your readiness to tackle Microsoft certifications. This evaluation should also help you understand what you need to know to master the topic of this book—namely, Exam 70-292 "Managing and Maintaining a Microsoft Windows Server 2003 Environment for an MCSA Certified on Windows 2000." But before you tackle this self-assessment, let's address concerns you might face when pursuing an MCSA (Microsoft Certified Systems Administrator) or MCSE (Microsoft Certified Systems Engineer) certification for the Windows Server 2003 platform and what an ideal MCSA candidate might look like.

MCSAs in the Real World

The next section describes an ideal MCSA candidate, but keep in mind that only a few real candidates will meet every aspect of this ideal. However, be keenly aware that it will take time, some expense, and experience with the various products, and it will also require real effort on your part to get through the process.

Increasing numbers of people are attaining Microsoft certifications, so the goal is within reach. You can get all the real-world motivation you need from knowing that many others have gone before, so you'll be able to follow in their footsteps. If you're willing to tackle the process seriously and do what it takes to obtain the necessary experience and knowledge, you can take—and pass—all the certification tests involved in obtaining an MCSA or MCSE.

Besides the MCSA, other Microsoft certifications include the following:

➤ **MCP (Microsoft Certified Professional)**—Passing one of the major Microsoft exams qualifies you for the MCP credential. An individual can demonstrate proficiency with additional Microsoft products by passing additional certification exams.

➤ **MCSE (Microsoft Certified Systems Engineer)**—Anyone who has a current MCSE is warranted to possess a high level of networking expertise with Microsoft operating systems and products. This credential is designed to prepare individuals to plan, implement, maintain, and support information systems, networks, and internetworks built around Microsoft Windows Server 2000/2003 and its BackOffice Server families of products. To obtain an MCSE, you must pass five core exams and two elective exams.

➤ **MCSD (Microsoft Certified Solutions Developer)**—These individuals are qualified to design and develop custom business solutions by using Microsoft development tools, technologies, and platforms. The new track includes certification exams that test users' abilities to build Web-based, distributed, and XML-based applications by using Microsoft products such as Microsoft SQL Server, Microsoft Visual Studio, and Microsoft Component Services. To become an MCSD, you must pass a total of four exams: one Web application exam, one Windows application exam, one XML Web Services and Server Components exam, and one Solution Architecture exam.

➤ **MCAD (Microsoft Certified Application Developer)**—This certification is aimed at software developers functioning at a departmental level with one to two years of applications-development experience. The MCAD certification requires two core exams, plus a third elective exam drawn from a limited pool of options.

➤ **MCDBA (Microsoft Certified Database Administrator)**—This is aimed at database administrators and developers who work with Microsoft SQL Server. The MCDBA certification requires three core exams and one elective exam.

➤ **Other Microsoft certifications**—The requirements for these certifications range from external training certificates (MCT) to blended multi-vendor certifications, including those provided by CompTIA (http://www.comptia.com). Microsoft has also added new certification concentrations, such as security-focused versions of the MCSE and MCSA. For more details about these and other certifications, take a look at Microsoft's training and certification Web site at http://www.microsoft.com/traincert/.

The Ideal MCSA Candidate

The MCSA program is designed for individuals who have experience in implementing and administering Microsoft Windows 2000 and Windows Server 2003 networks. This credential is designed to prepare individuals to plan, implement, troubleshoot, and maintain networks and inter-networks built around Microsoft Windows 2000 and Windows Server 2003 technologies within network environments of up to 26,000 users and 100 physical locations. To obtain an MCSA, an individual must pass three core exams and one elective exam.

The 70-292 exam covered within this self-assessment is intended to enable existing Windows 2000 MCSAs to upgrade their certification to include the new Windows Server 2003 family of servers and services—a significant improvement in functionality and ease of use for those familiar with both platforms.

Just to give you some idea of what an ideal MCSA candidate is like, here are some relevant statistics about the background and experience such an individual might have:

➤ Academic or professional training in network theory, concepts, and operations. That includes everything from networking media and transmission techniques through network operating systems, services, and applications.

➤ Three-plus years of professional networking experience, including experience with ethernet, token ring, modems, and other networking media. This should include installation, configuration, upgrade, and troubleshooting experience.

The Windows Server 2003 platform is somewhat different from previous versions of the Microsoft server platform, improving the functionality introduced with the Windows 2000 Server Active Directory platform. Therefore, you'll really need some hands-on experience with Active Directory to make the most of your skills.

➤ Two-plus years in a networked environment that includes hands-on experience with Windows Server 2003, Windows 2000, and Windows XP.

➤ A thorough understanding of key networking protocols, addressing, and name resolution, including TCP/IP and NetBEUI.

➤ A thorough understanding of NetBIOS naming, browsing, and file and print services.

➤ Familiarity with key Windows 2000 TCP/IP-based services, including Hypertext Transfer Protocol (HTTP), Dynamic Host Configuration Protocol (DHCP), Windows Internet Naming Service (WINS), Domain Name Service (DNS), and the Internet Information Server (IIS).

➤ An understanding of how to implement security and auditing for key network data in a Windows Server 2003 environment.

➤ A good working understanding of Active Directory concepts is critical to your success on this exam.

➤ A solid understanding of each system's architecture, installation, configuration, maintenance, and troubleshooting is also essential. The time you take practicing these skills will be time very well spent!

Don't worry if you don't meet these qualifications or don't even come that close—this is a far-from-ideal world, and where you fall short is simply where you have more work to do.

Fundamentally, this boils down to a bachelor's degree in computer science (or equivalent experience on the job), three years' experience working in a position involving network design, installation, configuration, and maintenance. We believe that well under half of all certification candidates meet these requirements and that, in fact, most meet less than half of these requirements—at least, when they begin the certification process. But because all the people who already have been certified have survived this ordeal, you can survive it too—especially if you heed what this self-assessment can tell you about what you already know and what you need to learn.

Put Yourself to the Test

The following series of questions and observations is designed to help you figure out how much work you must do to pursue Microsoft certification and what kinds of resources you should consult on your quest. Be absolutely honest in your answers; otherwise, you'll end up wasting money on exams that you're not yet ready to take. There are no right or wrong answers, only steps along the path to certification. Only you can decide where you really belong in the broad spectrum of aspiring candidates.

Two things should be clear from the outset, however:

➤ Even a modest background in computer science and programming will be helpful.

➤ Hands-on experience with Microsoft products and technologies is an essential ingredient to Microsoft certification success.

Educational Background

Following are questions related to your education:

1. Have you ever taken any computer-related classes? [Yes or No]

If Yes, proceed to question 2; if No, proceed to question 4.

2. Have you taken any classes on computer operating systems? [Yes or No]

If Yes, you'll probably be able to handle Microsoft's architecture and system component discussions. If you're rusty, brush up on basic operating system concepts and general computer security topics.

If No, consider some basic reading in this area. We strongly recommend a good general operating systems book, such as *Operating System Concepts, 6th Edition*, by Abraham Silberschatz, Peter Baer Galvin, and Greg Gagne (John Wiley & Sons, 2001). If this title doesn't appeal to you, check out reviews for other, similar titles at your favorite online bookstore.

3. Have you taken any networking concepts or technology classes? [Yes or No]

➤ If Yes, you'll probably be able to handle Microsoft's networking terminology, concepts, and technologies (brace yourself for frequent departures from normal usage). If you're rusty, brush up on basic networking concepts and terminology, especially networking media, transmission types, the OSI reference model, and networking technologies such as ethernet, FDDI, and WAN links.

➤ If No, you might want to read one or two books in this topic area. The two best books that we know of are *Computer Networks, 4th Edition*, by Andrew S. Tanenbaum (Prentice Hall, 2002) and *Computer Networks and Internets, 3rd Edition*, by Douglas E. Comer and Ralph E. Droms (Prentice Hall, 2001).

Skip to the next section, "Hands-on Experience."

4. Have you done any reading on operating systems or networks? [Yes or No]

If Yes, review the requirements stated in the first paragraphs after questions 2 and 3. If you meet those requirements, move on to the next section.

If No, consult the recommended reading for both topics. A strong background will help you prepare for the Microsoft exams better than anything else.

Hands-on Experience

The most important key to success on all the Microsoft tests is hands-on experience, especially with Windows Server 2003 Server and Windows XP, plus the many add-on services and components around which so many of the Microsoft certification exams revolve, such as the Group Policy Management Console (GPMC) discussed later in this book. After taking this self-assessment, you should learn at least this: There's no substitute for time spent installing, configuring, and using the various Microsoft products on which you'll be tested repeatedly and in depth.

 You can download objectives, practice exams, and other data about Microsoft exams from the Training and Certification page at **http://www.microsoft.com/ traincert/**. Use the Microsoft Certifications link to obtain specific exam information.

5. Have you installed, configured, and worked with Windows Server 2003? [Yes or No]

If Yes, make sure that you understand the basic concepts, TCP/IP interfaces, utilities, and services provided by the platform, as well as the procedures involved in implementing security features for Windows Server 2003, which is far superior to previous Microsoft products in this arena.

If No, you must get some experience. Read on for suggestions on how to do this.

Experience is a must with any Microsoft product exam, be it something as simple as FrontPage 2000 or as challenging as Microsoft Server 2003. We recommend that if at all possible, you obtain two computers—each with a network interface—and set up at least a two-node network on which to practice. With decent Windows 2003–capable computers selling for about $500 to $600 each these days, this shouldn't be too much of a financial hardship. If this isn't possible, you need to at least install the Windows Server 2003 software on the same computer on which you install sample tests. That way, you can go back and forth to see the software and determine why a particular answer is correct.

You might have to scrounge to come up with the necessary software, but if you scour the Microsoft Web site, you can usually find low-cost options to obtain evaluation copies of most of the software that you'll need. For trial evaluation copies of other software, search Microsoft's Web site using the name of the product as your search term. Also, search for bundles such as BackOffice and Small Business Server.

 If you have the funds, or your employer will pay your way, consider taking a class at a Microsoft Certified Training and Education Center (CTEC). In addition to classroom exposure to the topic of your choice, you usually get a copy of the software that is the focus of your course—along with a trial version of whatever operating system it needs—with the training materials for that class.

Before you even think about taking any Microsoft exam, make sure that you've spent enough time with the related software to understand how it may be installed, configured, and used. This will help you in the exam and in real life!

Testing Your Exam-Readiness

Whether you attend a formal class on a specific topic to get ready for an exam or use written materials to study on your own, some preparation for the Microsoft certification exams is essential. At $125 a try, pass or fail, you want to do everything you can to pass on your first try. That's where studying comes in.

We've included two practice exams in this book (Chapters 8 and 10), so if you don't score that well on the first, you can study more and then tackle the second. Que Certification also offers PrepLogic, Preview Edition as a solid practice exam engine. If you still don't hit a score of at least 75 to 80 percent after these tests, you'll want to investigate other practice test resources, such as http://www.preplogic.com and http://www.cramsessions.com where you can affordably purchase a good number of practice questions. Use these questions and extensive review study to brush up on your weak areas as you draw closer to passing your exam.

For any given subject, consider taking a class if you've tackled self-study materials, taken the test, and failed anyway. The opportunity to interact with an instructor and fellow students can make all the difference in the world, if you can afford that privilege. For information about Microsoft classes, visit the Training and Certification page at http://www.microsoft.com/education/partners/ctec.asp for Microsoft Certified Education Centers.

If you can't afford to take a class, visit the Training page at http://www.microsoft.com/traincert/training/find/ anyway because it also includes pointers to free practice exams and to Microsoft Certified Professional Approved Study Guides and other self-study tools. Even if you can't afford to spend much at all, you should still invest in some low-cost practice exams from commercial vendors.

6. Have you taken a practice exam on your chosen test subject? [Yes or No]

If Yes, and you scored 75–80% or better, you're probably ready to tackle the real thing. If your score isn't above that threshold, keep at it until you break that barrier.

If No, obtain all the free and low-budget practice tests you can find and get to work. Keep at it until you can break the passing threshold comfortably.

 When it comes to assessing your test readiness, there is no better way than to take a good-quality practice exam and pass with a score of 75–80% or better. When we're preparing, we shoot for 90% or more, just to leave room for the fact that you might encounter a question or two on the exam that makes little sense due to its wording. Such questions sometimes show up on Microsoft exams because of the newness of the testing environment or other unexpected factors.

Assessing Readiness for Exam 70-292

In addition to the general exam-readiness information in the previous section, there are several things you can do to prepare for the Managing and Maintaining a Microsoft Windows Server 2003 Environment exam. We suggest that you join an active Windows Server 2003 mailing list, frequently check the Microsoft Knowledge Base (integrated into the MSDN CD-ROM, or on the Microsoft Web site at http://support.microsoft.com/support/) for technical support issues that relate to your exam's topics, and become involved in local Microsoft product users groups that meet in your area. We've noticed some overlap between technical support questions on particular products and troubleshooting questions on the exams for those products.

What's Next?

After you've assessed your readiness, undertaken the right background studies, obtained the hands-on experience that will help you understand the products and technologies at work, and reviewed the many sources of information to help you prepare for a test, you're ready to take a round of practice tests. When your scores come back positive enough to get you through the exam, you're ready to go after the real thing. If you follow our assessment regime, you'll not only know what you need to study, but also when you're ready to make a test date at Prometric (http://www.prometric.com) or VUE (http://www.vue.com). Good fortune to you along your path to certification!

Microsoft Certification Exams

Terms you'll need to understand:

✓ Case study
✓ Multiple-choice question formats
✓ Build-list-and-reorder question format
✓ Create-a-tree question format
✓ Drag-and-connect question format
✓ Select-and-place question format
✓ Fixed-length tests
✓ Simulations
✓ Adaptive tests
✓ Short-form tests

Techniques you'll need to master:

✓ Assessing your exam-readiness
✓ Answering Microsoft's varying question types
✓ Altering your test strategy depending on the exam format
✓ Practicing (to make perfect)
✓ Making the best use of the testing software
✓ Budgeting your time
✓ Guessing (as a last resort)

Exam-taking is not something that most people anticipate eagerly, no matter how well prepared they are. In most cases, familiarity helps offset test anxiety. In plain English, that means you probably won't be as nervous when you take your fourth or fifth Microsoft certification exam as you'll be when you take your first one.

Whether it's your first exam or your tenth, understanding the details of taking the new exam (how much time to spend on questions, the environment you'll be in, and so on) and the new exam software will help you concentrate on the material rather than on the setting. Likewise, mastering a few basic exam-taking skills should help you recognize (and perhaps even outfox) some of the tricks and snares you're bound to find in some exam questions.

This chapter explains the exam environment and software and describes some proven exam-taking strategies that you can use to your advantage.

Assessing Exam-Readiness

I strongly recommend that you read through and take the self-assessment included with this book (it appears after the Introduction). It will help you compare your knowledge base to the requirements for obtaining an MCSA (Microsoft Certified Systems Administrator) or MCSE (Microsoft Certified Systems Engineer), and it will also help you identify parts of your background or experience that might need improvement or enhancement as well as where you need further learning. If you get the right set of basics under your belt, obtaining Microsoft certification will be that much easier.

After you've gone through the self-assessment, you can focus your studies on those topical areas in which your background or experience might be lacking. You can also tackle subject matter for individual tests at the same time, so you can continue making progress while you're catching up in some areas.

After you've worked through an *Exam Cram 2*, have read the supplementary materials, and have taken the practice test, you'll have a pretty clear idea of when you should be ready to take the real exam. Although I strongly recommend that you keep practicing until your scores top the 75% mark, 80% is a better goal because it gives some margin for error when you're in an actual, stressful exam situation. Keep taking practice tests and studying the materials until you attain that score. You'll find more pointers on how to study and prepare in the self-assessment.

What to Expect at the Testing Center

When you arrive at the testing center where you've scheduled your exam, you must sign in with an exam coordinator and show two forms of identification—one of which must be a photo ID. After you've signed in and your time slot arrives, you'll be asked to deposit any books, bags, pagers, calculators, cell phones, or other items you brought with you. Then you'll be escorted into a closed room for the actual exam.

All exams are completely closed book. Although you are not permitted to take anything with you into the testing area, you're furnished with a blank sheet of paper and a pen (in some cases, an erasable plastic sheet and an erasable pen). Immediately before entering the testing center, try to memorize as much of the important material as you can from the cram sheet so you can write that information on the blank sheet as soon as you're seated in front of the computer before starting your exam. You can refer to this piece of paper during the test, but you'll have to surrender the sheet when you leave the room. Because your timer does not start until you begin the testing process, it's best to do this first while the information is still fresh in your mind. You'll have some time to compose yourself, write down information on the paper you're given, and take a sample orientation exam before you begin the real thing. We suggest taking the orientation test before taking your first exam. Because the exams are generally identical in layout, behavior, and controls, you probably won't need to do this more than once.

The room typically has between one and six computers, where each workstation is separated from the others by dividers. Most test rooms feature a wall with a large picture window. This permits the exam coordinator to monitor the room, prevent exam-takers from talking to one another, and observe anything out of the ordinary. The exam coordinator will have preloaded the appropriate Microsoft certification exam (for this book, exam 70-292), and you'll be permitted to start as soon as you're seated in front of the computer.

All Microsoft certification exams allow a certain maximum amount of time in which to complete your work (this time is indicated on the exam by an onscreen counter/clock, so you can check the time remaining whenever you like). All Microsoft certification exams are computer generated. In addition to multiple choice, you might encounter select and place (drag and drop), create a tree (categorization and prioritization), drag and connect, and build-list-and-reorder (list prioritization) on some exams. The questions are constructed to check your mastery of basic facts and figures about the Microsoft Windows Server 2003 network environment and require you to evaluate one or more sets of circumstances or requirements. You'll often be asked to give more than one answer to a question. You might also be asked to select the best or most effective solution to a problem from a range of choices, all of which are technically correct.

Exam Layout and Design

The format of Microsoft exams varies. For example, many exams consist of a series of case studies, with six types of questions regarding each presented case. Other exams have the same six types of questions, but no complex multi-question case studies.

For design exams, each case study presents a detailed problem that you must read and analyze. Figure 1.1 shows an example of what a case study looks like. You must select the different tabs in the case study to view the entire case.

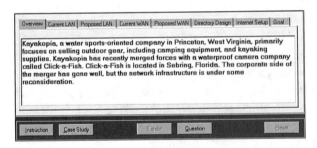

Figure 1.1   An example of a typical case study question.

Following each case study is a set of questions related to the case study. These questions can be one of several types (which are discussed next). Careful attention to the details provided in the case study is the key to success. Be prepared to toggle frequently between the case study and the questions as you work. Some of the case studies also include diagrams (called *exhibits*) that you'll need to examine closely to understand how to answer the questions.

After you complete a case study, you can review all the questions and your answers. Often, when you move on to the next case study, you cannot return to the previous case study and make any changes.

Following are the types of question formats:

➤ Multiple-choice, single answer

➤ Multiple-choice, multiple answers

➤ Build-list-and-reorder (list prioritization)

➤ Create a tree

➤ Drag and connect

➤ Select and place (drag and drop)

➤ Hot area

 The current form of the 70-292 exam is not presented in a case study format, although you should be familiar with all the various types of questions that could be found on Microsoft exams so that your later exams will be comfortable to you as well as your first.

Multiple-Choice Question Format

Some exam questions require you to select a single answer, whereas others ask you to select multiple correct answers. The following multiple-choice question requires you to select a single correct answer. Following the question is a brief summary of each potential answer and why it is either right or wrong.

Question 1

You have three domains connected to an empty root domain under one contiguous domain name: **tutu.com**. This organization is formed into a forest arrangement with a secondary domain called **frog.com**. How many Schema Masters are necessary for this arrangement?

○ A. One

○ B. Two

○ C. Three

○ D. Four

The correct answer is A. Only one Schema Master is necessary for a forest arrangement. The other answers (B, C, and D) are misleading because you're led to believe that Schema Masters may be in each domain or that you should have one for each contiguous domain namespace.

This sample question format corresponds closely to the Microsoft certification exam format (of course, questions are not followed by correct answer keys on the exam). To select an answer, you position the cursor over the radio button next to the answer and click the mouse button to select the answer.

Let's examine a question where one or more answers are possible. This type of question provides check boxes rather than radio buttons (circles) for marking all appropriate selections.

Question 2

How can you seize FSMO roles? (Choose two.)

❑ A. By using the Replication Monitor

❑ B. By using the **ntdsutil.exe** utility

❑ C. By using the **secedit.exe** utility

❑ D. By using Active Directory Domains and Trusts

Answers A and B are correct. You can seize FSMO roles from a server that is still running through the Replication Monitor, or in the case of a server failure, you can seize roles with the ntdsutil.exe utility. The secedit.exe utility is used to force group policies into play; therefore, answer C is incorrect. Active Directory Domains and Trusts is a combination of truth and fiction; therefore, answer D is incorrect.

For this particular question, two answers are required. Microsoft might sometimes give partial credit for partially correct answers. For question 2, you have to check the boxes next to answers A and B to obtain credit for a correct answer. Notice that picking the right answers also means knowing why the other answers are wrong.

Build-List-and-Reorder Question Format

Questions in the build-list-and-reorder format present two lists of items: one on the left and one on the right. To answer the question, you must move items from the list on the right to the list on the left. The final list must then be reordered into a specific order.

These questions are usually in the form, "From the following list of choices, pick the choices that answer the question. Then arrange the list in a certain order." To give you practice with this type of question, some questions of this type are included in this study guide. Here's an example of how they appear in this book; for an example of how they appear on the test, see Figure 1.2.

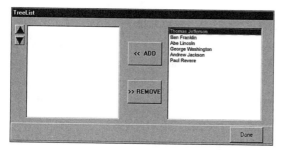

Figure 1.2   An example of how build-list-and-reorder questions appear.

Question 3

From the following list of famous people, pick those that have been elected President of the United States. Arrange the list in the order in which they served.

Thomas Jefferson

Ben Franklin

Abe Lincoln

George Washington

Andrew Jackson

Paul Revere

The correct answer is

George Washington

Thomas Jefferson

Andrew Jackson

Abe Lincoln

On an actual exam, the entire list of famous people would initially appear in the list on the right. You would move the four correct answers to the list on the left and then reorder the list on the left. Notice that the answer to the question did not include all items from the initial list. However, this might not always be the case.

To move an item from the right list to the left list, first select the item by clicking it and then clicking the Add button (left arrow). After you move an item from one list to the other, you can move the item back by first selecting the item and then clicking the appropriate button (either the Add button or the Remove button). After items have been moved to the left list, you can reorder the list by selecting an item and clicking the up or down button.

Create-a-Tree Question Format

Questions in the create-a-tree format also present two lists: one on the left and one on the right. The list on the right consists of individual items, and the list on the left consists of nodes in a tree. To answer the question, you must move items from the list on the right to the appropriate node in the tree.

These questions are basically a matching exercise. Items from the list on the right are placed under the appropriate category in the list on the left. Here's an example of how they appear in this book. For an example of how they appear on the test, see Figure 1.3.

Question 4

The calendar year is divided into four seasons:

Winter

Spring

Summer

Fall

Identify the season when each of the following holidays occurs:

Christmas

Fourth of July

Labor Day

Flag Day

Memorial Day

Washington's Birthday

Thanksgiving

Easter

The correct answer is

Winter

Christmas

Washington's Birthday

Spring

Flag Day

Memorial Day

Easter

Summer

 Fourth of July

 Labor Day

Fall

 Thanksgiving

In this case, all the items in the list were used. However, this might not always happen.

To move an item from the right list to its appropriate location in the tree, you must first select the appropriate tree node by clicking it. Then you select the item to be moved and click the Add button. If one or more items have been added to a tree node, the node is displayed with a plus sign (+) icon to the left of the node name. You can click this icon to expand the node and view whatever was added. If any item has been added to the wrong tree node, you can remove it by selecting it and clicking the Remove button (see Figure 1.3).

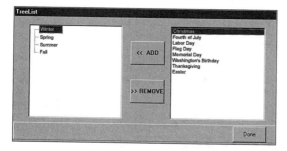

Figure 1.3 An example of how create-a-tree questions appear.

Drag-and-Connect Question Format

Questions in the drag-and-connect format present a group of objects and a list of connections. To answer the question, you must move the appropriate connections between the objects.

This type of question is best described using graphics. Here's an example.

Question 5

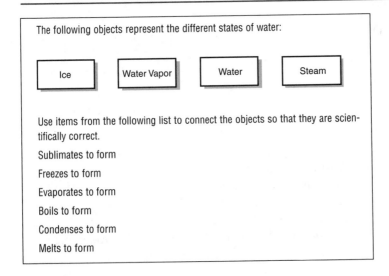

The correct answer is

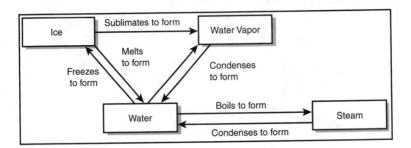

For this type of question, it's not necessary to use every object, but each connection can be used multiple times by dragging the answer to multiple locations. Dragging an answer away from its position removes it.

Select-and-Place Question Format

Questions in the select-and-place (drag-and-drop) format present a diagram with blank boxes and a list of labels that must be dragged to fill in the blank boxes. To answer the question, you must move the labels to their appropriate positions on the diagram.

This type of question is best described using graphics. Here's an example.

Question 6

Place the items in their proper order, by number, on the following flowchart. Some items may be used more than once, and some items might not be used at all.

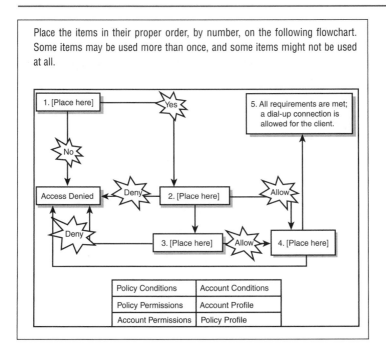

The correct answer is

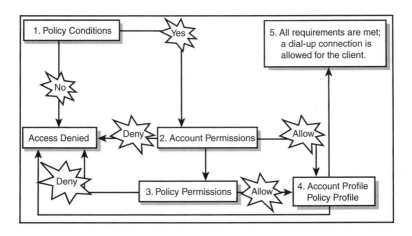

Hot Area

This type of question asks you to select one or more areas on a graphic to indicate the correct answer to a question. The hot spots on the graphic are shaded when you move the mouse over them, and are marked with an obvious border. To select or deselect an element, just click it.

A simple hot area question might present a screenshot of the Visual Studio .NET interface, and ask you to indicate the tab that allows you to retrieve information on particular databases. In that case, you'd click on the Server Explorer tab to answer the question.

Microsoft's Testing Formats

Currently, Microsoft uses four different testing formats:

➤ Case study

➤ Fixed length

➤ Adaptive

➤ Short form

 The current version of the 70-292 exam is of the fixed-length type, although you should at least be able to recognize the basic formats in case you encounter one on a later exam.

As mentioned earlier, the case study approach is used with many of the newer Microsoft exams. These exams consist of a set of case studies that you must first analyze to answer questions related to the case studies. Such exams include one or more case studies (tabbed topic areas), each of which is followed by 4 to 10 questions. The question types for exams will be multiple-choice, build-list-and-reorder, create a tree, drag and connect, and select and place. Depending on the test topic, some exams are totally case based, whereas others are not at all.

Other Microsoft exams employ advanced testing capabilities that might not be immediately apparent. Although the questions that appear are primarily multiple-choice, the logic in *fixed-length tests*, which use a fixed sequence of questions, is more complex than that in older Microsoft tests. Some questions employ a sophisticated user interface (which Microsoft calls a *simulation*) to test your knowledge of particular software and systems in a simulated live environment that behaves just like the original. The Testing Innovations article at http://www.microsoft.com/TRAINCERT/mcpexams/faq/innovations.asp includes a downloadable series of demonstrations and examples.

For some exams, Microsoft has turned to a well-known technique, called *adaptive testing*, to establish a test-taker's level of knowledge and product competence. Adaptive exams look the same as fixed-length exams, but they determine the level of difficulty at which an individual test-taker can correctly answer questions.

Adaptive tests work by evaluating the test-taker's most recent answer. A correct answer leads to a more difficult question and also raises the test software's estimate of the test-taker's knowledge and ability level. An incorrect answer leads to a less difficult question and also lowers the test software's estimate of the test-taker's knowledge and ability level). This process continues until the test targets the test-taker's true ability level. The exam ends when the test-taker's level of accuracy meets a statistically acceptable value (in other words, when his or her performance demonstrates an acceptable level of knowledge and ability) or when the maximum number of items has been presented (in which case, the test-taker is almost certain to fail).

Microsoft has also introduced a short-form test for its most popular tests. This test consists of 25 to 30 questions, with a time limit of exactly 60 minutes. This type of exam is similar to a fixed-length test because it allows readers to jump ahead or return to earlier questions and to cycle through the questions until the test is done. Microsoft does not use adaptive logic in this test; it claims that statistical analysis of the question pool is such that the 25 to 30 questions delivered during a short-form exam conclusively measure a test-taker's knowledge of the subject matter in much the same way as an adaptive test. The short-form test is like a "greatest hits exam" (that is, the most important questions are covered) version of an adaptive exam on the same topic.

Some of the Microsoft exams might contain a combination of adaptive and fixed-length questions.

Because you won't know in which form the Microsoft exam will be, you should be prepared for an adaptive exam instead of a fixed-length or a short-form exam because it weighs each question more heavily. Microsoft can at times present new versions of existing exams, which could be of a different format but cover the same knowledge domains. The penalties for answering incorrectly are built in to the test itself on an adaptive exam, whereas the layout remains the same for a fixed-length or short-form test, no matter how many questions you answer incorrectly.

The biggest difference between adaptive tests and fixed-length or short-form tests is that you can mark and revisit questions on fixed-length and short-form tests after you've read them. On an adaptive test, you must answer the question when it is presented and cannot go back to that question later.

Strategies for Different Testing Formats

Before you choose a test-taking strategy, you must determine what type of test it is—case study, fixed length, short form, or adaptive:

➤ Case study tests consist of a tabbed window that allows you to navigate easily through the sections of the case.

➤ Fixed-length tests consist of 50 to 70 questions with a check box for each question. You can return to these questions if you want.

➤ Short-form tests have 25 to 30 questions with a check box for each question. You can return to these questions if you want.

➤ Adaptive tests are identified in the introductory material of the test. Questions have no check boxes and can be visited (and answered) only once.

Some tests contain a variety of testing formats. For example, a test may start with a set of adaptive questions, followed by fixed-length questions.

 You'll be able to tell whether you're taking an adaptive, fixed-length, or short-form test by the first question. Fixed-length and short-form tests include a check box that allows you to mark the question for later review. Adaptive test questions include no such check box and can be visited (and answered) only once.

Case Study Exam Strategy

Although you won't find this kind of format for the 70-292 exam, you might find the test-taking strategies beneficial, and if you ever take a case study exam, you'll want to review this section. Most test-takers find that the case study type of exam seems the most difficult to master. When it comes to studying for a case study test, your best bet is to approach each case study as a standalone exam. The biggest challenge you'll encounter is that you'll feel you won't have enough time to get through all the cases presented.

Each case provides a lot of material you'll have to read and study before you can effectively answer the questions that follow. The trick to taking a case study exam is to first scan the case study to get the highlights. Make sure that you read the overview section of the case so that you understand the context of the problem at hand. Then quickly move on and scan the questions.

As you're scanning the questions, make mental notes to yourself or notes on your paper so that you'll remember which sections of the case study you should focus on. Some case studies might provide a fair amount of extra information that you don't really need to answer the questions. The goal with this scanning approach is to avoid having to study and analyze material that is not completely relevant.

I find it very useful to group all items from a particular case study together, and then draw a box around them as I move on to the next case study, to prevent accidentally including details from one case study into another. If at all possible, get multiple sheets of paper and two sharp pencils from the test center.

When studying a case, read the tabbed information carefully. It is important to answer each and every question. You'll be able to toggle back and forth from case to questions, and from question to question within a case testlet. However, after you leave a case and move on, you might not be able to return to it. We suggest that you take notes while reading useful information to help you when you tackle the test questions. It's hard to go wrong with this strategy when taking any kind of Microsoft certification test.

Fixed-Length and Short-Form Exam Strategy

A well-known principle when taking fixed-length or short-form exams is first to read through the entire exam from start to finish. Answer only those questions that you feel absolutely sure you know. On subsequent passes, you can dive into more complex questions more deeply, knowing how many such questions you have left and the amount of time remaining.

There's at least one potential benefit to reading the exam over completely before answering the trickier questions: Information supplied in later questions can sometimes provide an insight on earlier questions. At other times, information you read in later questions might jog your memory about facts, figures, or behavior that helps you answer earlier questions. Either way, you'll come out ahead if you answer only those questions on the first pass that you're absolutely confident about.

Fortunately, the Microsoft exam software for fixed-length and short-form tests makes the multiple-visit approach easy to implement. At the top-left corner of each question is a check box that permits you to mark that question for a later visit. This option is not available in the adaptive type format, so if the box is not present, you're most likely in an adaptive format block of questions.

NOTE Marking questions makes later review easier, but you can return to any question by clicking the Forward or Back button repeatedly.

Here are some question-handling strategies that apply to fixed-length and short-form tests. Use them if you have the chance:

➤ When returning to a question after your initial read-through, read every word again; otherwise, your mind can miss important details. Revisiting a question after turning your attention elsewhere sometimes enables you to see something you missed, but the strong tendency is to see what you've seen before. Try to avoid that tendency at all costs.

➤ If you return to a question more than twice, try to articulate to yourself what you don't understand about the question, why answers don't appear to make sense, or what appears to be missing. If you chew on the subject awhile, your subconscious might provide the missing details, or you might notice a "trick" that points to the right answer.

As you work your way through the exam, another counter that Microsoft provides comes in handy—the number of questions completed and questions outstanding. For fixed-length and short-form tests, it's wise to budget your time by making sure that you've completed roughly one-quarter of the questions one-quarter of the way through the exam period, and three-quarters of the questions three-quarters of the way through.

If you're not finished when only five minutes remain, use that time to guess your way through any remaining questions. Remember, guessing is potentially more valuable than not answering. Blank answers are always wrong, but a guess might turn out to be right. If you don't have a clue about any of the remaining questions, pick answers at random or choose all A's, B's, and so on. Questions left unanswered are counted as answered incorrectly, so a guess is better than nothing at all.

TIP At the very end of your exam period, you're better off guessing than leaving questions unanswered.

Adaptive Exam Strategy

This type of exam format will not appear in the current version of the 70-292 exam; however, an overview of how to approach adaptive exams might benefit you in a later exam. If there's one principle that applies to taking an adaptive test, it's "Get it right the first time." You cannot elect to skip a question and move on to the next one when taking an adaptive test because the testing software uses your answer to the current question to select whatever question it plans to present next. You also cannot return to a question because the software gives you only one chance to answer the question. However, you can take notes as you work through the test. Information supplied in earlier questions might sometimes help you answer later questions.

Also, when you answer a question correctly, you're presented with a more difficult question next, to help the software gauge your level of skill and ability. When you answer a question incorrectly, you're presented with a less difficult question, and the software lowers its current estimate of your skill and ability. This continues until the program settles into a reasonably accurate estimate of what you know and can do.

The good news is that if you know the material, you'll probably finish most adaptive tests in 30 minutes or so. The bad news is that you must really know the material well to do your best on an adaptive test. That's because some questions are so convoluted, complex, or hard to follow that you're bound to miss one or two, at a minimum. Therefore, the more you know, the better you'll do on an adaptive test, even accounting for the occasionally strange questions that appear on these exams.

 Because you can't always tell in advance whether a test is fixed length, short form, adaptive, or a combination of these, you should prepare for the exam as if it were adaptive. That way, you'll be prepared to pass, no matter what kind of test you take. If the test turns out to be fixed length or short form, remember the tips from the preceding section, which will help you improve on what you could do on an adaptive test.

If you encounter a question on an adaptive test that you can't answer, you must guess an answer quickly. (However, you might suffer for your guess on the next question if you guess correctly because the software will give you a more difficult question!)

Question-Handling Strategies

For those questions that have only one right answer, usually two or three of the answers will be obviously incorrect, and two of the answers will be plausible. Unless the answer leaps out at you (if it does, reread the question to look for a trick; sometimes those are the ones you're most likely to get wrong), begin the process of answering by eliminating those answers that are most obviously wrong.

At least one answer out of the possible choices for a question can usually be eliminated immediately because it matches one of these conditions:

➤ The answer does not apply to the situation.

➤ The answer describes a nonexistent issue, an invalid option, or an imaginary state.

After you eliminate all answers that are obviously wrong, you can apply your retained knowledge to eliminate further answers. Look for items that sound correct but refer to actions, commands, or features that are not present or not available in the situation that the question describes. In the 70-292 exam, be wary of options that were correct in Windows 2000 Server but might have changed in Windows Server 2003.

If you're still faced with a blind guess among two or more potentially correct answers, reread the question. Try to picture how each of the possible remaining answers would alter the situation. Be especially sensitive to terminology; sometimes the choice of words (*remove* instead of *disable*) can make the difference between a right answer and a wrong one.

You should guess at an answer only after you've exhausted your ability to eliminate answers and are still unclear about which of the remaining possibilities is correct. An unanswered question offers you no points, but guessing gives you at least some chance of getting a question right; just don't be too hasty when making a blind guess.

> **NOTE** If you're taking a fixed-length or a short-form test, you can wait until the last round of reviewing marked questions (just as you're about to run out of time or unanswered questions) before you start making guesses. You'll usually have the same option within each case study testlet (but after you leave a testlet, you might not be allowed to return to it). If you're taking an adaptive test, you'll have to guess to move on to the next question if you can't figure out an answer some other way. Either way, guessing should be your technique of last resort!

Numerous questions assume that the default behavior of a particular utility is in effect. If you know the defaults and understand what they mean, this knowledge will help you cut through many Gordian knots. Simple, final actions might be critical as well. If a utility must be restarted before proposed changes take effect, a correct answer might require this step as well.

Mastering the Inner Game

In the final analysis, knowledge gives confidence and confidence breeds success. If you study the materials in this book carefully and review all the practice questions at the end of each chapter, you should become aware of those areas where additional learning and study are required.

After you've worked your way through the book, take the practice exams in the back of the book. Taking these tests will provide a reality check and help you identify focus areas to study further. Make sure that you follow up and review materials related to the questions you miss on the practice exams before scheduling a real exam. Don't schedule your exam appointment until after you've thoroughly studied the material and feel comfortable with the whole scope of the practice exams. You should score 80% or better on the practice exams before proceeding to the real thing (otherwise, obtain some additional practice tests so that you can keep trying until you hit this magic number).

 If you take a practice exam and don't get at least 75% to 80% of the questions correct, keep practicing. Microsoft provides links to practice exam providers and also self-assessment exams at **http://www.microsoft.com/traincert/mcpexams/prepare/**.

Armed with the information in this book and with the determination to augment your knowledge, you should be able to pass the certification exam. However, you have to work at it or you'll spend the exam fee more than once before you finally pass. If you prepare seriously, you should do well.

The next section covers other sources you can use to prepare for the Microsoft certification exams.

Additional Resources

A good source of information about Microsoft certification exams comes from Microsoft itself. Because its products and technologies—and the exams that go with them—change frequently, the best place to go for exam-related information is online.

If you haven't already visited the Microsoft Certified Professional site, do so right now. The MCP home page resides at `http://www.microsoft.com/ traincert/` (see Figure 1.4).

Figure 1.4   The Microsoft Certified Professional Training and Certification home page.

Coping with Change on the Web

Sooner or later, all the information we've shared with you about the Microsoft Certified Professional pages and the other Web-based resources mentioned throughout the rest of this book will go stale or be replaced by newer information. In some cases, the URLs you find here might lead you to their replacements; in other cases, the URLs will go nowhere, leaving you with the dreaded "404 File not found" error message. When that happens, don't give up.

There's always a way to find what you want on the Web if you're willing to invest some time and energy. Most large or complex Web sites (such as the Microsoft site) offer a search engine. On all of Microsoft's Web pages, a Search button appears along the top edge of the page. As long as you can get to the Microsoft site (it should stay at **www.microsoft.com** for a long time), you can use this tool to help you find what you need.

The more focused you can make a search request, the more likely it is that the results will include information you can use. For example, you can search for the string

```
"training and certification"
```

to produce a lot of data about the subject in general, but if you're looking for the preparation guide for Exam 70-292, "Managing and Maintaining a Microsoft Windows Server 2003

Environment," you'll be more likely to get there quickly if you use a search string similar to the following:

```
"Exam 70-292" AND "preparation guide"
```

Likewise, if you want to find the Training and Certification downloads, try a search string such as this:

```
"training and certification" AND "download page"
```

Finally, feel free to use general search tools—such as **www.google.com**, **www.altavista.com**, and **www.excite.com**—to look for related information. Although Microsoft offers great information about its certification exams online, there are plenty of third-party sources of information and assistance that need not follow Microsoft's training strategy. Therefore, if you can't find something immediately, intensify your search.

Managing Users, Computers, and Groups

Terms you'll need to understand:

✓ csvde

✓ dsadd

✓ dsget

✓ dsmod

✓ dsmove

✓ dsquery

✓ dsrm

✓ ldifde

✓ Organizational Unit (OU)

✓ Group

✓ Identity

Techniques you'll need to master:

✓ Using the command-line tools to manipulate Active Directory objects

✓ Creating, modifying, and deleting user and computer accounts using both the Active Directory Users and Computers Microsoft Management Console (MMC) snap-in and the command-line utilities provided with Windows Server 2003

✓ Using Organizational Units (OUs) and groups to manage large numbers of accounts more efficiently

Management of resources and security principals within the Windows Server 2003 architecture requires an understanding of the process involved in the creation and manipulation of user, computer, and group objects. This chapter provides a brief review of the Windows forest and domain architecture and then delves into the changes that have been implemented between Windows 2000 and Windows Server 2003.

The Windows Server 2003 Network Architecture

The Windows Server 2003 network architecture extends the Active Directory schema present in Windows 2000 implementations to include several new features, along with a more integrated user interface for centralized administration over large and complex organizational implementations. Many of the interfaces appear similar to those in Windows Server 2000 with minor changes, as shown in Figure 2.1.

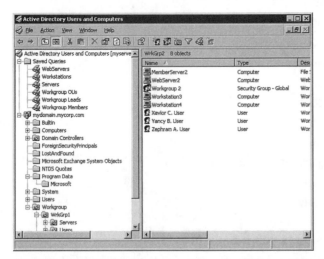

Figure 2.1 The Active Directory Users and Computers MMC snap-in showing the familiar organizational unit layout, along with the new capability to create stored search queries and items available through the Advanced Features view.

Many of the new Windows Server 2003 services also integrate more fully within the existing MMC snap-ins to centralize management over many tasks into a single interface. As shown in Figure 2.2, the installation of Microsoft's Exchange Server has added electronic mail–related options into the Properties dialog box brought up within the Active Directory Users and Computers MMC snap-in.

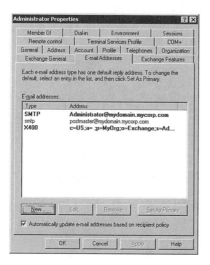

Figure 2.2   The Properties dialog box for the Administrator account opened within the Active Directory Users and Computers MMC snap-in to show the addition of mail-related items caused by the installation of Microsoft's Exchange Server.

The organization and layout of the overall user interface is also very similar to users of both Windows 2000 Server and Microsoft's Windows XP products. Familiar MMC snap-in utilities are arranged within similar groupings, with an overall feel that is more like that of the Windows XP interface, as shown in Figure 2.3.

Improved Functionality

The functionality of the user interface has been expanded in Windows Server 2003 to improve efficiency and ease of use. To move a security principal (user, group, or organizational unit) within the Windows 2000 Server environment, it was necessary to first right-click on the object within the Active Directory Users and Computers MMC snap-in, select Move from the options within the drop-down menu, and finally to navigate to the desired destination.

In Windows Server 2003, this process can be performed using a drag-and-drop mechanism that's familiar to users of Microsoft's Office suite of products. By left-clicking on an object and holding the mouse button, an administrator can simply move the cursor over the new destination and release the button to complete the same process that previously required several steps.

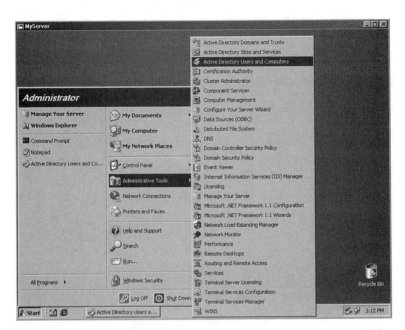

Figure 2.3   The user interface showing an XP-like layout that encapsulates familiar MMC snap-in utilities found also in Windows Server 2003.

Integration and Security

Windows Server 2003 is not only an updated version of Windows 2000 Server; it also includes features designed to allow more fluid integration with other operating systems and external functionality provided by many third-party vendors. One example of this is the inclusion of a new security principal type, the InetOrgPerson, which is used in migrating from or interfacing with other non-Microsoft LDAP and X.500 directory services.

Microsoft has improved the implementation of security options in many ways as well, starting with a more secure method of installation in which not every service possible is installed and activated by default. Each function a server is to implement must be enabled using the Manage Your Server Wizard, shown in Figure 2.4.

Microsoft has also added administrator-configurable security settings to control user access using advanced authentication methods, such as biometric authentication and smart cards. Accounts can be trusted for service-access delegation through the use of the setspn utility provided in the Windows

Support Tools, or can be restricted to prevent delegation, such as in the case of a Guest account. Windows Server 2003 includes support for the data encryption standard (DES) in many forms, as well as support for alternative implementations of the Kerberos protocol.

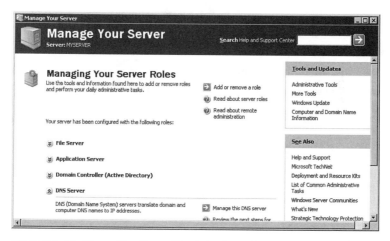

Figure 2.4   The Manage Your Server Wizard showing configured server roles for file server, application server, domain controller, and DNS server functionality.

Command-Line Utilities

Due to the scale and complexity of many Active Directory implementations, Microsoft has added many new command-line features to Windows Server 2003 to better support scripting of complex configuration tasks and bulk management initiatives.

 You should be able to perform the basic Active Directory object manipulation actions of creation, modification, and deletion using both graphical MMC snap-ins and command-line tools.

Table 2.1 details several new command-line tools included for Active Directory management, which we'll review in this chapter.

Table 2.1   Command-Line Tools for Manipulating Active Directory Objects

Tool	Description
csvde.exe	Used to import and export Active Directory data using a comma-separated file format (**.csv**)
dsadd.exe	Used to add a new object to the directory (user, computer, contact, group, or organizational unit)
dsget.exe	Used to display selected attributes of an object in the directory
dsmod.exe	Used to modify an existing object
dsmove.exe	Used to rename an object and move an object to a new location within the same domain
dsquery.exe	Used to display a list of objects within the directory that meet the specified search criteria
dsrm.exe	Used to delete an object from the directory
ldifde.exe	A powerful tool used to import and export Active Directory data and extend the schema, as well as to create, modify, and delete objects within the directory

Table 2.2 provides a listing of other important command-line tools included in Windows Server 2003.

Table 2.2   Additional Useful Command-Line Tools Provided for Scripting in Windows Server 2003

Tool	Description
Adprep	Used to prepare an existing Windows 2000 domain for upgrade to Windows Server 2003
Bootcfg	Used to configure, change, and review **BOOT.INI** settings
Choice	Used to prompt a user to select from a listing of choices
Clip	Used to send command-line output to the Windows Clipboard
Cmdkey	Used to review, create, and delete stored usernames and passwords
Diskpart	Used to manage disks, partitions, and volumes
Eventcreate	Used to create an event in a specified event log
Forfiles	Used to specify files to use in batch processing
Gettype	Used to identify the version of Windows being used
Gpresult	Used to review the Resultant Set of Policy (RSoP) data for a security principal
Inuse	Used to replace in-use operating system files
Logman	Used to schedule performance counter and trace log collection

(continued)

Table 2.2 Additional Useful Command-Line Tools Provided for Scripting in Windows Server 2003 *(continued)*	
Tool	**Description**
Openfiles	Used to review and disconnect currently open files
Prncnfg	Used to review and configure printer settings
Prnjobs	Used to review, pause, resume, and cancel pending print jobs
Sc	Used to review and configure services
Schtasks	Used to review, add, and delete scheduled tasks
Setx	Used to set environment variable values
Shutdown	Used to restart or turn off a computer
Systeminfo	Used to review system configuration details
Takeown	Used to take ownership of an existing file
Taskkill	Used to stop one or more processes
Tasklist	Used to review a listing of running processes
Waitfor	Used to synchronize networked computers on a common signal
Where	Used to review files that match the specified criteria
Whoami	Used to review user configuration information
WMIC	A command-line interface for Windows Management Instrumentation (WMI) scripting

Table 2.3 includes a listing of several useful command-line tools used to manage the Windows Internet Information Services (IIS).

Table 2.3 Command-Line Tools for Use with IIS 6.0	
Tool	**Description**
IISBack	Used to create and manage backups of the IIS configuration settings
IISCnfg	Used to import and export IIS configuration details
IISFtp	Used to start, stop, pause, resume, review, create, and delete FTP sites
IISFtpdr	Used to create and delete FTP site virtual directories
IISVdir	Used to create and delete Web site virtual directories
IISWeb	Used to start, stop, pause, resume, review, create, and delete Web sites

Because Windows Server 2003 has been designed to operate in large server-farm settings, almost any operation that can be managed at the console has a command-line equivalent. This eases remote and bulk scripted operations.

For more details on scripting for the Windows environment, you should look at the MSDN Windows Script site: **http://msdn.microsoft.com/library/default.asp?url=/nhp/Default.asp?contentid=28001169**.

As we'll discuss in later chapters, Microsoft Windows Server 2003 can also be remotely managed with the full capability of the graphical user interface (GUI) console by using Terminal Services in a Remote Management configuration, but you should be familiar with the command-line tools used for most basic operations in the chapters ahead.

Command-line operations can be performed by selecting Start, Run and then entering cmd before clicking the OK button. This opens the command-line shell interface, as shown in Figure 2.5.

Figure 2.5   The command-line shell environment opened by the Administrator account.

The **csvde** Utility

The csvde utility is provided to rapidly import from and export Active Directory data to a comma-separated file (.csv format). Programs such as Microsoft Excel can be used to export tabular data in .csv format, although it's also possible to generate a CSV file through scripted output or using Notepad, as shown in Figure 2.6.

Figure 2.6   Sample **.csv** file (**testdata.csv**) that includes Active Directory object data generated by use of the **csvde** utility.

The syntax of the **csvde.exe** utility is provided in the Microsoft help file:

```
csvde [-i] [-f FileName] [-s ServerName] [-c String1 String2]
[-v] [-j Path] [-t PortNumber] [-d BaseDN] [-r LDAPFilter] [-p
Scope] [-l LDAPAttributeList] [-o LDAPAttributeList] [-g] [-m]
[-n] [-k] [-a UserDistinguishedName Password] [-b UserName
Domain Password]
```

To see a listing of all the parameters and their meanings, type the following at the command-line shell prompt:

```
csvde /?
```

Exporting Data Using csvde

To perform a simple export of nonbinary information for User objects from the server MyServer, using the Active Directory port (3268) to the file MyUsers.csv in the current directory, perform the following steps:

1. Open the command-line shell interface by selecting Start, Run and entering cmd before clicking the OK button.

2. Input the following command:

   ```
   csvde -f MyUsers.csv -s MyServer -t 3268 -m -n -r (objectClass=User)
   ```

3. Open the file in Notepad to examine the result (see Figure 2.7).

Figure 2.7 Sample **.csv** data export of **MyUsers.csv** in Notepad.

Importing Data Using csvde

The csvde utility can also be used to import data into Active Directory from a .csv file, using a similar format:

```
csvde -i -f MyData.csv -s MyServer -r (objectClass=User)
```

This code imports (the -i parameter specifies an import) only the User type objects from the file MyData.csv into Active Directory using the default LDAP port on the MyServer domain controller.

The Idifde Utility

The ldifde utility provides a more complete command-line management tool that can be used to import or export Active Directory data against another directory service, to extend the schema, or to create, modify, and delete directory objects.

The syntax of the **Idifde** utility is provided in the Microsoft help file:

ldifde [**-i**] [**-f** *FileName*] [**-s** *ServerName*] [**-c** *String1 String2*] [**-v**] [**-j** *Path*] [**-t** *PortNumber*] [**-d** *BaseDN*] [**-r** *LDAPFilter*] [**-p** *Scope*] [**-l** *LDAPAttributeList*] [**-o** *LDAPAttributeList*] [**-g**] [**-m**] [**-n**] [**-k**] [**-a** *UserDistinguishedName Password*] [**-b** *UserName Domain Password*] [**-?**]

To see a listing of all the parameters and their meanings, type the following at the command-line shell prompt:

```
ldifde /?
```

Use of the `ldifde` utility is very similar to the `csvde` utility you're already familiar with, although the generated output file (`.ldf`) is very different in its final format. To generate an output file `MyUsers.ldf` in the current directory, exporting User data (`CN`, `DN`, `Object Class`, `givenname`, and `SAMAccountName`) from MyServer, execute the following command within the command-line shell:

```
ldifde -f MyUsers.ldf -s MyServer -r (objectClass=User)
➥-l "cn,givenName,samAccountName,objectClass"
```

Figure 2.8 displays part of the resulting file.

Figure 2.8   Sample **.ldf** data export **MyUsers.ldf** in Notepad.

 Because the **ldifde** utility can make fundamental modifications to the schema and Active Directory objects, it's best to practice using this command in a testing network rather than in a production environment.

Managing Objects in Active Directory

Objects within the directory can be managed through the use of the `ldifde` and `csvde` utilities described earlier in this chapter, as well as through the use of the Active Directory Users and Computers MMC snap-in and the command-line utilities detailed in Table 2.1. We'll review the use of the latter two options in the next section.

Managing User Objects

One of the most well-recognized security principals in the Active Directory environment is the User object, which is used to authenticate the identity of the user, authorize or deny access to resources, and administer other security settings. This object is granted privileges and permissions, can be used to start and stop services, can be configured for rights delegation, and is generally the object most familiar to users.

The user account is given a unique name and password, and can have many other options configured to allow or restrict its access to resources located throughout the directory's scope. A proper naming scheme must include planning for uniqueness within the expected scope of the account's creation, as well as planning for later extensibility in the event of business growth.

A user account has four types of associated names: the user logon name, the pre–Windows 2000 logon name, the principal logon name, and the Lightweight Directory Access Protocol (LDAP) relative distinguished name.

The user logon name is up to 20 characters in length (characters beyond 20 are ignored) and can be made up of uppercase (A–Z), lowercase (a–z), numerical (0–9), and symbol characters (with some symbols disallowed). Example: **dyuser**

The pre–Windows 2000 logon name is used for NetBIOS account logons, as a single name or the single-word (NetBIOS) domain name followed by the logon name. Example: **MYDOMAIN\SomeUser**

The principal logon name is composed of the user logon name and the fully qualified domain name (FQDN) of the domain to which it belongs in the directory. Example: **myuser@mydomain.mycorp.com**

The LDAP relative distinguished name uniquely identifies an account in terms of its location in the directory. Example: **CN=johnsmith,CN=Users,DC=mycorp,DC=com**

The user logon name must be unique within its container. The pre–Windows 2000 logon name must be unique within the domain. The principal logon name must be unique within the forest. And the LDAP relative distinguished name must be unique within its container (generally an OU, such as **Users** in the example given).

Several user accounts are created by default in Windows Server 2003:

▶ **Administrator**—This is the predefined master administration account. It is a member of the Administrators, Domain Admins, Domain Users, and Group Policy Creator Owners groups by default. It also inherits membership in the Enterprise Admins and Schema Admins groups if it's in the root domain of a new tree. This account cannot be deleted or disabled, although it can be renamed. Renaming the Administrator account is a recommended practice, with an unprivileged disabled account of the same name created to prevent some types of attack by automated hacking tools.

▶ **ASPNET**—This account is used by the .NET Framework to run ASP.NET processes. It is a member of the Domain Users group by default, and can perform all tasks available to a normal user.

➤ **Guest**—An unprivileged account created in a disabled condition. It is a member of the Domain Guests and Guests groups by default. If you decide to use this account for any purpose, it is recommended that you change its name and create a new, disabled, unprivileged account of the same name to prevent some types of account abuse.

➤ **Support**—An account used by the Help and Support service to run processes and batch jobs. It is a member of the HelpServices and Domain Users groups by default.

Additional applications and services can create specific service and access accounts, such as the IUSR_<computername> and IWAM_<computername> accounts created by the installation of IIS. There are also three predefined pseudo-accounts used by various processes running within the Windows environment:

➤ **LocalSystem**—This account is used to run many system services that only require local logon rights.

➤ **LocalService**—This account is used to run system services that need to generate system audit events in the Security log. Some services that use this account are the Alerter, Smart Card Helper, and WebClient services.

➤ **NetworkService**—This account is used to run services that also require network access, such as the DNS Client and the Performance Logs and Alerts service.

Creating a User Object

Before creating user accounts, it's important to plan a naming scheme and a password policy that ensures unique naming and adequate security. When creating new logons that will not be used for a while, it's generally a good idea to disable the accounts to prevent some types of misuse. Even disabled accounts can be exploited in some ways, so account cleanup and deletion of old expired accounts should also be a regular part of your maintenance plan.

We discuss Group Policy settings that are used to configure password policies in Chapter 3, "Managing Access to Resources," but you should be aware of several options that will be presented during account creation:

➤ **User Must Change Password at Next Logon**—When you reset a user's password, you'll also be provided this option at that time. Changing a user's password is discussed later in this chapter. It's considered a best practice by Microsoft to require users to change their password to something different at the first logon.

> ► **User Cannot Change Password**—This setting is useful when a public, shared, or guest account is used and you want to prevent users from changing the password. This configuration is often used for thin-client and kiosk auto-logon accounts. In addition, service accounts should be configured to prevent self-modification so that a secondary administrative account must be used to change its password.

> ► **Password Never Expires**—This option should be used very sparingly and only when absolutely necessary; any account set in this manner must be reviewed for misuse because a fixed password becomes more susceptible to brute force attacks at guessing a password, which are discussed in greater detail in Chapter 7, "Maintaining Network Security." Some service accounts are configured in this way to ease administrative effort, but at the cost of reduced overall security if the password is later compromised.

> ► **Account Is Disabled**—This isn't a password setting, but one that's used to restrict some forms of account misuse. When an account is disabled, the user cannot log in again. If a user is logged in at the time this setting is configured, he remains connected until his next logoff, and only then is he unable to log in again. If a user is on an extended leave of absence, the recommended practice is to disable that user's account during the absence.

A new user account can be created using the Active Directory Users and Computers MMC snap-in, as well as through the use of the dsadd.exe utility.

The syntax of the **dsadd.exe** utility is provided in the Microsoft help file:

```
dsadd user UserDN [-samid SAMName] [-upn UPN] [-fn FirstName]
[-mi Initial] [-ln LastName] [-display DisplayName] [-empid
EmployeeID] [-pwd {Password ¦ *}] [-desc Description]
[-memberof Group;...]
[-office Office] [-tel PhoneNumber] [-email Email]
[-hometel HomePhoneNumber] [-pager PagerNumber]
[-mobile CellPhoneNumber] [-fax FaxNumber] [-iptel
IPPhoneNumber] [-webpg WebPage] [-title Title] [-dept
Department] [-company Company] [-mgr Manager] [-hmdir
HomeDirectory] [-hmdrv DriveLetter:]
[-profile ProfilePath] [-loscr ScriptPath] [-mustchpwd {yes ¦
no}] [-canchpwd {yes ¦ no}] [-reversiblepwd {yes ¦ no}]
[-pwdneverexpires {yes ¦ no}] [-acctexpires NumberOfDays]
[-disabled {yes ¦ no}] [{-s Server ¦ -d Domain}] [-u UserName]
[-p {Password ¦ *}] [-q] [{-uc ¦ -uco ¦ -uci}]
```

To see a listing of all the many parameters and their meanings, type the following at the command-line shell prompt:

```
dsadd user /?
```

To create a new domain user using the Active Directory Users and Computers MMC snap-in, perform the following steps:

1. Select Start, Administrative Tools, Active Directory Users and Computers.

> If you need to create a local user account on a member server or standalone server, select the Computer Management MMC snap-in and navigate to Local Users and Groups to create local user and group accounts. Domain controllers will not have the Local Users and Groups node within this MMC.

2. Navigate to the desired container, right-click, and select New, User from the drop-down menu.

3. In the New Object - User dialog box, you'll be prompted to provide a first name, middle initial, and last name. The full name will be created for you using this information, although it can then be edited without affecting the original name field entries.

4. You must enter a user logon name and select the domain in which this user account will be created, which also creates a pre–Windows 2000 logon name.

5. After clicking the Next button, you will be prompted to provide a user password and to retype it in the Confirm Password box. Four options are provided as well: User Must Change Password at Next Logon, User Cannot Change Password, Password Never Expires, and Account Is Disabled.

> The User Cannot Change Password option is useful for kiosks and other public limited logons that multiple users might need to access but not be allowed to change the logon password. The Password Never Expires option can weaken security, so it should be used sparingly and only for well-audited service accounts or unprivileged public accounts.

6. After clicking Next, you might be presented with additional configuration options if you've installed other integrated .NET services. For example, if you have installed Microsoft's Exchange Server 2003, you'll be provided with the opportunity to create a new mailbox for the user, as shown in Figure 2.9.

7. After completing any additional integrated configuration items, you'll be presented with a confirmation screen where you must click the Finish button to create the new account.

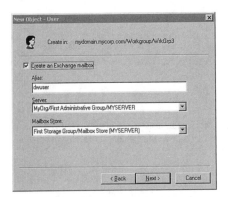

Figure 2.9 New Object - User dialog box showing Exchange mailbox setup options available due to a previously installed Exchange Server within the domain.

8. After creating the user account, you can double-click it within the MMC to open its Properties dialog box where additional details can be configured, such as the user's description, location, Terminal Services settings, COM+ partition, group membership, dial-in permissions, and email settings.

It's also possible to create a new user based on an existing user object by right-clicking the user account and selecting Copy, after which you'll be entered in the New Object - User dialog box, where you'll configure the details for the new account.

This has the advantage of propagating additional configuration settings such as location, description, and group membership from the original template account, making it possible to set up preconfigured role-based accounts very easily after the template accounts have been established.

You can also create a new domain user through the use of the dsadd utility. To create a new user called New User with a SAMid of nuser and a password of Pa55w0rd!, to be located in the Users container within the MyDomain.MyCorp.com domain, you can execute the following within the command-line shell:

```
dsadd user "CN=New User,CN=Users,DC=mydomain,DC=mycorp,DC=com"
          -samid nuser -s MyServer -pwd Pa55w0rd!
```

Because the distinguished name (DN) includes spaces, it is enclosed by quotation marks. This command could also be used to specify many more configuration details at the time of account creation.

When configuring a user account, several key items should be specified to better control the use of resources by the new account's logon, particularly the following:

> **Home folder**—The UNC path specifying the location in which the user's home file storage (the My Documents folder target location) will be located.

> **Logon script**—The UNC path and filename of a logon script (optional) if logon scripts are used.

> **Profile path**—The UNC path specifying the location to be used to store the user account's profile, which includes desktop and user interface settings and other application data.

When configuring these values, it's often desirable to be able to customize the path structure based on username or other environmental variables, including

> `%HomeDrive%`—The drive letter assigned to a user's home directory.

> `%HomePath%`—The full UNC path to the user's home directory.

> `%SystemRoot%`—The directory for the operating system installation, such as `C:\Windows\` or `C:\WinNT\`.

> `%UserName%`—The user account name, such as johndoe, which can be used to configure the home directory so that each user obtains her own folder within a common file store location.

On the Account tab within the properties of a user account, two buttons provide control over logon time and locations:

> **Logon Hours**—This button provides access to a graphical interface in which the logon permissible hours can be defined, such as only weekdays between the hours of 8 a.m. and 5 p.m., as shown in Figure 2.10.

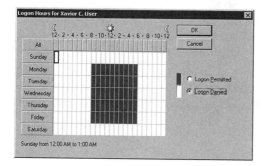

Figure 2.10 The graphical user interface selecting allowable logon hours for Xavior C. User.

➤ **Log On To**—This button provides access to a dialog box allowing specification of the particular computers that can be used by the user to log on. The default setting is All Computers.

Deleting User Objects

A user account can be deleted using the Active Directory Users and Computers MMC snap-in, as well as through the use of the dsrm.exe utility.

> The syntax of the **dsrm.exe** utility is provided in the Microsoft help file:
>
> ```
> dsrm ObjectDN ... [-subtree [-exclude]] [-noprompt]
> [{-s Server ¦ -d Domain}] [-u UserName] [-p {Password ¦ *}]
> [-c] [-q] [{-uc ¦ -uco ¦ -uci}]]
> ```
> To see a listing of all the parameters and their meanings, type the following at the command-line shell prompt:
> ```
> dsrm /?
> ```

To delete a domain user using the Active Directory Users and Computers MMC snap-in, you should perform the following steps:

1. Select Start, Administrative Tools, Active Directory Users and Computers.

2. Navigate to the desired container and account, right-click to select the target account, and select Delete from the drop-down menu. It's possible to select multiple accounts for deletion at the same time by holding down the Shift or Ctrl key while performing the selection operation.

3. You'll be prompted to confirm the deletion. If additional integrated services are present, such as Microsoft Exchange Server 2000 or later, you'll be given the chance to exclude contained objects, such as the electronic mailbox associated with the account.

You can also delete a domain user account through the use of the dsrm utility. To delete the user New User created in the previous exercise, execute the following within the command-line shell:

```
dsrm user "CN=New User,CN=Users,DC=mydomain,DC=mycorp,DC=com" -s MyServer
```

Managing User Objects

Two of the more common management actions you might be required to perform on user accounts are the resetting of passwords and the disabling or enabling of accounts. These actions can be performed using the Active

Directory Users and Computers MMC snap-in, as well as the command-line dsmod.exe utility.

The **dsmod.exe** utility operates in several configurations, allowing modification to the attribute values of user accounts (**dsmod user <*parameters*>**), computer accounts (**dsmod computer <*parameters*>**), group objects (**dsmod group <*parameters*>**), and other object types, including contacts, OUs, and servers. It's a good idea to review the various uses of this flexible command.

The syntax of the **dsmod.exe** utility used for modification to user accounts is provided in the Microsoft help file:

```
dsmod user UserDN ... [-upn UPN] [-fn FirstName] [-mi Initial]
[-ln LastName] [-display DisplayName] [-empid EmployeeID]
[-pwd (Password ¦ *)] [-desc Description] [-office Office]
[-tel PhoneNumber] [-email E-mailAddress] [-hometel
HomePhoneNumber] [-pager PagerNumber] [-mobile CellPhoneNumber]
[-fax FaxNumber]
[-iptel IPPhoneNumber] [-webpg WebPage] [-title Title]
[-dept Department] [-company Company] [-mgr Manager]
[-hmdir HomeDirectory] [-hmdrv DriveLetter:] [-profile
ProfilePath] [-loscr ScriptPath] [-mustchpwd {yes ¦ no}]
[-canchpwd {yes ¦ no}]
[-reversiblepwd {yes ¦ no}] [-pwdneverexpires {yes ¦ no}]
[-acctexpires NumberOfDays] [-disabled {yes ¦ no}]
[{-s Server ¦ -d Domain}] [-u UserName] [-p {Password ¦ *}]
[-c] [-q] [{-uc ¦ -uco ¦ -uci}]
```

To see a listing of all the many parameters and their meanings, type the following at the command-line shell prompt:

```
dsmod user /?
```

To modify the attributes of one or more domain user accounts using the Active Directory Users and Computers MMC snap-in, perform the following steps:

1. Select Start, Administrative Tools, Active Directory Users and Computers.

2. Navigate to the desired container and account, right-click to select the target account, and select Properties from the drop-down menu. It is possible to select multiple accounts for deletion at the same time by holding down the Shift or Ctrl key while performing the selection operation. When you do this, it opens a special dialog box that allows the selection of the specific attributes that will be modified across all selected accounts, as shown in Figure 2.11.

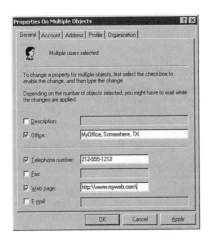

Figure 2.11 Properties on Multiple Objects dialog box showing several common values that will be applied to all selected objects.

3. By clicking the Apply button, the specified changes will be made to the selected user account or accounts.

To reset the password of a domain user account using the Active Directory Users and Computers MMC snap-in, perform the following steps:

1. Select Start, Administrative Tools, Active Directory Users and Computers. To change the password of a local user account on a member server or standalone server, select the Computer Management MMC snap-in here and navigate to Local Users and Groups.

2. Navigate to the desired container and account, right-click to select the target account, and select Reset Password from the drop-down list of options.

3. You're then prompted to enter the new password twice to confirm it, and presented with a check box to specify whether the user must change his password at the next logon.

4. After clicking the OK button, the new password is immediately replicated to all other authenticating domain controllers, rather than waiting for the next replication cycle. This ensures that password changes are available immediately, regardless of the server used to authenticate the user logon.

To disable or enable a domain user account using the Active Directory Users and Computers MMC snap-in, perform the following steps:

1. Select Start, Administrative Tools, Active Directory Users and Computers.

2. Navigate to the desired container and account, right-click to select the target account, and select Disable Account (or Enable Account for currently disabled accounts) from the drop-down list of options.

3. You will be notified that the account has been Disabled (or Enabled, if that is the case).

If an account has been locked out due to too many failed logon attempts for the currently configured password lockout policy settings, you'll need to unlock the account to allow the authorized user to be able to log on once more.

To unlock a domain user account using the Active Directory Users and Computers MMC snap-in, perform the following steps:

1. Select Start, Administrative Tools, Active Directory Users and Computers.

2. Navigate to the desired container and account, right-click to select the target account, and select Unlock Account from the drop-down list of options.

3. You will be notified that the account has been unlocked. It's a good idea to review your security logs to determine the source of the account lockout, in the event that the lockout was not accidental. Users should also be reminded to change their passwords regularly to ensure that repeated guessing does not eventually find the correct password.

Locating User Objects

In large organizations with complex multilevel organization unit structures, it's often very difficult to locate an individual user account by browsing through the OU hierarchy. Locating accounts that conform to a particular search criteria can be performed using the Active Directory Users and Computers MMC snap-in, as well as the command-line `dsquery.exe` utility. Common queries can also now be saved to simplify later recurring lookups.

The syntax of the **dsquery.exe** utility used to locate user accounts is provided in the Microsoft help file:

```
dsquery user [{StartNode ¦ forestroot ¦ domainroot}]
[-o {dn ¦ rdn ¦ upn ¦ samid}] [-scope {subtree ¦ onelevel ¦
base}] [-name Name] [-desc Description] [-upn UPN] [-samid
SAMName]
[-inactive NumberOfWeeks] [-stalepwd NumberOfDays] [-disabled]
[{-s Server ¦ -d Domain}] [-u UserName] [-p {Password ¦ *}]
[-q] [-r] [-gc] [-limit NumberOfObjects] [{-uc ¦ -uco ¦ -uci}]
```

To see a listing of all the many parameters and their meanings, type the following at the command-line shell prompt:

```
dsquery user /?
```

To locate one or more domain user accounts using the Find function within the Active Directory Users and Computers MMC snap-in, you should perform the following steps:

1. Select Start, Administrative Tools, Active Directory Users and Computers.

2. Navigate to the desired container, right-click to select the target container, and select Find from the drop-down menu.

3. Users, groups, and computers can be searched using Name or Description criteria. More advanced searches can be performed that allow for the location of accounts with a matching attribute value or values, or those with integrated service settings, such as Microsoft's Exchange Server. The use of the asterisk (*) defines a wildcard search.

4. After specifying the appropriate criteria, click the Find Now button to enact the search.

5. The resulting matched items will be displayed, as shown in Figure 2.12. These accounts can then be modified by right-clicking on them and selecting the options from the drop-down menu as if viewed in the full interface.

Windows Server 2003 adds a new feature to the Active Directory Users and Computers MMC snap-in in which saved queries can be stored for later reuse. This new folder tops the MMC's listing of containers, and new queries can be added by the following steps:

1. Select Start, Administrative Tools, Active Directory Users and Computers.

2. Navigate to the Saved Queries folder, right-click on the container, and select New, Query from the options provided.

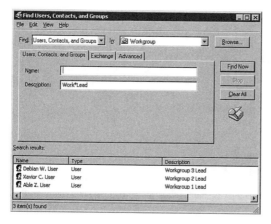

Figure 2.12   The results of a Find query on the Workgroup OU and its subordinate OUs with a Description field matching the wildcard specification **Work*Lead**.

3. You must provide a unique name for the new query, along with an optional description if desired. You can then navigate to the root container for the query, select whether the query will include subcontainers within the root container, and click the Define Query button.

4. You can then select the type of records to be included in the new query from the options provided:

  ➤ Users, Contacts, and Groups

  ➤ Computers

  ➤ Printers

  ➤ Shared Folders

  ➤ Organizational Units

  ➤ Custom Search

  ➤ Exchange Recipients (if Exchange is installed)

  ➤ Remote Installation Servers

  ➤ Common Queries

  ➤ Remote Installation Clients

5. After selecting the type of records, you'll be presented with a tabbed dialog box with the available search options for the selected type.

6. After selecting the desired search criteria, click the OK button to return to the New Query interface. (If you edit an existing query later, the same interface is used, as shown in Figure 2.13.)

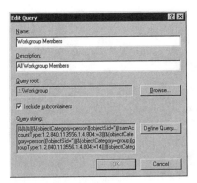

Figure 2.13   A saved query specifying criteria for accounts in the Workgroup OU container and all subcontainers.

7. Click the OK button to save the new query. To access the query on later occasions, all you have to do is highlight the target query and the results of the search will be displayed for access.

Managing Computer Objects

Computer account objects are managed using many of the same methods as for user account objects. Command-line utilities such as dsmod and dsquery have computer-specific uses, and the now-familiar Active Directory Users and Computers MMC snap-in carries all the same functionality for the creation and manipulation of computer objects.

One way to add a new computer to the directory is to select the Join This Computer to a Domain option during setup. This process adds the computer account to the default Computers container, where it can then be moved to the desired location. If an account is precreated within the directory, the newly joined computer will join in its destination container.

To precreate a new computer account using the Active Directory Users and Computers MMC snap-in, perform the following steps:

1. Select Start, Administrative Tools, Active Directory Users and Computers.

2. Navigate to the desired target container, right-click, and select New, Computer from the options provided.

3. You're presented with the New Object - Computer dialog box where a computer name can be entered, causing a pre-Windows 2000 computer name to be automatically generated. You also have the ability to select the user or group that will be allowed to join a computer with the

newly created name. Additional options can be selected to assign the computer as a pre–Windows 2000 computer or as a backup domain controller.

4. After clicking Next, you select whether the computer is a managed system with a pre-existing GUID that can then be entered in the dialog box.

5. After clicking Next and then Finish, the new account is created.

6. After creation, right-click on the account and select Properties to open its properties dialog box for additional configuration.

As with user accounts, you can enable and disable computer accounts to prevent users from logging in on the specified system. By right-clicking on a system and selecting Manage, you can open the Computer Management utility with a focus directed at the computer to be managed.

Organizing Objects

In large organizations, it isn't reasonable to leave all account objects in their default container locations. Applying privileges and permissions is also time-consuming when performed on each account individually. Fortunately, Windows Server 2003 manages both problems through structured containers (called *organizational units* [OU]s) and groups (through which member accounts inherit access rights and restrictions). Organizational unit membership can be used to assign GPO settings, whereas group membership is used to convey access rights or restrictions over distributed resources.

Using Organizational Units

The grouping of accounts into a structured hierarchy of containers and subcontainers (called organization units) makes it easier to manage very large numbers of account objects collected into logical groupings. By organizing the accounts along organizational lines, administrative control can be easily delegated in a restrictive manner, with administrators over a container sharing control over all subcontainers therein. A structured OU design allows local administrators to have access rights over only those elements under their control, which means that even a large organization could potentially use a single domain while still allowing for distributed administrative control.

It is possible to create a new OU using `dsadd.exe` as well as through the use of the Active Directory Users and Computers MMC snap-in. To create a new OU using the Active Directory Users and Computers MMC snap-in, perform the following steps:

1. Select Start, Administrative Tools, Active Directory Users and Computers.

2. Navigate to the desired OU parent container or the domain container and select New, Organizational Unit from the options provided. OUs cannot be created in the default Computers and Users containers, so the option is not provided when attempted there.

3. You are prompted to enter the name for the new OU and then to click OK to create the new OU.

4. After creation, select one or more OUs and right-click to access the Properties option in the drop-down menu. Doing so allows modification to the description and location information for the OU, along with the ability to configure security, management, COM+ partition, and Group Policy settings that apply to the objects within the OU and its subcontainers.

OUs can be placed within other OUs to create a structured container space in which accounts can be properly grouped along business or administrative lines. Objects can exist only within a single OU, and their LDAP relative distinguished name is derived from this location.

By configuring the Security settings, you can control what administrative rights are granted over objects within the OU, as shown in Figure 2.14.

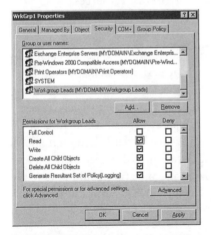

Figure 2.14   Security settings for the Workgroup Leads group over the WrkGrp1 organizational unit.

Using Groups

Unlike OUs, which are used to group objects into a structured set of containers where each object can be located in only a single OU, groups provide access rights and restrictions for member accounts and members of member groups. Through inheritance, member accounts can be granted additional privileges and access rights to distributed resources, or can be restricted from accessing the same. We discuss specific permissions in greater detail in Chapter 7, "Maintaining Network Security."

An account can be a member of multiple groups, each providing its own set of access rights and restrictions, with the final set of permissions and rights for the account being the aggregate of all inherited settings. Obviously, planning is key to providing access based on role or organizational needs while avoiding conflicts that might provide greater access than is desired or restrict necessary access.

The following two forms of groups are present in Windows 2000 and later forms of Active Directory:

➤ **Distribution**—These groups are used for email distribution lists when an integrated electronic mail service such as Exchange is present. They cannot be used to assign users rights and permissions.

➤ **Security**—Security groups are used to assign user rights (which define what members can do within the group's assigned scope) and permissions (which are used to access resources within the domain or forest). Security groups can also be used to restrict as well as grant permissions.

Groups are also assigned one of three possible scopes, which limit the extent to which rights are assigned by group membership:

➤ **Universal**—These groups are used to grant access to resources that span multiple domains. They are not available in Windows 2000 trees in Mixed mode, only in Windows 2000 Native mode and Windows 2003 directory implementations. Universal groups can include accounts, Global groups, and other Universal groups from any domain in the forest. Members of these groups should not change often because all changes will be replicated throughout the forest. Universal groups can be used to assign permissions over resources located in any domain.

➤ **Global**—These groups are used to manage accounts that require regular changes and upkeep. In Windows 2000 Mixed mode, Global groups can contain only accounts from the same domain. In Windows 2000 Native mode and Windows 2003 directories, they can contain accounts and other Global groups from the same domain. Global groups can be used to assign permissions over resources location in any domain.

➤ **Domain Local**—Domain Local groups are used to assign permissions over resources located only in their own domain. They can contain accounts, Global, and Universal groups from any domain, as well as other Domain Local groups from their own domain. Member servers and standalone servers also have Local groups, which are limited to providing access to resources on the local system and which cannot be added to domain and greater scoped groups.

A number of groups are created by default in the Built-In and Users containers. Groups created by default in the Built-In container include

➤ **Account Operators**—Members can create, modify, and delete computer and user accounts, with the exception of administrators, domain admins, and domain controllers.

➤ **Administrators**—Members have full control over the domain. The Administrator account, Domain Admins, and Enterprise Admins are members by default.

➤ **Backup Operators**—Members can log in to, shut down, and back up the files from any system in the domain, including domain controllers.

➤ **Guests**—Members are not granted rights by default. The Guest account and Domain Guests group are members by default.

➤ **Incoming Forest Trust Builders**—This group is present only in the root domain of a forest. Members can create a one-way incoming trust to another forest to provide access to resources in the other forest.

➤ **Network Configuration Operators**—Members can make changes to TCP/IP settings on any system in the domain, including domain controllers.

➤ **Performance Monitor Users**—Members can monitor performance counters locally and remotely on any computer in the domain, including domain controllers.

➤ **Performance Log Users**—Members can manage performance logs, counters, and alerts on any computer in the domain, including domain controllers.

➤ **Pre–Windows 2000 Compatible Access**—Members have Read access over all accounts and groups in the domain. The Everyone special identity is a member of this group by default.

➤ **Print Operators**—Members can create, delete, share, and manage printers and print queues, as well as log on and shut down any computer in the domain, including domain controllers.

➤ **Remote Desktop Users**—Members can remotely log onto any computer in the domain, including domain controllers.

➤ **Replicator**—This group is used by domain and file replication services and should not be assigned any new members.

➤ **Server Operators**—Members can log on to, shut down, and manage the local resources and services on any server computer in the domain, including domain controllers.

➤ **Users**—The default group to which domain users, authenticated users, and the Interactive special identity are assigned. Members can make use of domain resources.

Default groups in the Users container include the following:

➤ **Cert Publishers**—Members can publish security certificates for accounts.

➤ **DnsAdmins**—Present only if DNS is installed. Members can administer the DNS service.

➤ **DnsUpdateProxy**—Present only if DNS is installed. Members can perform dynamic DNS updates for other accounts.

➤ **Domain Admins**—Members have full rights over all resources in the domain and are members of the Administrators group on each computer in the domain. The Administrator account is a member of this group by default.

➤ **Domain Computers**—Automatically includes all computers joined to a domain and should not be assigned any new members manually.

➤ **Domain Controllers**—Automatically includes all domain controller computers joined to a domain and should not be assigned any new members manually.

➤ **Domain Guests**—Members have no rights assigned by default.

➤ **Domain Users**—Automatically includes all user accounts in a domain and should not be assigned any new members manually.

➤ **Enterprise Admins**—This group is present only in the root domain of a forest. Members have full control over all domains in a forest and inherit membership in the Administrators group on all domain controllers. The root domain's Administrator account is a member by default.

➤ **Group Policy Creator Owner**—Members of this group can create, delete, and modify Group Policy settings within the domain. The Administrator account is a member by default.

➤ **IIS_WPG**—Present only if IIS is installed. Used by the worker processes serving namespaces within IIS 6.0.

➤ **RAS and IAS Servers**—Member servers can access the dial-up and remote access properties on user account objects.

➤ **Schema Admins**—This group is present only in the root domain of a forest. Members can modify the Active Directory schema for a forest. The root domain's Administrator account is a member by default.

The following local groups might also be present:

➤ **DHCP Administrators**—Present only if the DHCP Server service is installed. Members can administer the DHCP service and its configuration.

➤ **DHCP Users**—Present only if the DHCP Server service is installed. Members can view the DHCP service settings and its configuration.

➤ **HelpServicesGroup**—Members can be granted any desired standard rights and permissions granted to support staff accounts and the Remote Assistance group.

➤ **Power Users**—Members of this group can fully administer local resources and accounts, except for members of the Adminstrators group. Power users cannot take ownership or backup files by default.

➤ **WINS Users**—Present only if the WINS service is installed. Members are able to view WINS database information.

Windows 2000 and later operating system variants include several special identities that can be used like groups to grant or deny access rights and permissions, though their membership cannot be changed manually. They are as follows:

➤ **Anonymous Logon**—Members automatically include anyone who accesses resources without using an authenticated logon and password.

➤ **Authenticated Users**—Members automatically include anyone who accesses resources through a logon process.

➤ **Batch**—Members automatically include all processes and accounts that access resources through a batch job.

- ➤ **Creator Group**—Members are inherited by sharing group membership with the account that created the resource.

- ➤ **Creator Owner**—The account that created a particular resource.

- ➤ **Dial-Up**—Members automatically include anyone who accesses resources through a dial-up connection.

- ➤ **Enterprise Domain Controllers**—Members automatically include any domain controller computers with enterprise-wide roles.

- ➤ **Everyone**—Members automatically include all accounts that log on to the network, even if from another domain.

- ➤ **Interactive**—Members automatically include any users logged in to a computer and accessing a particular local resource.

- ➤ **Network**—Members automatically include any users accessing a particular resource over the network.

- ➤ **Proxy**—Members automatically include any users accessing a particular resource through a proxy agent or delegate.

- ➤ **Restricted**—Members automatically include users with restricted access rights (non–power users on member servers, for example).

- ➤ **Self**—An object referencing itself.

- ➤ **Service**—A service referencing itself.

- ➤ **System**—The operating system referencing itself.

- ➤ **Terminal Server Users**—Members automatically include all users logging in through Terminal Services connections.

Because membership in some groups can be used to leverage additional administrative rights, it's important to restrict membership in the Account Operators, Administrators, Backup Operators, Domain Admins, Enterprise Admins, Power Users, Print Operators, and Server Operators groups.

To create a new group using the Active Directory Users and Computers MMC snap-in, perform the following steps:

1. Select Start, Administrative Tools, Active Directory Users and Computers.

2. Navigate to the desired target container, right-click and select New, Group from the drop-down options.

3. You are prompted to enter a name for the new group, which will automatically generate a pre–Windows 2000 name for the group as well. You will be provided with the options for the group scope and group type, as shown in Figure 2.15.

Figure 2.15   New Object - Group dialog box creating the 'My New Group' Global Security group.

4. After clicking the Next button, you're presented with the option to perform other configuration tasks for integrated services, such as Exchange email aliasing. After all such tasks, click Finish to create the new group, which will have no members by default.

5. After creation, right-clicking on a group and selecting its Properties allows manipulation of its members as well as its own membership in other groups using the Member Of tab.

To view and manipulate the membership of a particular user or computer account, you can use the Member Of tab within the properties of the account in the Active Directory Users and Computers MMC snap-in. In addition, the dsget.exe utility can be used to view the current membership of an object.

The syntax of the **dsget.exe** utility used for review of the group membership of user accounts is provided in the Microsoft help file:

```
dsget user UserDN ... [-dn] [-samid] [-sid] [-upn] [-fn] [-mi]
[-ln] [-display] [-empid] [-desc] [-office] [-tel] [-email]
[-hometel] [-pager] [-mobile] [-fax] [-iptel] [-webpg] [-title]
[-dept] [-company] [-mgr] [-hmdir] [-hmdrv] [-profile] [-loscr]
[-mustchpwd] [-canchpwd] [-pwdneverexpires] [-disabled]
[-acctexpires] [-reversiblepwd]
[{-uc ¦ -uco ¦ -uci}] [-part PartitionDN [-qlimit] [-qused]]

dsget user UserDN [-memberof] [-expand] [{-uc ¦ -uco ¦ -uci}]
```

To see a listing of all the parameters and their meanings, type the following at the command-line shell prompt:
```
dsget user /?
```

Groups can be used to assign a great many permissions and access rights throughout an Active Directory forest. You should be familiar with the user account Logon rights for Windows Server 2003:

➤ **Access This Computer from the Network**—Grants access to resources located on the system over the network.

➤ **Allow Logon Locally**—Grants access to log on through the local console.

➤ **Allow Logon Through Terminal Services**—Grants access to establish Terminal Service sessions.

➤ **Log On as a Batch Job**—Grants access to log on through batch jobs or scripts.

➤ **Log On as a Service**—Grants access to log on as a service or start up a service.

➤ **Deny Access to the Computer from the Network**—Specifies which accounts and groups cannot access resources over the network.

➤ **Deny Logon as Batch Job**—Restricts logon through batch jobs or scripts.

➤ **Deny Logon As Service**—Restricts service logon rights.

➤ **Deny Logon Locally**—Specifies which accounts and groups cannot log on through the local console.

➤ **Deny Logon Through Terminal Services**—Specifies which accounts and groups cannot establish Terminal Service sessions.

You should also be at least somewhat familiar with the available privileges that can be granted in Windows Server 2003:

➤ Act as part of the operating system

➤ Add workstations to a domain

➤ Adjust memory quotas for a process

➤ Back up files and directories

➤ Bypass traverse checking

➤ Change the system time

➤ Create a pagefile

➤ Create a token object

➤ Create permanent shared objects

➤ Debug programs

➤ Enable computer and user accounts to be trusted for delegation

➤ Force shutdown from a remote system

➤ Generate security audits

➤ Impersonate a client after authentication

➤ Increase scheduling priority

➤ Load and unload device drivers

➤ Lock pages in memory

➤ Manage auditing and security log

➤ Modify firmware environment values

➤ Profile a single process

➤ Profile system performance

➤ Remove computer from docking station

➤ Replace a process level token

➤ Restore files and directories

➤ Shut down the system

➤ Synchronize directory service data

➤ Take ownership of files or other objects

Exam Prep Questions

Question 1

You are the network administrator for BigCorp (**www.bigcorp.com**). After a reorganization following the acquisition of SmallCorp, you need to modify the location details of two public Web servers that have been relocated from the **smallcorp.com** Active Directory namespace to the **bigcorp.com** namespace. What action should you take to comply with this requirement?

○ A. Utilize the Active Directory Domains and Trusts MMC snap-in

○ B. Utilize the Active Directory Migration Tool MMC snap-in

○ C. Utilize the Active Directory Sites and Services MMC snap-in

○ D. Utilize the Active Directory Users and Computers MMC snap-in

Answer D is correct. The Active Directory Users and Computers MMC snap-in is used to configure various attribute values for both computer and user accounts, which would include the two already-migrated Web servers. The Location tab provides access to the location-specific information that you'll need to configure to meet the stated requirement.

Answer A is incorrect because the Active Directory Domains and Trusts MMC snap-in is used to manage domain-level description and trust relationships with other domains. Answer B is incorrect because the Active Directory Migration Tool (ADMT) is used to migrate accounts between domains, which has already been accomplished within this scenario. Answer C is also incorrect because the Active Directory Sites and Services MMC snap-in is used to configure site structure and replication connections to optimize directory replication.

Question 2

> You have three organizational units (Group1, Group2, and Group3) containing all the computer and user accounts for the three active program groups in the Marketing department. Marketing group #3 has completed its project and its members are being reassigned to group #1. To relocate the accounts, you have selected the Active Directory Users and Computers MMC snap-in as the best utility. What is the easiest way to relocate the accounts in the Group3 OU to Group1?
>
> O A. Select each of the accounts, right-click, select Move from the options provided, and then select the target organizational unit.
>
> O B. Select the Group1 Organization Unit, right-click, and open its properties. Navigate to the Members tab and select the accounts to be made members.
>
> O C. Select the accounts and drag them into the new organizational unit container.
>
> O D. Select the accounts, right-click to open their properties, select the Members Of tab, and select the target organizational unit.

Answer C is correct. One of the additions to the functionality of the Active Directory Users and Computers MMC snap-in is the ability to drag-and-drop accounts and containers to perform rapid reorganization of a domain's organizational structure. This functionality provides the easiest way to move the accounts present in one organizational unit to another.

Answer A is incorrect because although the option to move each account individually has been maintained from the Windows 2000 version of the Active Directory Users and Computers MMC snap-in, this isn't the most efficient way to move multiple accounts to a new location. Answers B and D are incorrect because the Members and Member Of selections are used to manage group membership, rather than organizational unit structure. Although the presented organizational units are named GroupX, it is important to remember the difference.

Question 3

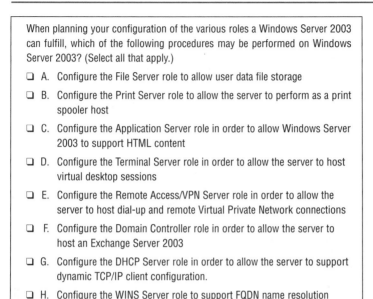

When planning your configuration of the various roles a Windows Server 2003 can fulfill, which of the following procedures may be performed on Windows Server 2003? (Select all that apply.)

- ❑ A. Configure the File Server role to allow user data file storage
- ❑ B. Configure the Print Server role to allow the server to perform as a print spooler host
- ❑ C. Configure the Application Server role in order to allow Windows Server 2003 to support HTML content
- ❑ D. Configure the Terminal Server role in order to allow the server to host virtual desktop sessions
- ❑ E. Configure the Remote Access/VPN Server role in order to allow the server to host dial-up and remote Virtual Private Network connections
- ❑ F. Configure the Domain Controller role in order to allow the server to host an Exchange Server 2003
- ❑ G. Configure the DHCP Server role in order to allow the server to support dynamic TCP/IP client configuration.
- ❑ H. Configure the WINS Server role to support FQDN name resolution

Answers A, B, D, E, and G are correct. A Windows Server 2003 can be configured for all of these roles, as well as other roles, such as Mail Server (POP3/SMTP), DNS Server, and Streaming Media Server. Some roles, such as Terminal Server, are unavailable in the Web Server version of Windows Server 2003, but the preceding list is applicable to the Enterprise Edition of Windows Server 2003 that is available for evaluation purposes and you should be familiar with each.

Answer C is incorrect because the Application Server role is provided to allow a server to host network applications, and is not directly related to the IIS 6.0 service required for HTML hosting. Answer F is incorrect because the Domain Controller role is required for logon authentication, script and GPO setting management, and replication of the AD database. Answer H is incorrect because the WINS Server role is used to provide support for NetBIOS naming, rather than fully qualified domain name (FQDN) resolution.

Question 4

You're the network administrator for NewCorp and are responsible for the creation of several hundred new accounts. You have the information for the new accounts stored in a file and want to use one of the command-line utilities provided with Windows Server 2003 to accomplish the requirement. Which option can be used for this purpose? (Choose two.)

❑ A. Utilize the **csvde** command-line utility to create the new accounts from the source file

❑ B. Utilize the **dsget** command-line utility to create the new accounts from the source file

❑ C. Utilize the **dsrm** command-line utility to create the new accounts from the source file

❑ D. Utilize the **mkacct** command-line utility to create the new accounts from the source file

❑ E. Utilize the **ldifde** command-line utility to create the new accounts from the source file

Answers A and E are correct. Both the csvde and ldifde command-line utilities can be used to import account details from an external file for mass creation of new accounts.

Answer B is incorrect because the dsget utility is used to display selected attributes of a pre-existing object within the directory and is not used to create a new account object. Answer C is also incorrect because the dsrm command-line utility is used to delete an existing object rather than to create one. Answer D is incorrect because there is not an mkacct utility provided.

Question 5

You're the network administrator for SmallCorp and are responsible for documentation of the Active Directory domain used by SmallCorp for its information technology needs. As a part of this documentation, you need to provide a comma-separated (**.csv**) file that details the attributes for Active Directory accounts. Which option should be performed for this purpose?

- ○ A. Utilize the **csvde** command-line utility to produce the comma-separated file
- ○ B. Utilize the **dsget** command-line utility to produce the comma-separated file
- ○ C. Utilize the **dsmod** command-line utility to produce the comma-separated file
- ○ D. Utilize the **dsquery** command-line utility to produce the comma-separated file
- ○ E. Utilize the **ldifde** command-line utility to produce the comma-separated file

Answer A is correct. The csvde command-line utility is used to import and export the attributes of Active Directory objects using a comma-separated (.csv) file type.

Answer B is incorrect because the dsget utility is used to display selected attributes of a pre-existing object within the directory and is not used for import or export of the attributes of Active Directory objects using .csv files. Answer C is incorrect because the dsmod utility is used to modify the attributes of an existing object. Answer D is incorrect because the dsquery utility is used to list active directory objects that meet a specified set of criteria. Answer E is incorrect because the ldifde utility is not used in conjunction with .csv files, but rather with its own .ldf format.

Question 6

You have been tasked with the creation of a new script that will process a comma-separated file to create user accounts on a server named MyServer using the Active Directory connector. Which of the following parameters would be used to specify the type of connection?

- ○ A. **-b**
- ○ B. **-f**
- ○ C. **-s**
- ○ D. **-t**
- ○ E. **/?**

Answer D is correct. The -t parameter is used to specify the connection port (in this case, port 3268 for the Active Directory connection specified). Answer A is incorrect because the -b parameter is used to specify the username, domain, and password to be used for authentication on the target server. Answer B is incorrect because the -f parameter is used to specify the source .csv file that will be used. Answer C is incorrect because the -s parameter is used to specify the name of the target server. Finally, answer E is incorrect because the /? switch is used to query the command's help file for its available parameters.

Question 7

You are the network administrator for NewCorp and are responsible for deleting usernames from in-place systems using a scripted solution. Which of the following solutions should be used to fulfill this requirement?

- ○ A. Utilize the **adprep** utility to delete the target user accounts
- ○ B. Utilize the **bootcfg** utility to delete the target user accounts
- ○ C. Utilize the **cmdkey** utility to delete the target user accounts
- ○ D. Utilize the **diskpart** utility to delete the target user accounts
- ○ E. Utilize the **gpresult** utility to delete the target user accounts

Answer C is correct. The cmdkey utility can be used to create, review, or delete stored usernames and passwords.

Answer A is incorrect because the adprep utility is used to prepare an in-place Windows 2000 domain for upgrade to Windows Server 2003. Answer B is incorrect because the bootcfg utility is used to manipulate the boot.ini file. Answer D is incorrect because the diskpart utility is used to manage disk partitions rather than user accounts. Answer E is incorrect because the gpresult utility is used to review the Resultant Set of Policy (RSoP) for a selected security principal rather than manipulating or deleting the account itself.

Question 8

You've just been hired as the administrator for OldCorp, which has many servers configured for various tasks. Because the previous administrator failed to document his configuration details, you need to generate documentation detailing the services currently running on all the servers. Because they are so numerous, you decide to script this effort. Which option should be used for this purpose?

○ A. Use the **choice** command-line utility to generate the required documentation

○ B. Use the **forfiles** command-line utility to generate the required documentation

○ C. Use the **prncnfg** command-line utility to generate the required documentation

○ D. Use the **sc** command-line utility to generate the required documentation

○ E. Use the **setx** command-line utility to generate the required documentation

Answer D is correct. The sc utility is used to review and configure services. Answer A is incorrect because the choice tool is used to prompt a user to select from a listing of choices before proceeding through a script. Answer B is incorrect because the forfiles utility is used to specify files that will be used in batch processing. Answer C is incorrect because the prncnfg utility is used to review and configure printer object settings. Answer E is also incorrect because the setx utility is used to set the various environment variables.

Question 9

You've been tasked with creating a script that can stop and restart the IIS services (FTP and Web) each night. Which two options can be used for this purpose?

❑ A. Utilize the **IISCnfg** command-line utility to restart both IIS services

❑ B. Utilize the **IISFtp** command-line utility to restart the FTP service

❑ C. Utilize the **IISFtpdr** command-line utility to restart the FTP service

❑ D. Utilize the **IISVdir** command-line utility to restart the Web service

❑ E. Utilize the **IISWeb** command-line utility to restart the Web service

Answers B and E are correct. The IISFtp and IISWeb utilities can be used to start, stop, pause, resume, review, create, and delete the FTP or Web sites supported by Microsoft's IIS service.

Answer A is incorrect because the iisCnfg utility is used to import and export IIS configuration details. Answers C and D are incorrect because the iisFtpdr utility is used to create or delete FTP site virtual directories, and the iisVdir utility is used for the same regarding Web site virtual directories.

Question 10

You want to open a command-line prompt for testing a new script that takes advantage of the newer features of Microsoft Windows Server 2003, what must you do from the logon default desktop?

○ A. Select Start, Run, type **cmd**, and press Enter

○ B. Select Start, Run, type **cmdln**, and press Enter

○ C. Select Start, Run, type **command**, and press Enter

○ D. Select Start, Run, type **comln**, and press Enter

○ E. Select Start, Run, type **prompt**, and press Enter

Answer A is correct. The proper command to open a 32-bit command-line prompt is cmd. Answers B, D, and E are incorrect because there is no executable command with the default name of cmdln, comln, or prompt. Answer C is incorrect because the invocation of command.com opens a 16-bit command-line interpreter used for legacy command invocation.

Need to Know More?

 70-292 Training Guide: Managing and Maintaining a Microsoft Windows Server 2003 Environment for an MCSA Certified on Windows 2000. Indianapolis, IN: Que Certification, 2003.

 Microsoft Windows Server 2003 Administrator's Pocket Consultant. Redmond, WA: Microsoft Press, 2003.

 Introducing Microsoft Windows Server 2003. Redmond, WA: Microsoft Press, 2003.

 Microsoft Windows Server 2003 Web site: `http://www.microsoft.com/windowsserver2003/default.mspx`

 Microsoft Server 2003 MSDN Web site: `http://msdn.microsoft.com/library/default.asp?url=/nhp/default.asp?contentid=28001691`

3

Managing Access to Resources

Terms you'll need to understand:

✓ Shares
✓ Share permissions
✓ NTFS permissions
✓ GPMC
✓ RSoP
✓ **Gpupdate**
✓ Remote Desktop
✓ Terminal Server

Techniques you'll need to master:

✓ Determining effective permissions combining both share and NT File System (NTFS) permissions
✓ Knowing how to back up, restore, import, and copy GPO settings using the GPMC
✓ Understanding how to configure a server for Remote Access using the Remote Desktop for Administration and Terminal Server service

r accounts have been created, available networked resources can be configured to allow or deny access for each user based on permissions assignment and group policy settings. Remote users can also access application resources through Microsoft's Terminal Services. This chapter provides a brief review of the use of NTFS and share permissions, and reviews the Windows Server 2003 implementations of group policy and terminal services access control.

Creating Shares and Granting Permissions

Access to remote resources within the Windows Server 2003 environment has many qualities in common with the Windows 2000 Server environment, with new features and functionality added to improve utility, as illustrated in Figure 3.1.

Figure 3.1 An example of the new Remote Desktops MMC snap-in that provides multi-console functionality similar to the earlier Terminal Services client of Windows 2000.

Creating Shares

Creating network folder shares remains similar to the implementation in Windows Server 2000, with all available shares listed within the Shares subfolder of the Shared Folders node presented in the Computer Management MMC snap-in, as shown in Figure 3.2.

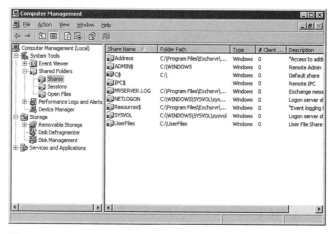

Figure 3.2   The Computer Management MMC snap-in showing file shares present on a Windows Server 2003 running Microsoft Exchange.

Creating a New Share Using the Computer Management MMC Snap-in

New file shares can be created within the Computer Management MMC snap-in by performing the following steps:

1. Open the Computer Management MMC snap-in located within the Administrative Tools folder.

2. Navigate to the Shared Folders node, highlighting the Shares subfolder if you want to view the existing shares.

3. Right-click on the Shares folder and select New Share from the options provided. Click Next.

4. Provide the local Folder Path that will be shared as the newly created share. By clicking the Browse button, you can create a new folder if the desired target does not yet exist. Click Next.

5. Provide a share name and optional description, and configure the offline file settings for this share, which will be discussed later in this chapter. Click Next.

6. Select the permissions to be granted by default to the share. The options available are as follows:

   ➤ All users have read-only access.

   ➤ Administrators have full access; other users have read-only access.

> Administrators have full access; other users have read and write access.

> User custom share and folder permissions—this allows selection of detailed allow and grant permissions.

7. After clicking Next, you'll be notified of the success of the sharing action and provided the option to close the Share a Folder Wizard or to run the wizard again to share another folder.

Creating a New Share Using Windows Explorer

New file shares can also be created within the Windows Explorer interface by the following procedure:

1. Open Windows Explorer by double-clicking on the My Computer icon, and then navigating to the desired target folder.

2. Right-click on the target folder to be shared and select Sharing and Security from the drop-down list of options. This opens the Properties dialog box for the selected folder with its focus set to the Sharing tab.

3. You'll be prompted to provide a share name, an optional description, and the number of users who can connect to the share at one time. By clicking the Permissions button, you can configure the Share Permissions for the newly created share, as shown in Figure 3.3.

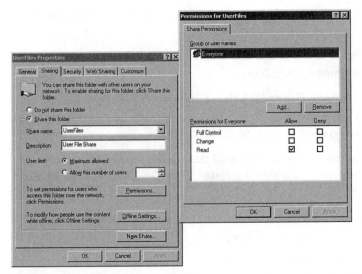

Figure 3.3 The Sharing and Share Permissions dialog boxes for a newly created share named UserFiles.

4. Click Apply to create the new share or click the Security tab, where you configure the NTFS permissions for the shared folder as shown in Figure 3.4.

Figure 3.4   The Security tab for a newly created share whose target is the UserFiles folder.

5. Click the Advanced button to open the Advanced Security Settings dialog box for the folder, which is the standard dialog box used for advanced NTFS files and folder permissions, as shown in Figure 3.5. Here, you can select whether the parent container object will be propagated to the child object.

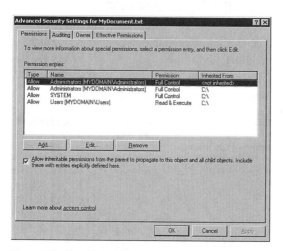

Figure 3.5   The Advanced Security Settings dialog box for the **MyDocument.txt** file.

6. You can evaluate the effective permissions based on the overall inherited and directly applied permissions by selecting the Effective Permissions tab, as shown in Figure 3.6.

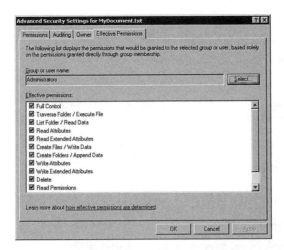

Figure 3.6 The Effective Permissions tab within the Advanced Security Settings dialog box.

7. After all permissions have been configured, click the Apply button to apply the new settings. When fully configured, click OK to close the Permissions dialog box.

Creating a New Share Using the Command Line

New file shares can also be created within the command line using the `net share` command, which is one of the many available `net` services commands present within Windows Server 2003.

The syntax of the **net share** command is provided in the Microsoft help file:

```
net share [ShareName]
net share [ShareName=Drive:Path [{/users:Number | /unlimited}]
[/remark:"Text"] [/cache: {manual | automatic | no}]]
net share [ShareName [{/users:Number | unlimited}]
[/remark:"Text"] [/cache: {manual | automatic | no}]]
net share [{ShareName | Drive:Path} /delete]
```

To see a listing of all the parameters and their meanings, type the following at the command line:

```
net share /?
```

Table 3.1 lists a few of the more common commands you should be familiar with.

Table 3.1	Some Common net Services Commands in Windows Server 2003
Command	**Description**
net accounts	Used to modify password and logon settings for all accounts
net config	Displays or modifies the settings of available configurable services
net file	Displays a listing of shared files and can close open files
net help	Displays a listing of network commands
net send	Sends a message to other users or computers
net session	Displays a listing of current network sessions
net share	Used to display, create, and modify file shares
net start	Used to display a listing of running services or to start an individual service
net stop	Used to stop a running service
net use	Used to connect or disconnect from a shared resource

Shares created through the use of the **net share** command are created with the Everyone group having Read permissions.

Creating a New Share Using the Server Management Wizard and File Server Management MMC Snap-in

New file shares can also be created within the Server Management Wizard if the File Server role has been configured for the computer as well as the File Server Management MMC snap-in, which is also accessible from within the Server Management Wizard, as shown in Figure 3.7.

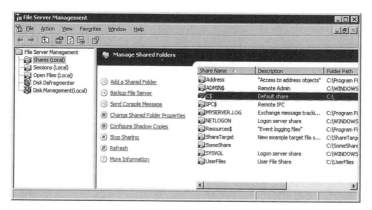

Figure 3.7   The File Server Management MMC snap-in showing existing shares.

Creating file shares using the Server Management Wizard and File Server Management MMC snap-in invokes the same Share a Folder Wizard invoked from the Computer Management and Windows Explorer utilities.

Offline Settings for Shared Resources

Shares configured for offline storage are copied into a local cache so that users can continue utilizing, editing, and otherwise manipulating files even while disconnected from the network. This is an advantage to mobile users, whose files are copied to the offline cache when they're in the office and then later used while disconnected. The files are later synchronized with their original counterparts on the next connection to the network.

Configuring the offline settings for a particular share can be accomplished by clicking the Offline Settings button on the Sharing tab of the share's properties page, as was shown in Figure 3.3. The share can be configured so that files and programs from the share will not be available offline, so that only those specified by the user will be available offline, or so that all files and folders the user opens from the share will be cached for offline access. The last option can be used to select to optimize for performance, which caches program executables locally, improving shared application performance over slow networks.

This configuration can also be accomplished using the net share command-line utility with the /cache parameter in the following format:

```
net share <sharename> /cache:<manual/documents/programs/none>
```

Granting Permissions

The final permissions that are granted when accessing shared resources are determined based on the NTFS permissions assigned to a resource or inherited by an account through its group membership, in addition to the share permissions configured for a particular share.

 It's possible to have different access rights over the same file or folder when accessed through separate shares. Although the NTFS permissions over the file (for example: **C:\USER\New\myfile.txt**) remain the same, the share permissions for one share (for example: UserFiles, mapped to **C:\USER**) can be very different from those granted through another (for example: NewFiles, mapped to **C:\USER\New**).

Assigning Share-Level Permissions

Share-level permissions are more limited than NTFS permissions because they define only the level of shared folder access that is granted or denied when accessing resources through the share. The available share permissions are as follows:

➤ Full Control—Allows both Read and Change permissions, in addition to the ability to later change the Permissions on the share.

➤ Change—Allows the ability to create, modify, and delete resources within the share.

➤ Read—Allows the ability to view filenames and folder names within the share, as well as the ability to view and execute files located within the shared folder.

It is not possible to grant Change permission over a share without also granting the Read permission.

NTFS Permissions

Files and folders can be provided with detailed assignments of access rights and restrictions through the use of NT File System (NTFS) permissions, as was shown in Figure 3.4. These permissions can be assigned directly to a particular file or folder, or inherited from its parent container. The effective permissions combining both directly assigned and inherited permissions (with regard to a particular user or group) can also be viewed as shown earlier in Figure 3.6.

NTFS permissions are available only when a volume or partition has been formatted using NTFS. FAT32-formatted volumes have only folder (share-level) permission configuration.

When planning for file access control, it's important to include NTFS permission assignment and restrictions. Users accessing local files will only be restricted by the NTFS permissions, whereas users accessing shared resources will encounter a combination of both share and NTFS permissions. Table 3.2 details the basic NTFS permissions available.

Table 3.2	Basic NTFS Permissions
Permission	**Description**
Full Control	Includes all other NTFS permissions configured, as well as the ability to take ownership of files or other containers within the target location.
Modify	Allows the creation, modification, and deletion of files and folders.
Read & Execute	Includes the rights of the Read permission in addition to the ability to traverse a folder and execute a file.
Read	Allows the ability to read file and folder attributes, list folder contents, view files, and synchronize files access.
Write	Includes the rights of the Read permission in addition to the ability to create new files and folders, modify existing files, and write file and folder attributes.
Special Permissions	This option is available only when advanced permission settings have been configured. Allows control over the application of Advanced permission settings.

The Advanced NTFS permissions available in Windows Server 2003 include the following:

➤ Traverse Folder/Execute File

➤ List Folder/Read Data

➤ Read Attributes

➤ Read Extended Attributes

➤ Create Files/Write Data

➤ Create Folders/Append Data

➤ Write Attributes

➤ Write Extended Attributes

➤ Delete Subfolders and Files

➤ Delete

➤ Read Permissions

➤ Change Permissions

➤ Take Ownership

➤ Synchronize

Calculating Final Permissions

To plan the final set of permissions that result from assigned and inherited permissions, the NTFS and share permissions should be calculated using the least restrictive set of permissions for each. Then the aggregate of the resulting NTFS and share permissions is determined by using the most restrictive combination of the aggregate NTFS and share permissions. In all cases, an assignment of a Deny setting overrides all assignments of Allow settings. The process is as follows:

1. Determine the least restrictive combination of NTFS permissions over the resource based on direct assignment and inheritance. Any permission configured as Deny will be denied, even if set to Allow elsewhere.

2. Determine the least restrictive combination of share permissions over the resource based on direct assignment and inheritance. Any permission configured as Deny will be denied, even if set to Allow elsewhere.

3. Determine the most restrictive combination of the aggregate NTFS and share permissions from steps 1 and 2. Any permission configured as Deny through either aggregate will be denied. This is the final set of access permissions available through a particular share.

Using Group Policy

Centralized management of computer and user configuration settings within Windows Server 2003 is accomplished through Group Policy management, which was introduced in Windows Server 2000. Group Policy settings are configured within Group Policy Objects (GPOs), which can be linked to container locations throughout the Active Directory. The container objects will inherit the proper GPO settings based on object location within the site, domain, or OU to which the GPO has been linked. Group Policy settings are grouped into the following general categories:

➤ **Registry-Based Policy**—These settings are used for Registry-based configurations such as the automatic removal of the Run option within the Start menu.

➤ **Security Settings**—These settings include security settings for local, domain, and network connections as well as software restriction management based on access path.

➤ **Software Restrictions**—These settings can be used to configure the accessibility of individual software packages throughout the directory, limiting the damage that virus programs or undesirable software can cause.

➤ **Software Distribution and Installation**—These settings are used to manage the installation, update, and removal of approved software packages based on organizational factors and group membership.

➤ **Computer and User Scripts**—Scripts can be written for automatic configuration of the local environment at computer startup and shutdown, or user logon and logoff.

➤ **Roaming User Profiles and Redirected Folders**—These settings can be used to configure user environment storage locations, such as the location of the My Documents folder path, along with details for users with roaming profiles.

➤ **Offline Folders**—These settings can be used to configure the synchronization options and details for offline file management.

➤ **Internet Explorer Maintenance**—These settings can be used to configure user environment details when utilizing the Internet Explorer browser, such as security zones and privacy settings.

Configuration of individual settings is managed within the Group Policy Object Editor (see Figure 3.8), which is almost identical to its Windows Server 2000 equivalent. Windows Server 2003 has added more than 200 new settings that can be configured using this tool.

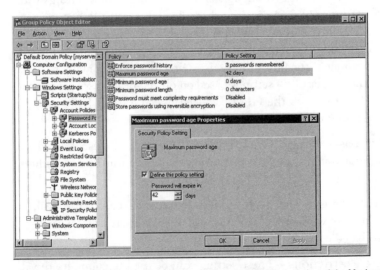

Figure 3.8   The Group Policy Object Editor showing current manipulation of the Maximum Password Age policy setting.

Using the Group Policy Management Console

One key technology introduced in Windows Server 2003 is the Group Policy Management Console (GPMC), which brings together many standard management functions for the manipulation of GPOs and their links into a single utility.

The GPMC utility is not included in the Windows Server 2003 Administrative Tools package (**Adminpak.msi**), but is available as a free download (**gpmc.msi**) from Microsoft's download site: **http://www.microsoft.com/downloads/details. aspx?FamilyID=f39e9d60-7e41-4947-82f5-3330f37adfeb&DisplayLang=en**.

Using this utility, individual GPOs can be configured and linked, and each link's enforcement managed through a simple user interface, as shown in Figure 3.9.

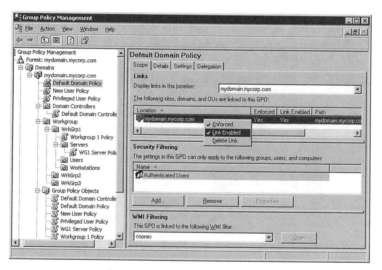

Figure 3.9 The Group Policy Management Console showing a current manipulation of the enforcement status of the Default Domain Policy link to the **mydomain.mycorp.com** domain.

The current status of each GPO can be manipulated using the GPMC, as shown in Figure 3.10.

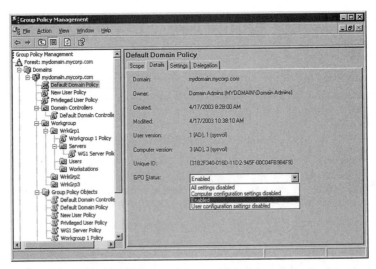

Figure 3.10 The Group Policy Management Console showing a current manipulation of the GPO status of the Default MyDomain Policy.

The GPMC also includes a well-developed reporting capability, which can be used to display the settings of an individual GPO, as shown in Figure 3.11.

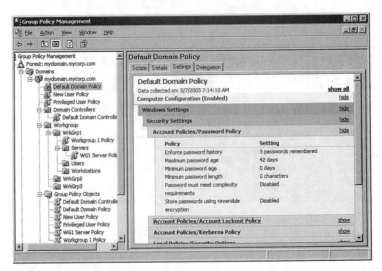

Figure 3.11 The Group Policy Management Console showing a report of the current Default MyDomain Policy GPO settings.

Because accounts and groups inherit Group Policy settings based on their access privileges, the GPMC includes the capability to manipulate GPO delegation, as shown in Figure 3.12.

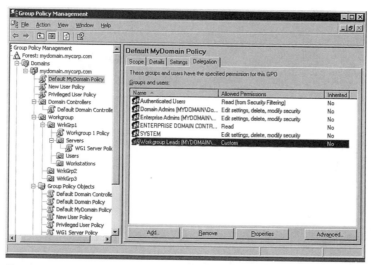

Figure 3.12   The Group Policy Management Console showing the current delegation settings for the groups and users with permissions to the Default MyDomain Policy.

By manipulating the privileges for each group or user, it's possible to further refine the application of Group Policy settings based on as complex a scheme of inheritance as is desirable. To block the application of a particular GPO's settings to a group or user, the rights to Read and Apply Group Policy can be denied, as shown in Figure 3.13.

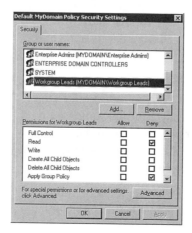

Figure 3.13   Restricting the Read and Apply Group Policy rights of the Workgroup Leads group with regard to the Default MyDomain Policy.

The GPMC provides a convenient method for the review of all linked GPOs for a particular container, including the order in which the links will be evaluated, as shown in Figure 3.14.

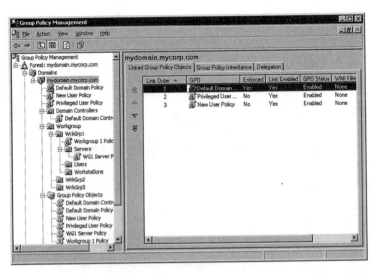

Figure 3.14 The Group Policy Management Console showing all linked GPOs and their evaluation order for the **mydomain.myserver.com** domain.

Copying a GPO

The GPMC can be used to copy an existing GPO to any trusted domain in which the administrator using the GPMC utility has the right to create new GPOs. This can be accomplished by the following:

1. After adding the source and target domains to the GPMC and ensuring that the necessary rights have been granted to the account performing the migration, expand the Group Policy Objects node of the source domain.

2. It's possible to drag and drop a particular GPO listed in the source domain's Group Policy Objects container to the Group Policy Objects container in the target domain. Alternatively, right-clicking on the source GPO, selecting Copy, and then right-clicking on the container in the target domain and selecting Paste also provides the same result: opening the Cross-Domain Copying Wizard. Click Next.

3. Specify whether the copied GPO will use the default permissions for new GPOs or if the original GPO's permissions should be migrated and preserved.

4. After the wizard has performed a scan of the new GPO's application, specify a migration map for the specification of local security principal references. Clicking Next enables you to select a default migration mapping or the specification of unique by-item migration tables.

5. After the selection of all migration mapping, you can review the pending migration and then click the Finish button to complete the copying process.

Backing Up and Restoring GPOs

In addition to the ability to copy GPOs between domains, the GPMC can also be used to back up existing GPOs so that they can be recovered later through a restore procedure. Backing up a GPO stores a copy of the GPO's settings to a selected file location, which can be used to store multiple versions of the same GPO, allowing for versioned recovery to prior GPO settings through a simple restoration of the earlier form. A GPO backup can be accomplished by performing the following steps:

1. Within the GPMC, right-click the desired GPO and select the option to Back-up from the drop-down list provided.

2. Provide a location in which to store the GPO backup and an optional unique description for the backup.

3. Click the Backup button.

 It's possible to back up all GPOs by right-clicking on the Group Policy Objects node and selecting Back Up All from the options provided.

Restoration of an existing backup can be accomplished by the following procedure:

1. Within the GPMC, right-click the desired GPO and select the option to Restore from Backup from the drop-down list provided.

2. Provide the backup location used previously to store the GPO backups.

3. Select the desired backup file and choose to view the settings of the highlighted backup before restoration, if desired.

4. Provide the details of the pending operation; click Finish to perform the restoration.

It's also possible to manage all existing backups by right-clicking on the Group Policy Objects node and selecting Manage Backups from the drop-down list of options. Within the Manage Backups dialog box, you can view a listing of existing backups that can be restored and deleted from this interface; you can also view the settings for each.

Importing GPO Settings

Previous GPO backups can also be used for migration of settings when inter-forest GPO copying is not convenient, such as between testing and production environments. The following procedure can be used to perform an importation of GPO settings from an available backup:

1. Within the GPMC, you should create a new GPO or you can use an existing one as the target for the imported settings.

2. Right-click on the target GPO and select Import Settings from the drop-down list of options provided to open the Import Settings Wizard.

3. You'll be prompted with the option to backup the current settings of the existing GPO before performing the import operation.

4. After selecting the backup source location and specific GPO backup, a scan will be performed. If any local security principals or UNC paths must be migrated, you'll be prompted to provide a migration mapping before the import procedure begins.

5. Click the Finish button to allow the importation of previously backed up settings to the target GPO, overwriting its current settings.

Configuring the Resultant Set of Policy

The GPMC includes several features beyond the manipulation of individual GPO links, such as the ability to evaluate the overall Resultant Set of Policy (RSoP) with regard to a particular account or group, as shown in Figure 3.15.

This capability is invaluable for troubleshooting the resulting settings that are produced through the application of GPO links across many levels of container inheritance. Each resulting setting and the GPO link that is its source can be displayed, as shown in Figure 3.16.

In addition to static information such as GPO settings, the GPMC's reporting capability for modeling Resulting Set of Policy details can also be used to review policy-related events generated within the target system's event logs, as shown in Figure 3.17.

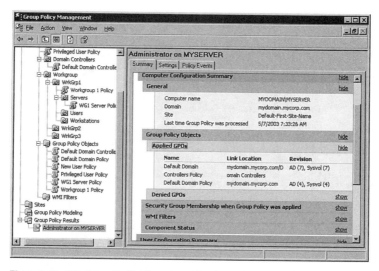

Figure 3.15   The Group Policy Management Console showing an evaluation of the RSoP for the Administrator account.

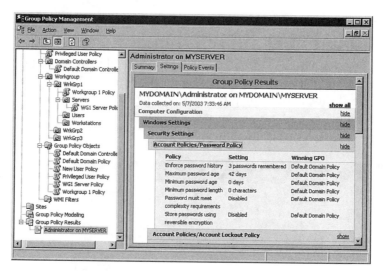

Figure 3.16   The Group Policy Management Console showing each setting and the Winning GPO that produces the configuration result.

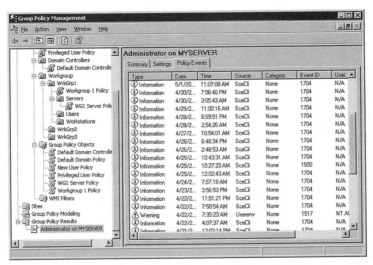

Figure 3.17   The Group Policy Management Console showing policy-related events queried from the target server's event logs.

Performing Policy Simulation

The GPMC also includes the capability to perform an evaluative simulation of the effect of a particular GPO's application to the current GPO configuration through the use of the Group Policy Modeling subcomponent, which includes the ability to perform a simulated application of a GPO's settings based on a detailed query specification, as shown in Figure 3.18.

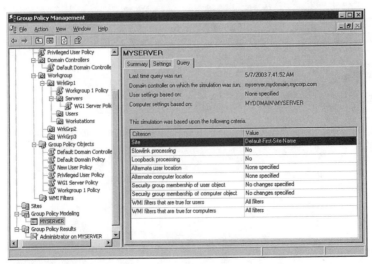

Figure 3.18   The Group Policy Management Console showing the query settings for an evaluation of GPO application.

Group Policy settings can be evaluated within this testing environment before rolling out the results within the production environment. This feature, along with others present within the GPMC, make it possible to perform complex troubleshooting and testing of planned changes to policy settings to facilitate centralized management over even very extensive and complex directory structures.

Configuring Security Policy Management

Microsoft Windows Server 2003 provides many different means by which individual settings can be configured, including the Group Policy Management Console as well as the Active Directory Users and Computers, Active Directory Domains and Trusts, and Active Directory Sites and Services MMC snap-ins. After the Group Policy Management Console has been installed, the Group Policy tab (displayed in the Properties pages of sites, domains, and OUs when the MMC is started in Author mode) displays an Open button that redirects GPO access attempts to the GPMC, making this utility a one-stop solution for all categories of GPO manipulation.

The Group Policy Object Editor accessible through the aforementioned MMC snap-ins (refer to Figure 3.8) provides the ability to manipulate all possible settings for a particular GPO. Additionally, Microsoft Windows Server 2003 also includes more focused utilities, such as the Local Security Policy, Domain Security Policy, and Domain Controllers Security Policy MMC snap-ins. These utilities allow the manipulation of security settings within the appropriate GPO, where templates can be used to apply standard configuration settings based on the intended role of the target system.

A number of preconfigured security templates are stored in `%systemroot%\Security\Templates` and include the following:

➤ `Compatws.inf`—The compatibility template is used to relax security settings to allow users to make use of applications that do not conform to the requirements for the Windows Logo Program for Software.

➤ `DC Security.inf`—The default security template for domain controllers.

➤ `Hisecdc.inf`—The highly secure template for domain controllers.

➤ `Hisecws.inf`—The highly secure template for workstations.

➤ `Rootsec.inf`—The root directory permissions template.

➤ `Securedc.inf`—The secure template for domain controllers.

➤ `Securews.inf`—The secure template for workstations.

➤ `Setup security.inf`—The default security settings for a system created during initial installation.

Using Security Policy MMC Snap-ins

Windows Server 2003 includes several MMC snap-ins that can be added to custom MMCs. Two in particular are useful in the manipulation of security template settings: the Security Configuration and Analysis MMC snap-in and the Security Templates MMC snap-in. The following steps can be used to create a custom MMC with these snap-ins configured:

1. Select Start, Run, and then type MMC in the Open box. After clicking OK, a new blank MMC console opens.

2. From the Console main menu, select File and then Add/Remove Snap-in from the list of options provided. Select the console to which the snap-ins will be added, then click the Add button to open the Add Standalone Snap-in dialog box.

3. From the list of options provided, create a custom MMC that includes many standard tasks. For the purposes of this example, highlight the Security Configuration and Analysis option and click Add, highlight the Security Templates option, and click Add again.

4. Click the Close button and then the OK button to return to the custom console, as shown in Figure 3.19.

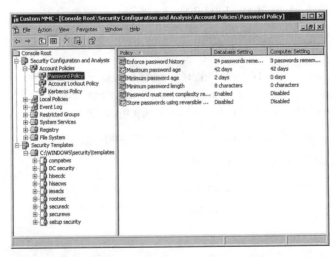

Figure 3.19 A custom MMC console with the Security Templates and the Security Configuration and Analysis MMC snap-ins added.

5. Save this custom MMC for later reuse by selecting File, Save As. After selecting the container location and name for the new custom MMC, save the console with its current settings.

The Security Templates MMC snap-in can be used to create and modify templates, which can then be modeled and applied within the Security Configuration and Analysis MMC snap-in using the same techniques described within the Group Policy Editor MMC snap-in accessed through the GPMC.

When a target template is analyzed against current security settings, the Security Configuration and Analysis MMC snap-in produces a comparative analysis of each setting, as shown in Figure 3.19.

Managing Policies Through the Command Line

Microsoft Windows Server 2003 includes command-line utilities that mirror much of the same functionality present in the graphical user interface utilities previously discussed in this chapter, including

➤ Secedit.exe—A utility used to analyze and configure security settings based on templates. This is a command-line close equivalent to the Security Configuration and Analysis MMC snap-in, which was also present in Windows Server 2000. In the Windows Server 2003 version of the utility, the /refreshpolicy option is no longer present.

➤ Gpupdate.exe—This utility is used to refresh Group Policy settings, replacing the /refreshpolicy option within the secedit utility. This utility can be used to force a logoff or reboot when the update is complete to ensure that new policy settings are applied immediately.

➤ Gpresult.exe—A utility that can be used to display Group Policy settings and the RSoP of a target user or computer account. This utility is a command-line close equivalent to the reporting and analysis functions within the GPMC.

You should be able to use the **gpupdate** utility to refresh a GPO. The syntax of the **gpupdate.exe** utility is provided in the Microsoft help file:

```
gpupdate [/target:{computer ¦ user}] [/force] [/wait:Value]
[/logoff] [/boot]
```

To see a listing of all the parameters and their meanings, type the following at the command-line shell prompt:

```
gpupdate /?
```

The GPMC's Software Development Kit (SDK) includes a number of scripts that can be used to automate GPO troubleshooting, including the following:

➤ `ListAllGPOs.wsf`—Used to list all GPOs within a domain

➤ `FindDisabledGPOs.wsf`—Used to list any GPOs currently disabled

➤ `DumpGPOInfo.wsf`—Used to display information about a particular GPO

➤ `QueryBackupLocation.wsf`—Used to list all GPOs stored within the specified target backup location

➤ `FindUnlinkedGPOs.wsf`—Used to list all unlinked GPOs within a domain

Using Remote Desktop Access

Windows NT Server 4.0 introduced the Terminal Services capability that allows Windows Server to host multiple virtual terminal sessions, accessed by remote clients able to run on downlevel (earlier) versions of the Windows operating system. Applications running within each virtual terminal session operate on the server system; the mouse and keyboard of the client system provides input to the server while the video output is routed back to the client.

Starting with Windows Server 2000, Terminal Services was implemented in two versions: application mode could be configured to allow multiple client systems to access a virtual terminal running under a licensed Terminal Services session, whereas a limited-access version of the Terminal Services connectivity could be used by up to two concurrent users for the purposes of remote administration. This administrative mode did not require a Terminal Services Licensing server to function, and was loaded within the Add/Remove Programs wizard after server setup.

In Windows XP, Microsoft introduced a client-accessible version called the Remote Desktop. This is a single-user modified version of the Terminal Services capability, enabling a user to connect to an existing console session on a remote Windows XP system.

Windows Server 2003 introduces a more refined version of the Remote Desktop capability, merging enhancements from the Windows XP Remote Desktop Protocol (version 5.1) into the multiple-terminal capability of the full Terminal Services server. The new implementation of the Remote Desktop Protocol (version 5.2) adds a number of new options, such as

➤ Color depth—The ability to control the color depth of the video output to optimize operation based on available bandwidth

➤ Audio redirection—The ability to bring audio output from the RDP session on the server to the client system

➤ Console connection—The ability to connect to the current console session, rather than a Terminal Services virtual session

➤ Local resource access—The ability of an RDP user to access local client-system resources, such as printers and drives from within the Remote Desktop session, as shown in Figure 3.20

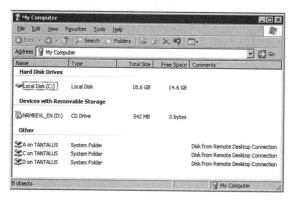

Figure 3.20   An example of local drives from the client system (TANTALUS) being made accessible to an existing Remote Desktop connection.

Terminal Services

Microsoft makes use of several components running on the Terminal Services host server to manage remote access, including

➤ Remote Desktop for Administration—This replaces Terminal Services running in Remote Administration mode. It's installed by default on all Windows Server 2003 products, although connections cannot be established until Remote Access has been enabled.

➤ Terminal Server—This service provides virtual terminal access for Windows-based and non–Windows-based clients using the Remote Desktop Protocol (RDP). This mode is not available on Windows Server 2003, Web Edition.

➤ Terminal Server Session Directory—This service enables a client to reconnect to a disconnected session running within a Terminal Services server farm. In previous versions of Microsoft Terminal Services, clients who experienced a loss of connectivity with a server farm would most often connect to an entirely new TS session when reconnecting, losing access to pending work from the previously established session and in some configurations, tying up a new connection license.

> Terminal Services connections are accomplished using the standard RDP port (3389) and are created using an encrypted session to avoid passing clear text information across an unsecured network. This improves security of all proper communications, while also creating a potential reduction in security due to the encrypted console connectivity.
>
> Someone seeking unauthorized access can create Remote Desktop/Terminal Server–encrypted connections and use brute-force hacking techniques over the encrypted connection, preventing intrusion detection services (IDSs) from noticing the attack. If you're going to use these services, it's important to enact strong password and account lockout policies to maintain security and prevent this type of attack from being successful.

Microsoft has also included many new remote access options within the MMC snap-in utilities, as well as many policy settings. One security policy setting you might have noticed in Chapter 2 is Allow Login to Terminal Services Only, which restricts users to Remote Desktop connections only, rather than the Log on Locally permission that was mandated in Windows Server 2000 implementations.

Remote Desktop Connections

Clients can connect to a Microsoft Windows Server 2003 Terminal Server or Remote Desktop for Administration connection using the Remote Desktop client, shown in Figure 3.21, which is familiar to anyone who has used the interface between Windows XP systems.

Figure 3.21   The Remote Desktop client in its basic form.

By expanding the Options button on the RDC, it's possible to configure the connection's settings and then save the RDC settings as a shortcut that can be easily used by clients to open the preconfigured session, as shown in Figure 3.22.

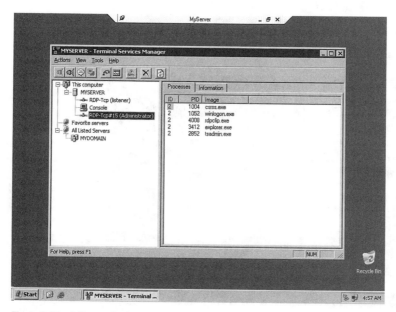

Figure 3.22   A Remote Desktop session to MyServer displaying the Terminal Services Configuration MMC snap-in showing this connection.

In addition to the single-console RDC (mstsc.exe), Windows Server 2003 also includes the multi-connection Remote Desktops MMC snap-in utility (refer to Figure 3.1), as well as an ActiveX Web-based connection utility that can be used to open a Terminal Services connection using Internet Explorer, as shown in Figure 3.23.

The Remote Desktop Web Connection component is not installed by default, but can be added through the Add/Remove Programs Wizard, where it is a subcomponent of the IIS installation option. After it's installed, the client can be accessed at **http://<*ServerName*>/TSWeb/**.

Microsoft has also provided an add-in to the Active Directory Users and Computers MMC snap-in that extends the Remote Control functionality to this administration utility, as shown in Figure 3.24. This additional component can be downloaded at the following Web site: http://www.microsoft.com/ downloads/details.aspx?FamilyID=0a91d2e7-7594-4abb-8239-7a7eca6a6cb1&DisplayLang=en.

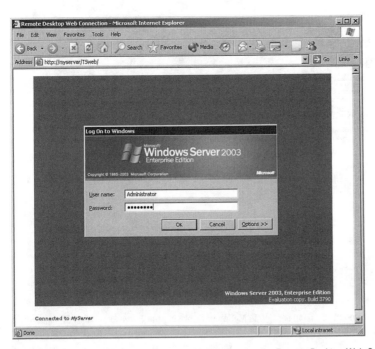

Figure 3.23 A Remote Desktop session to MyServer using the Remote Desktop Web Connection ActiveX component.

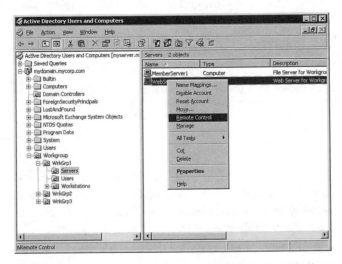

Figure 3.24 The Remote Control option added to the Active Directory Users and Computers MMC snap-in.

Allowing Remote Connections

Before any remote terminal sessions can be created, it's first necessary to allow users to connect remotely to your computer, which is accomplished on the Remote tab of a server's System Properties dialog box, as shown in Figure 3.25.

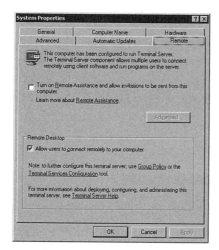

Figure 3.25 The Remote tab of the System Properties dialog box.

User accounts must be granted the proper permissions to connect via Remote Access, which can be accomplished by inheritance from membership in the Remote Desktop Users group. Additional Terminal Server settings can be configured within the Active Directory Users and Computers MMC snap-in for a user or group, through the RDP's advanced options (see Figure 3.26), through Group Policy settings (see Figure 3.27), and within the Terminal Server Configuration MMC snap-in (see Figure 3.28).

Data encryption options for each connection can be configured at the client as well as at the host server, with the server's settings winning in case of conflict. The FIPS Compliant option provides connection encryption using the Federal Information Processing Standard (FIPS).

Figure 3.26 Remote Desktop client environment options.

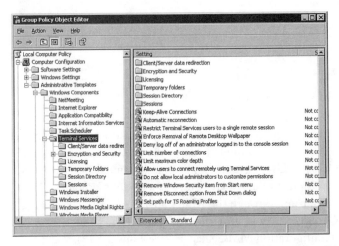

Figure 3.27 Terminal Services GPO settings node within the Group Policy Object Editor.

Configuring Terminal Services

When Terminal Services will be used in Application mode, it is necessary to install the Terminal Services Configuration utility (see Figure 3.29) from within the Add/Remove Programs Wizard. The Terminal Services Licensing service (see Figure 3.30) can also be installed here if this server will be used to provide licensing for servers running the Terminal Services service within your enterprise, forest, or domain.

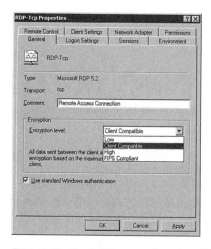

Figure 3.28   Terminal Server configuration within the Terminal Server Configuration MMC snap-in.

Figure 3.29   The Terminal Services Configuration MMC snap-in.

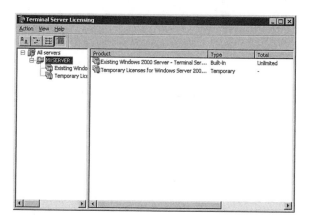

Figure 3.30   The Terminal Services Licensing MMC snap-in.

After installation of the Terminal Services Configuration MMC snap-in, you can configure the properties of each connection available on a host server running the Terminal Server service. To utilize the licensing capability of a Terminal Services Licensing server, the server must first be activated within the Terminal Services Licensing MMC snap-in by right-clicking the target server and selecting Activate Server. Activation can be accomplished automatically, via HTTP connection, or by telephone.

Connections that are not associated with Terminal Server licenses, such as those used for remote administration, will be displayed within the Temporary Licensing node of the Terminal Server Licensing MMC snap-in. When licenses are added, the type and quantity of each set of licenses must be provided (see Figure 3.31) along with the appropriate licensing key.

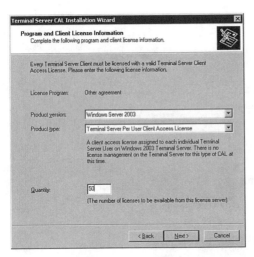

Figure 3.31   The Terminal Server CAL Installation Wizard showing the installation of 50 licenses for Windows Server 2003 per-user licensing.

When Terminal Server Licensing problems arise, it is possible to easily diagnose the current license allocation within this MMC snap-in as well.

Exam Prep Questions

Question 1

> You're the network administrator for BigCorp (**www.bigcorp.com**). You need to create several new file shares on your server (**bigserver.bigcorp.com**). Which of the following options can be used for this purpose in a default installation of Windows Server 2003? (Choose three.)
>
> ❑ A. Utilize the Computer Management MMC snap-in
>
> ❑ B. Create the file shares within the Windows Explorer
>
> ❑ C. Utilize the **net share** command-line utility
>
> ❑ D. Utilize the Server Management MMC snap-in
>
> ❑ E. Create the file shares within the Internet Explorer
>
> ❑ F. Utilize the File Server Management MMC snap-in

Answers A, B, and C are correct. New file shares can be created using the Computer Management and Windows Explorer graphical user interface tools, as well as the command line net share utility.

Answers D and F are incorrect within a default installation of Windows Server 2003 because the File Server role is not installed by default. After this role has been added, the Server Management and File Server Management MMC snap-ins would then be able to be used to create new file shares. Answer E is incorrect because Internet Explorer is used to browse the Web, rather than to manipulate local resource access.

Question 2

> What permissions are granted to the Everyone group over the share created by the following code?
>
> net share MyShare=C:\MyFiles\MyShare
>
> ○ A. Change
>
> ○ B. Full Control
>
> ○ C. None
>
> ○ D. Read

Answer D is correct. Newly created shares in Windows Server 2003 grant only the Read permission to the Everyone group by default, making Answer A incorrect. Answer B is incorrect in Windows Server 2003, although this was the default behavior in Windows Server 2000. Answer C is incorrect because the Read permission remains in Windows Server 2003 in a default permission share creation.

Question 3

> You're the network administrator responsible for review of shared resources on several servers within a corporate domain. To accomplish this task, you've decided to use an automated script that will run several times per day to determine what shared resources are being used. Which of the following options would be most useful in meeting this requirement?
>
> ○ A. Utilize the **net accounts** command to review the shared resources
>
> ○ B. Utilize the **net config** command to review the shared resources
>
> ○ C. Utilize the **net file** command to review the shared resources
>
> ○ D. Utilize the **net session** command to review the shared resources

Answer C is correct. The net file command can be used to enumerate shared files as well as to close an open file by specifying the process ID and the /close option.

Answer A is incorrect because the net accounts command is used to review and configure the password and logon settings that are applied to all local accounts. Answer B is incorrect because the net config command is used to review and configure the settings of configurable services, such as the Workstation and Server services. Answer D is incorrect because the net session command can display only the current session connections established by remote users, rather than the specific resources they are accessing.

Question 4

> You're writing a logon script that will be used to automatically link a remote file share as the home directory for the current logon account. Which option would be best used to create a link for the home file share?
>
> ○ A. Utilize the **net send** command to create the home file share link
>
> ○ B. Utilize the **net share** command to create the home file share link
>
> ○ C. Utilize the **net start** command to create the home file share link
>
> ○ D. Utilize the **net use** command to create the home file share link

Answer D is correct. The net use command is used to connect to remote shared resources and can be used with the /home option to designate a home file share.

Answer A is incorrect because the net send command is used to send a text message to the specified target computer, user, or domain. Answer B is incorrect because the net share command is used to create or modify file shares, rather than to remotely connect to shared resources elsewhere. Answer C is incorrect as well because the net start command is used to display currently running services or to start a specified service.

Question 5

You're the network administrator responsible for setting up and configuring several file shares that will be used by mobile users. When in the office, these shares will be accessed through a logon script that utilizes the **net share** command. You need to configure the **/cache** option so that the salesforce application will automatically remain available when your users are in the field. Which of the following settings will have the desired result?

○ A. Documents

○ B. Manual

○ C. None

○ D. Programs

Answer D is correct. The /cache:programs configuration setting results in executables and other share-accessed files being automatically cached to the local client system.

Answer A is incorrect because the /cache:documents setting does not automatically cache program executables. Answer B is incorrect because the /cache:manual setting requires a manual synchronization action by your users and does not meet the specified requirement. The /cache:none setting disables automatic caching of the shared resources, making answer C incorrect as well.

Question 6

If GroupA is granted the Change permission over a file share \\someserver\someshare\, it will definitely have which of the following permissions as well by default?

○ A. Full Control

○ B. Modify

○ C. None

○ D. Read

Answer D is correct. The Change permission also grants the Read share permission, making Answer C incorrect. Answer A is incorrect because the Full Control permission includes additional rights not automatically granted by the Change assignment. Answer B is incorrect because the Modify permission is an NTFS permission, rather than a share-access right.

Question 7

Which of the following statements are true regarding access permissions? (Choose three.)

- ❑ A. NTFS permissions are available for files stored on FAT32-formatted partitions.
- ❑ B. NTFS permissions are available for files stored on NTFS-formatted partitions.
- ❑ C. NTFS permissions are available for files stored on CDFS-formatted partitions.
- ❑ D. NTFS permissions are available for files stored on removable DAT media.
- ❑ E. Share permissions are available for shared folders on FAT32-formatted partitions.
- ❑ F. Share permissions are available for shared folders on NTFS-formatted partitions.

Answers B, E, and F are correct. NTFS file-level permissions can only be managed within NTFS-formatted storage locations, making answer A incorrect. Share-level access permissions can be assigned for file shares on both FAT32- and NTFS-formatted file storage locations. Answers C and D are incorrect because CD-ROM (CDFS) and mounted digital tape (DAT) media storage will not support NTFS file-level permission assignment.

Question 8

When calculating final permissions over a file accessed through a remote share, what is the resulting combination composed of? (Choose two.)

- ❑ A. The most restrictive combination of NTFS permissions
- ❑ B. The least restrictive combination of NTFS permissions
- ❑ C. The most restrictive combination of Share permissions
- ❑ D. The most restrictive combination of Share and NTFS permissions
- ❑ E. The least restrictive combination of Share and NTFS permissions

Answers B and D are correct. The final set of access rights is determined by first aggregating the least restrictive set of NTFS and Share permissions, and then combined them as the most restrictive set of the aggregates together, making answers A, C, and E incorrect as well.

Question 9

A share called \\myserver\files\ has been created for the user file location **C:\somefiles** on server **myserver.mycorp.com**. The NTFS access permissions for **C:\somefiles** allow Full Control to the Authenticated Users group, whereas the share permissions Deny access to the share for members of the Sales group. Bob is a member of the Sales group and is attempting to access files within the affected location while logged in to **myserver.mycorp.com** using his normal account. What are his effective permissions over the files in the target location?

- ○ A. None
- ○ B. Full Control
- ○ C. Read
- ○ D. Undetermined

Answer B is correct. Because Bob is logged in locally, only the NTFS permissions apply and so Bob has Full Control rights, making Answer D incorrect. Answer A is incorrect because the denial of access rights is configured over the share, which Bob does not need to use to access the local `c:\some-files\` folder. Answer C is incorrect because the Full Control permission includes not only the Read permission, but also other rights such as those granted through the Change permission.

Question 10

A GPO named AccessRights has been created and linked to the domain container and separately to the SalesDepartment OU. The link at the domain level has been filtered to exclude access for the Management group, whereas the link at the SalesDept Organizational Unit allows all members of the SalesDept Read and Apply Group Policy permissions. Sally is a member of both the Sales and Management groups, and her account is located in the SalesDept OU. How will the AccessRights GPO's settings be applied for Sally's account?

- ○ A. The GPO's settings will not be applied to Sally's account.
- ○ B. The GPO's settings will be applied to Sally's account at the domain level.
- ○ C. The GPO's settings will be applied to Sally's account at the OU level.
- ○ D. The GPO's settings will be applied to Sally's account at both the domain and OU levels.

Answer C is correct. Unlike NTFS permissions, each link to a GPO can be configured with a different set of access rights and filtering of one link does not affect others of the same GPO, allowing the GPO's settings to be applied to Sally's account through her OU membership, making Answers A, B, and D incorrect as well. Sally's account will be excluded from the domain-level GPO assignment because of the imposed filtering, but the second link to the same GPO at the OU level will result in the settings being applied to members of that OU even if they did not inherit the settings from the domain-level assignment.

Need to Know More?

 Microsoft Windows Server 2003 Administrator's Pocket Consultant, ISBN 0-7356-1354-0, Microsoft Press, Redmond, Washington, 2003.

 Introducing Microsoft Windows Server 2003, ISBN 0-7356-1570-5, Microsoft Press, Redmond, Washington, 2003.

 Microsoft Windows Server 2003 site: `http://www.microsoft.com/ windowsserver2003/default.mspx`

 Microsoft Windows Server 2003 MSDN site: `http://msdn. microsoft.com/library/default.asp?url=/nhp/default.asp?con- tentid=28001691`

 Windows Server 2003 Terminal Services Technology site: `http://support.microsoft.com/default.aspx?scid=fh;EN- US;winsvr2003term`

Managing a Server Environment

Terms you'll need to understand:

✓ Software Update Service (SUS)
✓ Automatic Updates
✓ WUAU.ADM
✓ Microsoft Management Console (MMC)
✓ Remote Desktop Protocol (RDP)
✓ Web server extensions
✓ Application pooling
✓ Metabase
✓ Windows Management Instrumentation (WMI)

Techniques you'll need to master:

✓ Configuring Automatic Updates
✓ Knowing how to manage, back up, restore, and test SUS
✓ Connecting to a remote server using MMC and the Remote Desktop Connection utility
✓ Configuring options in the Remote Desktop Connection utility
✓ Installing, configuring, and managing IIS 6.0
✓ Installing and managing ASP.NET
✓ Implementing Web applications and application pooling

System administrators are increasingly overburdened with a wide variety of management tasks. In this chapter, you'll learn about several new and enhanced management tools designed to save time and simplify and reduce total cost of ownership (TCO).

Managing a Windows Server 2003 environment includes using Microsoft's Software Update Service (SUS) to automate the retrieval of security patches and operating system fixes from a server on your corporate intranet. Administrators can test the patches and then schedule the security updates to install on targeted computers automatically.

Mobile users need secure access to information stored on their private networks. Remote Access Server uses the latest remote access technologies, including integrated dial-up and virtual private networking (VPN), to manage remote client access to corporate networks using secure practices.

Terminal Server Services is another improved remote service that can deliver Windows-based applications to client desktops. Similar to earlier versions of Terminal Server, it operates in either application or remote administration mode. Operating in remote desktop for administration mode, Terminal Services uses the Remote Desktop Protocol (RDP), allowing administrators to take control of the user's desktop console session.

Internet Information Services (IIS) 6.0 is now locked down by default and has improved authentication, easier management, and increased reliability. IIS Web services enables companies to deploy Web sites and provide a secure platform for applications built using Microsoft's ASP.NET framework.

Using SUS to Manage a Software Update Infrastructure

System administrators need to check the Windows Update Web site frequently to obtain the latest security patches and operating system stability fixes. The Windows Update site automates the process by scanning your hard drive for previous installed patches before displaying a list of the latest recommended patches. Administrators, however, must still download and test the latest patches before manually distributing and applying them.

 Traditional enterprise software tools such as Microsoft's Systems Management Server (SMS) are also used to update clients' computers. If you're using electronic software distribution solutions for complete software management, Microsoft recommends that you continue to do so.

Many companies implement policies to prevent users from browsing the Internet for updates. The Software Update Service (SUS) provides a solution to the problem of managing and deploying Windows patches by dynamic notification of critical updates at scheduled times to Windows client computers. Updates can be tested by the administrator and then scheduled to automatically update selected client computers.

SUS is installed on a Windows 2000 Server (SP2 or later) or Windows Server 2003 inside the company's firewall. After it's installed, the SUS server downloads all critical updates and security roll-ups when they're posted to the Windows Update Web site. The administrator also has the option of receiving email notification when new updates are posted.

SUS contains the following features:

➤ Software Update Services Server—The SUS server on your internal intranet synchronizes with the Windows Update Web site whenever new critical updates for Windows 2000, Windows 2003, or Windows XP are available. The synchronization can be performed manually by the administrator or automatically. After all updates are downloaded to your SUS server, you can test and decide which updates you want to publish to the client computers. The SUS server is supported for Windows 2000 Server (SP2 or later) and the Windows Server 2003 family.

➤ Client Automatic Updates—This is the client component that is usually configured to connect to your SUS server for updates. Administrators control which clients connect and can also schedule when to deploy the critical updates, either manually or by using Active Directory Service Group Policy. The Automatic Updates client software is supported for Windows 2000 Server (SP2 or later), Windows Server 2003, Windows 2000 Professional (SP2 or later), and Windows XP Professional and Home Editions.

NOTE

The Automatic Updates client software is included with Windows 2000 Service Pack 3, Windows XP Service Pack 1, and the Windows Server 2003 family of operating systems. Other clients can obtain the Automatic Updates client at

http://www.microsoft.com/windows2000/downloads/recommended/susclient/ default.asp

Installing and Configuring SUS on a Server

The minimum configuration requirements are as follows:

➤ Pentium III 700MHz or higher processor

➤ 512MB of RAM

➤ 6GB of free hard disk space

➤ Internet Explorer, version 5.5 or higher

➤ Internet Information Server installed

Perform the following steps to install SUS with default settings:

1. Download the SUS Package—Using Internet Explorer version 5.5 or higher, browse to the following Web site and download the Software Update Services setup package from the SUS page:

   `http://www.microsoft.com/downloads/details.aspx?FamilyId=A7AA96E4-6E41-4F54-972C-AE66A4E4BF6C&displaylang=en`.

2. Install SUS SP1—Double-click the `sus10sp1.exe` file and click Next on the Welcome screen of the SUS Setup Wizard. Read and accept the End User License Agreement and click Next.

3. Select Typical if you want to have all the defaults applied or select Custom to configure the SUS options now. Select Custom and click the Next button.

4. Choose file locations—You can store the updates locally or have clients update their files from a Microsoft Windows Update Server. In the Update Storage section, select the radio button Save the Updates to This Local Folder (by default, `c:\sus\content`) and then click Next.

5. Language settings—By default, the All Available Languages radio button is selected, which results in more than 600MB of updates. If you don't need additional languages, select English Only (about 150MB of updates) or the Specific Languages radio button. Select the English Only button and click Next (see Figure 4.1).

Figure 4.1 You can conserve disk space by specifying a language on the Language Settings screen.

6. Handing new versions of previously approved updates—You can manually or automatically approve new versions. Select the Automatically Approve New Versions of Previously Approved Updates radio button and click Next to continue.

7. SUS installs and applies the IIS lockdown tool to Windows 2000 SP2 Server, Advanced Server and earlier versions. Note the IIS lockdown tool is included with Windows 2000 Server (SP3 and later) and the Windows Server 2003 family.

8. Click the Finish button to complete the installation. SUS setup adds a Start menu shortcut in the Administrative Tools folder and opens the SUS administration Web site in Internet Explorer at `http://`
`<yourservername>/SUSAdmin`.

 You must be a local administrator on the SUS Server to install and view the Administration Web page. If you try to connect to the Administration Web site with a version of IE older than version 5.5, you'll see an error page reminding you to upgrade to IE 5.5 or greater.

If your network uses a proxy server to connect to the Internet, configure your proxy server settings on the SUS Administration Web page under the Select a Proxy Server Configuration section.

Configuring Client Automatic Updates

To use the SUS server for updates, client computers must be running the updated Automatic Updates client. Windows 2000 Professional and Server (SP2 or earlier), and Windows XP Home and Professional clients must update their operating system to use SUS. The update is available at `http://www.microsoft.com/windows2000/downloads/recommended/susclient/default.asp`.

The administrator can configure Windows XP or Windows 2000 automatic client updates either by using the Automatic Updates tab in the System Properties dialog box of the System applet in the Control Panel, or by connecting to a wizard after waiting at least 24 hours after connectivity to the update service has been established. The System Properties Automatic Updates tab configuration options are shown in Figure 4.2.

The following options are used to control how updates are applied:

➤ Notify before updates are downloaded and notify again before the updates are installed

➤ Download the updates automatically and notify before the updates are installed

➤ Download the updates automatically and install the updates based on a specified schedule

Figure 4.2 You configure the Automatic Updates options in the System applet from the Control Panel.

Using Group Policy to Configure SUS Clients

Using Group Policy is the preferred way of applying updates to your clients. Policies can also be configured using Windows NT 4 System Policy or by manually setting Registry keys.

 Remember that Active Directory (AD) Group Policy settings always take precedence over Local Group Policies or user-defined options.

To set up a Group Policy using Active Directory installed on Windows 2000 or Windows Server 2003, perform the following steps:

1. Click Start, All Programs, Administrative Tools, Active Directory Users and Computers to open the Active Directory Users and Computers MMC interface.

2. Right-click the organizational unit (OU) or the domain where you want to create the policy and then click Properties.

3. Click the Group Policy tab and then click New. Type a name for your policy, and then click the Edit button. The Group Policy editor opens.

4. Navigate to and expand the computer configuration folder. Right-click Administrative Templates, choose Add/Remove Templates, and then click Add.

5. In the Policy Templates dialog box, select the `wuau.adm` template and click the Open button. Verify your template has been added and then close the Add/Remove Templates dialog box. Steps 4 and 5 are not necessary to perform on a Windows Server 2003 server because `wuau.adm` is already installed by default.

6. Under Computer Configuration, expand the Administrative Templates folder, expand the Windows Components folder, and then select the Windows Update folder.

7. In the right pane, four policies are displayed that you can configure. Configure Automatic Updates, Specify Intranet Microsoft Updates Service Location, Reschedule Automatic Updates Scheduled Installations, and No Auto-Restart for Scheduled Automatic Updates Installations.

8. Double-click Configure Automatic Updates and select the Enabled option radio button.

9. In the Configure Automatic Update section, select one of the following options from the drop-down list box:

   ➤ Notify for download and notify for install

   ➤ Auto-download and notify for install (default setting)

   ➤ Auto-download and schedule the install

10. When you finish, click the OK button.

11. Next, in the right pane, double-click Specify Intranet Microsoft Updates Service Location and select the Enabled option radio button as shown in Figure 4.3.

12. To specify a location for the SUS server that your Windows clients will be redirected to, type the URL in the Set the Intranet Update Service for Detecting Updates text box. Click the OK button when complete.

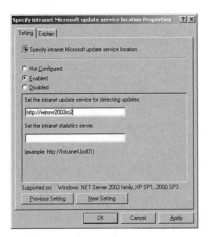

Figure 4.3 You can enable automatic updates via the Specify Intranet Microsoft Updates Service Location Properties screen.

Managing a Software Update Infrastructure

Common administrative tasks for managing SUS include synchronizing content, approving updates and timing issues, and reviewing server actions and server health. To synchronize your SUS server with the Microsoft Update Services, perform the following steps:

1. On the navigation bar of the SUS administrator Web page, click Synchronize Server.

2. Click Synchronize Now. After synchronization completes, a list of updates appears on the Approve Update page.

To set up automatic synchronization, click Synchronize Server in the navigation bar and then click the Synchronize Now button. Updates start downloading with a progress bar displayed as shown in Figure 4.4. When downloads have completed, you'll receive a notification that your SUS server has successfully synchronized with the Microsoft Windows Update server. Click the OK button to confirm.

Next, click the Synchronization Schedule button. To approve updates for deploying to your computers, click Approve Updates Server in the navigation bar, select the updates you want to deploy, and then click Approve. Every 22 hours or so, your targeted client computers will poll the SUS server for approved updates to install.

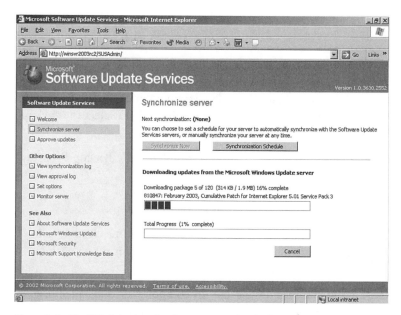

Figure 4.4   The SUS dialog box showing server synchronization progress.

    If you subsequently unapprove an update after it has been installed on client computers, it does not automatically uninstall from the client.

A synchronizing log and the approval log are provided for review. The synchronizing log maintains and keeps track of your content synchronizations. The approval log tracks both approved and unapproved contents. Both of these logs can be accessed from the SUS administration Web page navigation pane.

Backing Up and Restoring an SUS Server

To restore a fully functional SUS server in the event of an SUS failure, you need to back up the administration site SUS directory that contains the content, the Web site directory that the administration site was created in, and the Internet Information Server metabase. Open the IIS MMC Snap-in console and perform the following actions to back up the IIS metabase:

1. From the Action menu, select All Tasks, and then Backup/Restore Configuration.

2. Click Create Backup in the Configuration Backup/Restore dialog box, type a name for the backup, and then click OK.

3. Verify that your backup is listed and then click Close to close the Configuration Backup/Restore dialog box and exit IIS Manager.

4. Run NTBackup (Start, All Programs, Accessories, System Tools, Backup) and in the left pane under Inetpub, click to select the wwwroot (default Web site) and the SUS (system content) folder. Next, navigate to \WINDOWS\system32\inetsrv\Metaback folder and select the backup of the IIS metabase you created and saved.

5. Click Start Backup. When the backup completes, the Backup Progress dialog box displays with completed results.

To restore a failed SUS server, perform the following steps:

1. Disconnect the server from the network and perform a clean install of Windows Server 2003, making sure to give the server the same computer name it originally had.

2. Make sure that you install the same IIS components as installed originally.

3. Apply the latest service packs and security fixes as originally installed.

4. Install SUS in the same directory.

5. Run NT Backup to restore your most recent backup. Include the SUS content directory, the IIS site containing the SUSAdmin and AutoUpdate virtual directories, and the IIS metabase backup on the server running SUS.

Testing Content for SUS Implementation

There are two methods for testing content:

➤ In a test lab, set up both a test Windows Server 2003 SUS server and a client computer running either Windows 2000 Professional with SP3 installed or Windows XP with SP1. Both clients already have the Automatic Updates client software installed. Set up the client computer to download and install your approved updates from your SUS server.

➤ Using your browser, connect the test client computer to the Windows Update site and apply the patches you want to test on the client. The Windows Update site is located at http://windowsupdate.microsoft.com.

Managing Servers Remotely

Networks today are becoming more difficult and complex to manage. System administrators often need access to their corporate wide area networks (WANs) from wherever they are. The Windows Server 2003 family includes many new remote access features that enable administrators to remotely manage their servers.

The runas command, first introduced in Windows 2000, enables an administrator to perform a secondary logon that enables her to perform administrative tasks with a particular tool while still being primarily logged on as a typical user. New timesaving enhancements in Windows Server 2003 include the capability to create desktops shortcuts using the runas command.

This chapter includes several methods used to connect to a remote server. One method is to use the improved MMC Routing and Remote Access (RRAS) snap-in tools. Another way is to use the Remote Desktop Connection (the new Terminal Services client) utility included with Terminal Server. Remote Desktop uses the new Remote Desktop Protocol (RDP) and displays the actual console session of a remote-accessed server. Configurations settings such as dynamically configuring the remote connection to match the available bandwidth and automatic reconnection improve the reliability of the administrator's remote session.

Creating Desktop Shortcuts That Process the runas Command

Administrators are always on the lookout for timesaving and more efficient ways to perform their duties. Administrators can remotely log in to their networks with administrative credentials using the runas command tool. Remote Computer Management and Active Directory Users and Computers management with administrative credentials can also be accomplished by using this tool.

To create a desktop shortcut using the runas command, perform the following steps:

1. Right-click an empty area on your desktop, choose New, and then click Shortcut.

2. In the Create Shortcut Dialog box, type the location of the Item text box, and type runas along with the command parameters you want to use. See Table 4.1 for examples and parameters.

3. Click the Next button, type a descriptive name for the shortcut, and click the Finish button.

Table 4.1 shows some examples of the `runas` command.

Table 4.1 Examples Using the runas Command	
To Create a Shortcut To	**Type**
A command prompt with administrative credentials	`runas /user:ComputerName\administrator cmd`
Computer Management with administrative credentials	`runas /user:ComputerName\administrator "mmc%windir%\system32\compmgmt.msc"`
AD Users and Computers with domain administrative credentials	`runas /user:ComputerName\administrator "mmc%windir%\system32\dsa.msc"`
AD Users and Computers in another forest	`runas /netonly /user:DomainName\UserName "mmc%windir%\system32\dsa.msc"`

For example, if you want to connect to a remote server to perform computer management as administrator on a computer named winsvr2003rc2, you type the following in the Type the Location of the Item text box. The following syntax works if the domain or local machine name is winsvr2003rc2:

```
runas /user:winsvr2003rc2\administrator "mmc%windir%\system32\compmgmt.msc"
```

The **runas** command isn't limited to just administrator accounts. Use this command when you're logged on as a member on another group. Also note that some programs do not support the **runas** command.

When running the Microsoft Management Console (MMC), the user's credentials are not displayed. Exercise caution.

Connecting to a Remote Server Using the MMC Snap-Ins

Another method to remotely manage Windows 2000 Server and Windows Server 2003 is to use the Microsoft Management Console snap-in tools. Windows Server 2003 includes many built-in tools saved with an .msc extension. For example, Computer Management and AD Users and Computers are available in the Administrative Tools folder located in both the Control Panel and the Start, All Programs menu.

To perform remote administrative management tasks on server computers using an MMC console, follow these steps:

1. Click Start, click Run, type mmc in the Open text box, and then click OK.

2. From the menu in the Console1 window, click File, Add/Remove Snap-in, and then click the Add button in the Add/Remove Snap-in dialog box.

3. In the Add Standalone Snap-in dialog box, double-click the snap-in you want to use. For example, double-click the Computer Management snap-in. Figure 4.5 shows the resulting Computer Management dialog box with the Another Computer radio button selected.

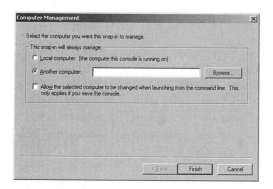

Figure 4.5   You can select another computer to manage via the Computer Management console.

4. Click another computer, browse, or type the name of the server you want this snap-in to manage remotely, and click the Finish button.

 You can save typing time by clicking the Browse button that displays the Select Computer dialog box. Click the Locations button to display the entire directory. Next, expand the Entire Directory folder, select and expand the desired domain, select and expand either the Domain Controllers or Computers folders, and select the server you want to manage remotely.

To perform remote administrative management tasks on server computers using a saved MMC console, perform the following steps:

1. Click Start, Run, and type mmc in the Open text box.

2. Select Open from the Console Programs menu.

3. Browse to the folder that contains your saved console and then double-click the console to open.

Connecting to a Remote Server Using the Remote Desktop Connection Utility

Windows 2000 Terminal Services operates in either application mode or remote administration mode. In Windows 2003 Terminal Server, the remote administration mode is referred to as *Remote Desktop for Administration*. Terminal Services for Windows Server 2003 uses the Remote Desktop Protocol for communication to remotely display the actual console session of the remote server. New Remote Desktop Connection features include an improved user interface, the ability to easily switch between windowed and full-screen mode, and dynamic allocation of network bandwidth to match the client's remote session.

The Remote Desktop Connection snap-in is used to manage Remote Desktop connections to the Windows 2003 family of server operating systems. This tool is an invaluable aid to administrators who manage several Windows 2000 or Windows 2003 servers or terminal servers. Administrators can easily switch between active server connections using the standard navigation tree in the Remote Desktop MMC snap-in.

 Make sure that you know the best tool to use for remotely managing servers. For managing and administering several servers, the Remote Desktop Connection utility is the best tool. The **runas** command-line utility is best used to manage one server and administer one activity when logged on to a user's PC. The MMC snap-in tools are best utilized to manage several activities on one server.

Using a RDP client, such as Windows XP Professional, to connect to a terminal server includes the capability to use many of the local resources within the remote session, such as client file system, smart cards, audio, clipboard, printers (both local and network), and serial ports. This redirection of resources gives users many new advantages.

To connect to a remote server using the Remote Desktop MMC snap-in utility in Windows 2003, perform the following steps:

1. Click Start, All Programs, Administrative Tools, Remote Desktops. The Remote Desktops MMC console opens.

2. In the left pane, right-click the Remote Desktops icon and select Add New Connection from the shortcut menu. Figure 4.6 shows the resulting Add New Connection dialog box.

Figure 4.6 You can configure a remote server via the Add New Connection dialog box.

3. In the Add New Connection dialog box, type the terminal server name or IP address or click the Browse button. Type a meaningful connection name in the Connection Name text box. Make sure that the Connect to Console check box is checked. Enter your user logon name, password, and domain in the logon information text boxes, and click OK to continue.

Server-side Remote Desktop client configuration options are available in the Terminal Services configuration program. To configure client remote session settings using Windows 2003 Terminal Server:

1. Click Start, All Programs, Administrative tools, and then Terminal Services Configuration.

2. In the left pane, select the Connections folder. In the right pane, right-click the RDP-TCP connection icon and choose Properties.

3. Click the Remote Control tab, as shown in Figure 4.7, and select one of the following three options:

➤ Use Remote Control with Default User Settings

➤ Do Not Allow Remote Control

➤ Use Remote Control with the Following Settings—With this option, you can request the user's permission for viewing or interacting with the remote session.

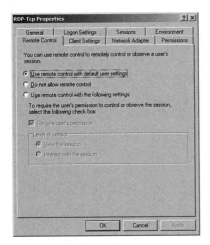

Figure 4.7   You can configure client remote session settings via the RDP-TCP Properties dialog box.

4. Click the Client Settings tab. The Client Settings tab contains the Use Connections Settings from User Settings check box, various settings for controlling the degree of color depth, and check boxes to disable various mappings.

Client-side Remote Desktop client configuration options are accessed in the Remote Desktop Connection dialog box by clicking the Options button. To start a client remote session using Windows XP Professional, perform the following steps:

1. Click Start, All Programs, Accessories, Communications, Remote Desktop Connection.

2. In the Remote Desktop Connection dialog box, type the computer name of the Terminal Server you want to connect to.

3. Click the Connect button to connect to the Windows 2000 or Windows 2003 Terminal Server.

4. Type in your username and password and click the OK button. When complete, click the OK button.

5. Your remote session is full screen and high color by default. The connection bar appears at the top of your full-screen session. Double–click in the pinned connection bar area to display your server's GUI in Windows screen mode. Click the maximize button in the window to return to pinned mode. Click the Windows X button to close the session. You're prompted to confirm closing the Terminal Services session. Click the OK button to close the session.

Lower-speed bandwidth connections can be optimized to improve performance by choosing the proper connection speed on the Experience tab located in the Remote Desktop Connection dialog box. To configure client connection speed using the Remote Desktop utility, perform the following steps:

1. Click Start, All Programs, Accessories, Communications, Remote Desktop Connection.

2. In the Remote Desktop Connection dialog box, click the Options button to display client configuration options.

3. Click the Experience tab and select the appropriate connection speed by clicking on the drop-down list box as shown in Figure 4.8. You can also uncheck unneeded components for your remote session in the Allow the Following check box lists.

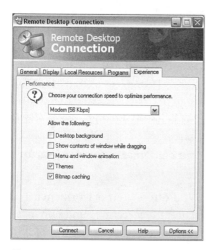

Figure 4.8 You can configure the proper connection settings for the remote connection via the Experience tab of the Remote Desktop Connection dialog box.

What happens if your remote session unexpectedly terminates? RDC will automatically try to reconnect to the Terminal Server when a network connection is lost.

One last point worth mentioning is the new Remote Desktop Users group. Instead of adding individual users to a list in the Terminal Services configuration program, you can simply make them members of the Remote Desktop Users group.

Add the Everyone group to the Remote Desktop Users group to allow everyone access to Terminal Server sessions.

Managing Internet Information Services Web Server

Previous versions of Internet Information Services were installed by default on Windows NT Server and the Windows 2000 Server family. Furthermore, in earlier versions (that is, IIS 5.0), IIS servers were not locked down by default. Many unnecessary settings were on by default. This opened the door to widespread vulnerability and attacks. Locking down IIS server was tedious and had to be performed manually.

Installing any of the Windows Server 2003 family of products, except Windows 2003 Web Server Edition, does not install IIS 6.0 by default. Administrators must explicitly select and install IIS 6.0 on all but the Web Server Edition. Also note that IIS 6.0 is disabled by default when a Windows server is upgraded to Windows Server 2003. When IIS 6.0 is installed, it is configured by default in a locked-down state. After installation, IIS 6.0 accepts requests for static files only until you configure it to serve dynamic content.

IIS 6.0 is more reliable, easier to manage, and offers high performance and scalability along with being much more secure. New features and enhancements include server consolidation, lower total cost of ownership (TCO), and less planned and unplanned downtime.

The following section shows you how to install and configure IIS 6.0, install and manage ASP.NET, implement Web applications and application pooling, manage the metabase and remote locations, and how to monitor and optimize IIS 6.0.

Installing IIS 6.0

One of two methods is used to install IIS 6.0 on Windows Server 2003. Use either the Configure Your Server Wizard or the Add/Remove applet in the Control Panel. The following steps will install IIS 6.0 from the Add/Remove applet:

1. Click Start, Control Panel. Double-click the Add/Remove applet and then click the Add/Remove Windows Components button.

2. In the Windows Components dialog box, check the Application Server check box, and then click the Details button.

3. Click the Internet Information Services (IIS) check box and then click the Details button.

4. Notice that Common Files, Internet Information Services Manager, and World Wide Web Service (WWW) are the only items checked. Select World Wide Web Service and click the Details button. Notice that only the WWW service and Active Server Pages are selected by default. Click the Cancel button to return to the IIS dialog box. Click the Cancel button to return to the Application Server dialog box.

5. Because we will be learning about ASP.NET features, check the ASP.NET check box in the Application Server dialog box, and then click the OK button to continue.

6. Click the Next button in the Windows Components dialog box.

7. Click the Finish button to complete the installation.

Configuring IIS Authentication

Windows Server 2003 offers improved authentication and authorization. Although you're familiar with the Windows authentication process, you probably do not thoroughly understand what authorization is all about. Authorization allows or denies a user permission to perform a process or task. Windows Server 2003 now supports .NET Passport as a method to authenticate. Authorization in Windows 2000 IIS 5.0 has been enhanced in IIS 6.0 to include the use of a new authorization framework. Web applications can make use of URL authorization along with Authorization Manager to control user access. Domain administrators can make use of constrained, delegated authorization to delegate control to individual computers and services only.

To start IIS 6.0 Manager, click Start, All Programs, Administrative Tools, Internet Information Services (IIS) Manager. IIS opens. User authentication can be set up for your Web resources by configuring property sheets at the Web site, directory, or file level. Table 4.2 offers a summary of Web site authentication methods along with a brief description of each.

Table 4.2 Summary of Web Site Authentication Methods

Method	Description
Anonymous Authentication	No username or password required. Best used to grant public access to information that requires no security.
Basic Authentication	Requires a user account and password. Has a low level of security because passwords are sent across the network in plain text.
Digest Authentication	Similar to Basic Authentication. Requires a user account and password. Has a medium level of security because user credentials are sent across the network in a hashed message digest.
Advanced Digest Authentication	Similar to Digest Authentication. Requires a user account and password. Has a medium level of security. A domain controller (DC) stores the user credentials as an MD5 hash.
Integrated Windows Authentication	Uses Kerberos as the authentication protocol, provides a high level of security, and is best used on your organization's intranet.
Certificate Authentication	Establishes secure connection between client and server by using Secure Sockets Layer (SSL). Provides a high level of security and is the preferred method used for conducting business over the Internet.
.NET Passport Authentication	Provides single unified logon through SSL, HHTP redirects, cookies, and JavaScript. Passwords are encrypted and the level of security is high.
UNC Authentication	Used to verify user credentials for access to shared folders and files on a remote computer.

Installing and Adding ASP.NET to Web Server Extensions

The .NET Framework and ASP.NET offer high functionality with rapid application development (RAD) and improved request-processor architecture integration with IIS 6.0. By default, ASP.NET is not installed. When you install ASP.NET, it adds the ASP.NET to the Web Server extensions list with the allowed status as shown in Figure 4.9.

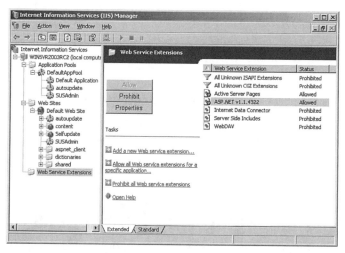

Figure 4.9   You can verify the status of ASP.NET Web Server Extensions via IIS Manager.

The ASP.NET configuration system has great flexibility in defining configuration settings. You can define configuration settings when your applications are first deployed and later add or revise the configuration. Any standard text editor or XML parser can be used to create, edit, and manage configuration information because the configuration information is stored in XML-based text files.

An ASP.NET application server can store many configuration files, all named Web.config, in multiple directories. The Web.config file applies configuration settings to its own directory and all child directories below it. To protect the configuration information files, ASP.NET configures IIS to prevent direct browser access.

Command Line Administration

IIS 6.0 includes many new management tools to reduce time and management duties. For example, the XML configuration file can be modified while the server is still up and running. Command-line administration using supported scripts is designed to do most common Web management administration tasks from the command prompt. These scripts use the Windows Management Instrumentation (WMI) service to retrieve and write information to IIS's metabase. The following command-line scripts are included:

➤ IISweb.vbs—Used to start, stop, create, delete, and list Web sites

➤ IISftp.vbs—Used to start, stop, create, delete, and list file sites

➤ IISvdir.vbs—Used to create, delete, and display virtual directories

➤ IISftpdr.vbs—Used to create, delete, and display virtual directories under a root

➤ IISconfg.vbs—Used to import and export IIS configuration to an XML file

➤ IISback.vbs—Used to back up and restore IIS configuration

➤ IISapp.vbs—Used to list application pool and process IDs for started worker processes

➤ IISweb.vbs—Used to configure Web service extensions

Creating and Managing Web Applications

To create an application, you need to designate a directory (called the *application root*) as a starting point. You can give it a friendly name that appears in IIS Manager.

By default, Web sites are root-level applications. When you create a Web site, a default application is created at the same time. You can use the default created application, delete it, or replace it with a new application.

You must be a member of the local Administrators group on the local computer to create Web applications. If you're logged on with only user permissions, you could use the runas command discussed earlier to log on with Administrative privileges to create a Web application.

To create a new Web site and the default application, perform the following steps:

1. Open IIS Manager, expand your local computer, right-click the Default Web Site, choose New, and then choose Web Site. The Web Site Creation Wizard opens. Click the Next button to continue.

2. Type a name for your Web site in the Web Site Description text box and then click the Next button to continue.

3. Select your IIS server's IP address for the Web site and then click the Next button.

4. Type or browse to the path for your home directory in the Path text box. Check or uncheck the Allow Anonymous Access to This Web Site check box and then click the Next button to continue.

5. Assign the appropriate Web site access permissions as shown in Figure 4.10 and click the Next button.

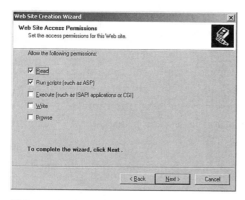

Figure 4.10 You configure permissions via the Web Site Access Permissions dialog box.

6. Click the Finish button. The new Web site is created along with the default application.

7. Using IIS Manager, browse to the newly created Web site directory, right-click it, and choose Properties.

8. On the Web site Properties sheet, click the Home directory tab. Notice the default application is listed in the Application Name text box.

9. You can either accept the default application or click the Remove button to create a new application.

If you see the Remove button instead of the Create button, an application is already created.

10. In the Execute Permissions list box, set your permissions by performing one of the following actions and then click the OK button:

➤ Click None to prevent scripts from running.

➤ Click Scripts Only to enable scripts to run.

➤ Click Scripts and Executables to allow any application to run.

Implementing Application Pooling

Web sites and applications use self-contained units called *application pools* as part of their fault-tolerant process architecture. Application pools are separated by boundaries so that applications run unaffected with other applications.

After an application is created, you can isolate it to run in a process separate from the Web server and other applications. You isolate the application in one of the two following modes: worker process isolation mode or IIS 5.0 isolation mode. To isolate an application in worker process mode, perform the following steps:

1. In IIS Manager, right-click the application you want to isolate and choose Properties. Select the Home Directory tab.

2. Under the Application Settings section in the Application Pool list box, click an application pool. Click the Apply button and the OK button.

 NOTE To create application pools, you must be running in work process isolation mode and be a member of the Administrators group.

To create application pools, perform the following steps:

1. In IIS Manager, expand the local computer, right-click Application Pools, select New, and then click Application Pool. Figure 4.11 shows the Add New Application Pool dialog box.

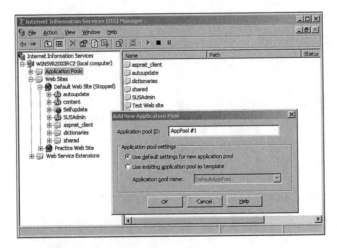

Figure 4.11 Add New Application Pool dialog box.

2. Type in a name for the application pool in the application pool IIS text box.

3. Select either Use Default Settings for New Application Pool or Use Existing Application Pool as Template, and then click the OK button.

To assign an application to an application pool, perform the following steps:

1. Right-click the application you want to assign to an application pool and click Properties.

2. Click the Home Directory tab, verify that application name displays or create a new application.

3. In the Application Pool list box, select the application pool name (refer to Figure 4.11).

Managing the IIS 6.0 Metabase

The metabase configuration file, `Metabase.xml`, stores the IIS configuration settings in a hierarchical structure. When IIS starts, `Metabase.xml` configuration settings are read and copied into IIS cache memory, referred to as *in-memory metabase*. `Metabase.xml` is a plain-text file that is easily read and configured using a text editor like Notepad.

After your Web site and application are up and running, you can save the metabase configuration as a backup copy. Each time the metabase changes, IIS automatically creates a backup of the metabase configuration and schema files.

To create a manual metabase configuration backup, perform the following steps:

1. In IIS Manager, right-click your local computer, select All Tasks, and then click Backup/Restore Configuration.

2. Click Create Backup.

3. Type the name for your backup in the Configuration Backup Name text box. Optionally check the Encrypt Backup Using Password check box. Click OK, and then click Close.

Metabase backup files contain only configuration settings. They do not include content such as .asp files.

Managing an IIS Server Remotely

IIS 6.0 includes a new Web-based administration console called the Remote Administration tool for remotely managing other IIS servers. Using your Web browser on either your company's intranet or Internet connection, the Remote Administration tool enables you to remotely configure and manage a server from a remote client. You can configure network settings, set disk quotas, manage local user accounts, create and delete Web sites, and restart the remote Web server using the Web interface for Remote Administration tool. You can also use IIS Manager to remotely manage your company's intranet or Terminal Services to connect to your IIS Manager.

To install and add the Remote Administration tool, perform the following steps:

1. Click Start, Control Panel, click the Add or Remove Programs applet, and select Add/Remove Windows Components.

2. Select Application Server and click the Details button.

3. Select Internet Information Server (IIS) and click Details.

4. Select World Wide Web Publishing Service and click Details.

5. Select the Remote Administration (HTML) check box.

6. Click the OK button three times, click Next, and Finish.

To view the Remote Administration tool, expand your local computer, expand the Web Sites folder, right-click on the Administration Web Site folder, and click Browse.

To administer an IIS Web server using the Remote Administration tool, open your intranet site using your Web browser and type the following in the address bar: `http://hostname:8099`, where *hostname* is the name of the IIS computer you want to manage.

Monitoring IIS 6.0

The WWW Service Administration and Monitoring component pings worker processes periodically to determine whether they're blocked. If a process is completely blocked, the WWW service terminates the process and creates a new worker process to replace it. IIS 6.0 also periodically checks the status of application pools and will automatically restart the Web site and applications in the event of a failure. Web sites that fail to open in a short time period are automatically disabled, offering further stability and protection.

Introduced in Windows 2000, the Windows Management Instrumentation (WMI) tool provides access to important data and statistics such as performance counters and system configuration. IIS 6.0 now includes WMI for monitoring performance. Administrators can now manage query support and associations between objects using the WMI tool included with IIS 6.0.

To manage servers remotely, you need to be a member of the local Administrators group. The one exception is using the **runas** command.

Exam Prep Questions

Question 1

> Sara has a Windows XP Professional computer. Her administrator told her about the importance of keeping her computer system up-to-date by using the Automatic Updates client software. Sara needs to install this update but cannot find it on her computer. What are two methods that Sara can use to install the Automatic Updates client software? (Select two choices.)
>
> ❑ A. Select Start, Control Panel, and click the Automatic Updates applet.
>
> ❑ B. Install Windows XP Service Pack 1.
>
> ❑ C. Select Start, Settings, Control Panel, and click the Automatic Updates applet.
>
> ❑ D. Run Internet Explorer and type **http://www.microsoft.com/windows2000/downloads/recommended/susclient/default.asp** in the Address bar.
>
> ❑ E. Select Start and click the Automatic Updates icon.

Answers B and D are correct. Windows XP Professional does not include the Automatic Updates client software. Sara can obtain the updates by either browsing to the automatic client updates site or by installing Service Pack 1, which includes the update. There is no Automatic Updates icon or applet on Sara's computer.

Question 2

> Alex has just finished installing Windows Server 2003 on a new computer that has a 4GB hard drive. Alex decides to install the Software Update Services (SUS). He downloads the SUS package, double-clicks the SUS10sp1.exe file, and begins the installation. He selects the Typical installation button, and the installation successfully completes. Next, Alex connects to the Windows Update site and downloads all the updates. Afterward, Alex notices the Updates folder contains almost 600MB of files. Another administrator told Alex that this folder would contain about 150MB of files. What did Alex do wrong?
>
> ○ A. Alex downloaded the wrong file.
>
> ○ B. During the installation, Alex selected Typical instead of Custom.
>
> ○ C. Alex obtained the wrong patches and updates.
>
> ○ D. Alex's Windows 2003 server already has SUS and the updates installed in the same folders.

Answer B is correct. During the installation process, Alex should have selected Custom to select English and one or two other languages that he might need. By default, Typical installs all the language files, consuming more than 600MB of hard disk space. Alex did download the correct file and updates. Therefore, answers A and C are incorrect. Windows 2003 does not include the SUS software program or the updates; therefore, answer D is incorrect.

Question 3

Using Internet Explorer 5.0, Sara, a local administrator, attempts to view the SUS Administration Web page from her Windows 2000 Professional computer, but she cannot. Why can't Sara view the SUS Administration Web page?

○ A. Sara is not a member of the Power Users group.

○ B. Sara is not a member of the Domain Administrators group.

○ C. Sara needs to use IE version 5.5 or greater.

○ D. Sara does not have Windows 2000 Professional with SP3 installed on her computer.

Answer C is correct. Using IE 5.0 causes an error page to display, reminding you to update to IE 5.5 or greater. Answers A and B are incorrect because you must be a member of the local Administrators group to view the SUS Administration Web page. Answer D is not correct because Windows 2000 SP3 has nothing to do with viewing the SUS Administration Web page.

Question 4

Alex is a local administrator and needs to use the MMC snap-in tools to connect to a remote server. He clicks Start, Run, types mmc in the Run text box, and Console1 opens. Next he selects File, Add/Remove Snap-in from the menu, and clicks the Add button. He selects the Computer Management snap-in and clicks the Add button, and the Finish button. The MMC console displays Computer Management (local). What did Alex do wrong?

○ A. Alex is not a member of the Power Users group.

○ B. Alex is not a member of the Domain Administrators group.

○ C. After Alex selects Computer Management snap-in and clicks the Add button, Alex needs to select the Another Computer radio button in the Computer Management dialog box.

○ D. From the Console File menu, select File, Connect to Another Computer.

Answer C is correct. After Alex selects Computer Management snap-in and clicks the Add button, he needs to select the Another Computer radio button in the Computer Management dialog box and then either browse or type in the remote server's name in the text box. Answers A and B are incorrect because you only need to be a member of the local Administrators group. Answer D is incorrect because there is no such command available.

Question 5

Sara needs to manage several servers remotely. What is the best tool for Sara to use?

- ○ A. The **runas** command
- ○ B. The Remote Desktop connection utility
- ○ C. MMC snap-in tools
- ○ D. AD Users and Computers

Answer B is correct. The Remote Desktop connection utility tool is best used for managing several servers. The runas command is used to manage one server. The MMC snap-in tools are best used to manage one server performing several activities. AD Users and Computers cannot be used to manage remote computers.

Question 6

Using Remote Desktop Connection on a Windows XP Professional computer, Sara sends an invitation to her administrator to view her desktop remotely and then disconnects from the Internet. Her administrator receives the invitation but cannot access Sara's computer. What does the administrator need to do to manage Sara's desktop remotely?

- ○ A. Tell Sara to reconnect to the Internet.
- ○ B. Instruct Sara to reinstall the Remote Desktop connection utility.
- ○ C. Make Sara a member of the local Administrators group.
- ○ D. Instruct Sara to check the Allow This Computer to Be Controlled Remotely check box in the Remote tab of her computer's Properties box.

Answer A is correct. Sara needs to reconnect to the Internet, send another invitation, and remain on the Internet. Instructing Sara to reinstall the Remote Desktop connection utility or making Sara a member of the local Administrators group would not solve the problem. Instructing Sara to check the Allow This Computer to Be Controlled Remotely check box in the Remote tab of her computer's Properties box would allow the administrator to take control of and manage her desktop when a connection is established.

Question 7

Alex manages a Windows Server 2003 computer at his company's branch office. Using Terminal Server Remote Desktops MMC console, he successfully connects to his company's main office Terminal Server. He needs to change the Terminal Server's main office User Remote Control configuration settings—how is this accomplished?

○ A. Alex needs to run Terminal Services Manager.

○ B. Alex needs to run Terminal Services Configuration.

○ C. Alex cannot do this task remotely.

○ D. Alex needs to check the Allow This Computer To Be Controlled Remotely check box in the Remote tab of his computer's Properties box.

Answer B is correct. Alex needs to run Terminal Services Configuration, select the Connections folder, right-click the RDP-TCP connection icon, and choose Properties. In the RDP-TCP properties box, he should select the Remote Control tab and make his changes. Neither Terminal Services Manager nor checking the Allow This Computer to Be Controlled Remotely check box will help Alex change users remote control configuration settings.

Question 8

Clara is a local administrator managing a Windows Server 2000 computer with SP3 applied and Active Directory installed at her company's main office. Clara installs the Software Update Services on the Windows 2000 Server. Clara wants to create a group policy to apply updates for the main office clients. She right-clicks the main office OU in AD Users and computers, chooses Properties, and clicks the Group Policy tab. She then clicks New, types in SUS Policy for the policy name, and then clicks the Edit button. The Group Policy Editor opens. Clara navigates and expands the Computer Configuration, Administrative Templates, and Windows components folders, but does not see The Windows Update folder listed. Why not?

○ A. Clara needs to apply SP4 to the Windows 2000 Server.

○ B. Clara needs to reinstall SUS.

○ C. Clara needs to right-click the Administrative Templates folder and choose add Add/Remove Templates.

○ D. Clara needs to download the wuau.adm template from Microsoft's Web site.

Answer C is correct. Clara needs to right-click Administrative Templates, choose Add/Remove Templates, and then click Add. In the Policy Templates dialog box, she should select the wuau.adm template and click the Open button. The SUS wuau.adm template is only added to the Administrative Templates folder on Windows 2003 Server by default. Neither applying SP4, reinstalling SUS, nor downloading the wuau.adm template is necessary because the template was added to the Policy Templates folder during the initial SUS installation.

Question 9

Which IIS Web site authentication method is similar to basic authentication, requires a user account and password and has a medium level of security because user credentials are sent across the network in a hashed message digest?

○ A. Advanced digest authentication

○ B. Digest authentication

○ C. Integrated Windows authentication

○ D. .NET Passport authentication

Answer B is correct. Digest authentication requires a user account and password and has a medium level of security because user credentials are sent across the network in a hashed message digest. Advanced digest authentication is similar to digest authentication, requires a user account and password and has a medium level of security. A domain controller (DC) stores the user credentials as an MD5 hash. Integrated Windows authentication uses Kerberos as the authentication protocol and provides a high level of security. .NET Passport authentication provides a single, unified logon, passwords are encrypted, and the level of security is high.

Question 10

Sara needs to add a Web application to her IIS 6.0 Server. She opens IIS Manager, navigates to her Web site, and opens the Web site property page. She clicks on the Home Directory tab to add the application in the Settings text box and sees the Remove button instead of the Create button. What must be done for Sara to add her Web application?

○ A. Add Sara to the Power Users group.

○ B. Add Sara to the domain administrators group.

○ C. Instruct Sara to click the remove button, type he application name in the text box, and then click the Create button.

○ D. Change the default application pool.

Answer C is correct. An application is already installed if the Remove button is visible instead of the Create button. Instruct Sara to click the Remove button, type the application name in the text box, and then click the Create button. Because Sara has already opened IIS Manager and the Web site's properties page, she is a local administrator. Changing the default application pool has to do with isolating the Web application into a separate process.

Need to Know More?

 Microsoft Software Update Services: Flash Demo: `http://www.microsoft.com/windows2000/windowsupdate/sus/flashpage.asp`

 Software Update Services Components and Features: `http://www.microsoft.com/windows2000/windowsupdate/sus/suscomponents.asp`

 What's New in Internet Information Services 6.0: `http://www.microsoft.com/windowsserver2003/evaluation/overview/technologies/iis.mspx`

 IIS 6.0 Mature at Last: Microsoft's Internet Information Server: `http://mcpmag.com/features/article.asp?editorialsid=330.`

 White paper—*Technical overview of management services*: `http://www.microsoft.com/windowsserver2003/docs/Manageover.doc`

 TechNet Windows 2003 Resources: `http://www.microsoft.com/technet/treeview/default.asp?url=/technet/prodtechnol/windows2000serv/default.asp`

 Microsoft Training and Certifications—Exams: `http://www.microsoft.com/traincert/mcpexams/default.asp`

 Microsoft Training and Certifications—View new and upcoming exams at `http://www.microsoft.com/traincert/mcpexams/status/new.asp`

 Preparation Guide for Exam 70-292: `http://www.microsoft.com/traincert/exams/70-292.asp`

Implementing Disaster Recovery

Terms you need to understand:

✓ ASR

✓ Shadow Copies of Shared Folders

✓ System State

✓ Differential versus incremental

✓ EFS

✓ Digital signature

✓ Safe mode

✓ Last known good configuration

✓ Driver rollback

Techniques you need to master:

✓ Using Automatic System Recovery (ASR) to back up and restore Windows Server 2003

✓ Learning how to restore data from Shadow Copies of Shared Folders

✓ Learning device driver rollback features

✓ Configuring security for backup actions

✓ Troubleshooting restoring data problems

✓ Troubleshooting boot process failures and problems

The Windows Server 2003 family includes many new features and enhancements for better storage management. Managing and maintaining hard disk drives and storage volumes and backing up and restoring data are more reliable and easier to do. Improvements in storage management help reduce total cost of ownership (TCO) while making Windows Server 2003 more secure, robust, and reliable. Planned downtime and maintenance are reduced. Backup operations can be completed with open file backup. Backup uses shadow copies, ensuring that any open files accessed by users are also backed up.

In this chapter, you'll learn how to use Automatic System Recovery (ASR) to back up and restore a Windows Server 2003 installation in the event of a catastrophic failure. You'll also learn how to restore user data versions using Shadow Copies of Shared Folders.

Updating device drivers sometimes results in system instability or even the famous Blue Screen of Death. With the new Device Driver Rollback feature, you can easily uninstall the errant driver, restore your previous driver, and get back to work.

Backing up, restoring, and maintaining security for backup operations are discussed along with troubleshooting problems with restoring data. Finally, troubleshooting boot startup process failures using the Windows Server 2003 variety of troubleshooting tools and utilities is analyzed.

Using Automatic System Recovery

Fortunately, server devastation, such as catastrophic hardware failure, does not occur often. Fire, earthquakes, and malicious vandalism are good reasons to use the new Automatic System Recovery (ASR) feature included in Windows Server 2003. When disaster strikes, using ASR enables you to recover a Windows Server 2003 without difficulty, including the server's System State and hardware configuration and all applications. ASR was introduced with the Windows XP operating system. Using the Windows Server 2003 Backup application, you can easily configure ASR for disaster recovery.

Using Windows 2000 Server, recovering from a disaster is a long, tedious, and manual process. You need to install Windows 2000 Server, manually configure storage hardware to match pre-disaster hardware, restore operating system settings, and restore all applications and users' data.

Instead of using the time-consuming manual methods, ASR provides an uncomplicated solution by automatically bringing a failed, nonbootable Windows Server 2003 back to its former state. ASR restores the operating system and all applications and settings. ASR configures new storage with the same settings as the pre-disaster server. You only need to use Backup afterward to restore all users' data.

To use ASR, you must first create a complete backup of all the server's system files and also create an ASR floppy disk that will be used in the recovery process. The floppy disk contains important system storage configuration information. Perform the following steps to create a full backup and an ASR floppy:

1. Click Start, All Programs, Accessories, System Tools, Backup. Next, click the Advanced Mode hyperlink on the Backup Wizard Welcome screen.

2. Click the Automated System Recovery Wizard button. The Welcome to the Automated System Recovery Wizard dialog box appears.

3. Click the Next button to proceed. In the Backup Destination dialog box, select your media type from the drop-down list box. Browse or type the backup media or filename in the Backup Media or File Name text box and click the Next button to continue.

4. Click the Finish button to start the ASR backup. A dialog box appears and informs you that ASR is saving your storage configuration settings. ASR then prepares to back up your files using Shadow Copies of Shared Folders (these features are discussed next in this chapter). The backup dialog box displays time, a progress bar, status, and file and bytes processed and estimated. On my Windows Server 2003 with Word 2000 installed, about 2.6GB of data (about 22,000 files) was backed up.

5. When the backup completes, you're prompted to insert a floppy disk for the ASR storage file information as shown in Figure 5.1.

Figure 5.1   Backup Utility dialog box.

6. Insert a formatted floppy into your floppy drive and click the OK button to write the ASR storage file information. A reminder dialog box appears when complete to remind you to store your ASR floppy in a safe place. Click the OK button, click the Close button, and then exit the Backup application.

To restore your Windows Server 2003 using ASR, perform the following steps:

1. Boot your Windows Server 2003 Installation CD-ROM and choose Automated System Recovery on the Welcome menu.

2. If you have a manufacturer's driver disk for the mass storage controller, press your F6 function key when prompted and insert your manufacturer's driver disk.

3. Press your F2 function key when prompted at the start of the 16-bit text-mode section of Setup.

4. Insert your ASR floppy disk when prompted.

5. ASR recovery begins. Grab a cup of coffee or soda and take a break. When ASR finishes, your Windows Server 2003 will have the operating system and all applications installed.

6. Run Backup to restore the latest backup of users' data.

 If you make major hardware changes to the server after you've created an ASR backup, it's a good idea to delete your original ASR and make a new ASR backup. Windows Server 2003 ASR provides fully extensible third-party support for backup solution vendors.

Restoring Data from Shadow Copies of Shared Folders

According to a recent survey, companies lose an estimated 12 billion dollars per year due to accidental file corruption and file deletion! When a user accidentally deletes a file, he or she must either re-create the file from scratch or have the network administrator search the tape backup library and try to restore the file from the latest backup. Even if the file is restored from tape backup, the user still needs to re-create the data lost prior to the latest backup. Either method is extremely frustrating and time-consuming.

Shadow Copies of Shared Folders, a new feature added to Windows 2003, provides point-in time copies of files located in shared folders on Windows

Server 2003. Users can view, copy, and restore previous versions of their shared files as they existed at points-of-times in the past. With Shadow Copies of Shared Folders, you can

➤ Recover accidentally deleted and corrupted files without assistance from network support

➤ Recover files that were accidentally overwritten by using the Save command instead of the Save As file command

➤ Compare or use previous versions of files

➤ Recover files that are open and used by several users, such as Access database files

Shadow Copies of Shared Folders benefits include the following:

➤ Applications can continue to write data during backup.

➤ Open files are no longer omitted during backup.

➤ Backups can be performed at any time, without locking out files and users.

➤ Users can view, copy, and restore their own previous file versions, saving administrators time.

Creating Shadow Copies of Shared Folders is not a replacement for regular backups.

Microsoft likes to ask exam questions that involve permissions. Restoring a file from a regular backup restores all file permissions previously assigned. Recovering a file that was accidentally deleted resets the file to its original default permissions.

Here's how Shadow Copies of Shared Folders works. Shadow Copies stores only the changes that occur in files from the last time they were copied. By copying only changes between points in time, file sizes should be reduced, saving both time and hard disk space. Four key decisions must be addressed before you begin installing the server-side software for Shadow Copies of Shared Folders:

➤ Source files—Volume containing files that need shadow copying

➤ Disk Space—Amount of space allocated for shadow copies

➤ Location of copies—Location of volume on hard disk drives

➤ Schedule—Schedule frequency of shadow copies

> **TIP**
>
> Planning ahead and making these decisions before you set up the server for Shadow Copies of Shared Folders saves time and unnecessary work for you afterward.

To set up server-side components and enable Shadow Copies of Shared Folders, perform the following steps:

1. On the file server, share the volume drive you want to make available for shadow copying.

2. Using Windows Explorer, right-click the volume, choose Sharing and Security from the context menu. From the Local Disk Properties page, click the Shadow Copies tab. The shared volume drive's properties are displayed as shown in Figure 5.2.

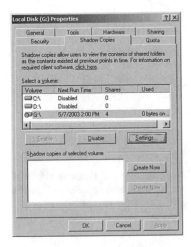

Figure 5.2 Shadow Copies main tab.

3. Under Select a Volume, select the volume you want Shadow Copies installed on, and then click Enable as shown in Figure 5.2. A message appears indicating that if you enable Shadow Copies, Windows will use the default schedule and settings, and create a shadow copy of the selected volumes(s) now—a warning that the default settings are not appropriate for servers that have high I/O load and asks Do You Want to Enable Shadow Copies? Click the Yes button to enable Shadow

Copies of Shared Folders. The Shadow Copies of Shared Folders service is initiated.

4. When Shadow Copies for Shared Folders creates shadow backups,
they're listed under Shadow Copies of Selected Volume as shown in
Figure 5.2. You can click the Create Now button to create a shadow
copy backup immediately. You can also click the Settings button to create a backup schedule.

5. To change the default schedule for Shadow Copies on the volume,
click the Settings button. The Settings dialog box opens, as shown in
Figure 5.3.

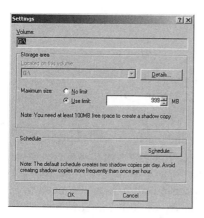

Figure 5.3 Shadow Copies volume settings.

6. In the Settings dialog box, click the Schedule button. Two default
schedules are listed in the Schedule drop-down list box: Monday
through Friday at 7 AM and Monday through Friday at Noon. You can
select one of the default schedules or click the New button and create a
new schedule.

7. To specify and set up a new schedule task, click the Schedule Task
drop-down list box and select one of the following options: Daily,
Weekly, Monthly, Once, At System Startup, At Logon, or When Idle.
If the task is scheduled for daily, weekly, monthly, or only once, select
the start time using the spinner controls. Click the scheduled task
weekly spinner controls to select how often in weeks you want to
scheduled task to run. To run the task, you can select multiple days of
the week. Check off the appropriate days in the week(s) on check
boxes. Finally, click the New button to create the additional scheduled
task and display it in the Scheduled Task drop-down list box as shown
in Figure 5.4.

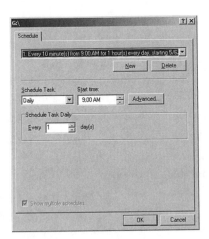

Figure 5.4 Shadow Copies Schedule settings tab.

8. Click the Advanced button shown in Figure 5.4 if you need to set a start date, end date, or repeat the task. Click the OK button to return to the Volume Settings dialog box.

9. You can also configure storage limits. Clicking the Details button displays the Shadow Copies volume storage area and free disk space statistics. Use the radio buttons to set either no storage limit or use limit for the storage volume. Use the radio buttons on the Setting Properties page to set either No Storage Limit or Use Limit for the Storage Volume.

 If the storage limit is reached, Shadow Copies will start deleting Shadow Copies backups, beginning with the oldest one. This bit of information would fit nicely into a Microsoft scenario-type question.

Shadow Copies of Shared Folders is built into the Windows Server 2003 family of products. Windows 98, Windows NT, Windows 2000 Server and Professional (SP3 and above), and Windows XP Professional clients have to install Shadow Copies of Shared Folders. You can download the client at http://www.microsoft.com/windowsserver2003/downloads/shadowcopyclient.mspx.

To set up client-side components and enable Shadow Copies of Shared Folders, perform the following steps:

1. Install the downloaded file ShadowCopyClient.msi file on your computer.

2. Using Windows Explorer, right-click the Shadow Copy Shared folder, choose Properties, and click the Previous Versions tab as shown in Figure 5.5.

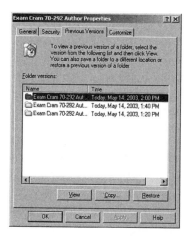

Figure 5.5   Shadow Copies' Previous Versions tab displaying folder versions.

To view, copy, or restore a folder, you must select the folder version that you want to view, copy, or restore. To open the folder, click View. To copy the folder to a different location, click Copy. To restore the entire previous version folder, click Restore.

To recover data and restore a deleted file, perform the following steps:

1. Select the Previous Versions tab as shown in Figure 5.5.

2. Select the folder version containing the deleted file and click the View button.

3. Select the version of the folder that contains the file (before deletion) and click the View button.

4. Select the folder and select the file to be recovered.

5. Drag and drop the file to your desktop or folder.

Restoring a corrupted or overwritten file is easier because you click the file itself and not the folder. To restore an overwritten or corrupted file, perform the following steps:

1. Select the Previous Versions tab as shown in Figure 5.5.

2. Select the folder version containing the overwritten or corrupted file and click the View button.

3. Right-click the overwritten or corrupted file and choose Properties.

4. Select the Previous Versions tab and click View to view the old version.

5. Click Copy to copy the old version to a different location, or click Restore to replace the current version with the older version.

 Learn the difference between restoring a folder and restoring a file. Know the difference between recovering and restoring a deleted file and restoring a corrupted or overwritten file.

Shadow Copies for Shared Folders—Best Practices

The following lists some tips for receiving the full benefit from employing Shadow Copies for Shared Folders:

➤ Consider user usage and scheduling before you enable shadow copies on the server.

➤ Do not use shadow copies on dual-boot computers or volumes containing mount points.

➤ For better performance, select a different volume on another disk for the storage area.

➤ Perform your regular daily backups.

➤ Do not schedule shadow copies to occur more than once an hour.

➤ If you need to delete the shadow volume, you should delete the scheduled task for creating shadow copies first.

Using Device Manager Driver Rollback Feature

First introduced in Windows XP, Driver Rollback enables you to uninstall or roll back the current drivers to the previous installed drivers. If a device you install fails or if your computer becomes unstable after you install a device, Driver Rollback enables you to restore the previous driver version.

To restore a previous version of a device driver, perform the following steps:

1. Click Start, All Programs, Administrative Tools, Computer Management.

2. In the Console tree, select System Tools, and then click Device Manager.

3. In the right-pane, double-click the type of device you want to roll back.

4. Right-click the device you want to restore to a previous state and then choose Properties.

5. Click the Driver tab, and then click the Roll Back Driver button as shown in Figure 5.6.

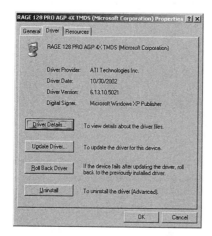

Figure 5.6   Click the Roll Back Driver button to use a previous driver.

You cannot use the rollback feature to restore previous versions of printer drivers.

Backing Up Files, Including System State Data

Backup has come a long way! Because Backup contains no built-in scheduling capabilities in Windows NT Server, the only methods for backing up your data files are to manually back them up or use tedious AT commands from a Command Prompt window. Also, NT Server's backup enables you to back up only to tape media.

Windows 2000 Server and Windows Server 2003 enable you to schedule backups, back up to many different media types, and also backup important system configuration files, including the Registry.

You perform backups and restores using either the Backup and Restore Wizard or by manually backing up and restoring data. You can back up the entire contents of a volume, selected files and folders, or just the System

State. You can also setup and schedule full, copy, differential, and incremental backups.

The importance of backing up the System State files at regular intervals cannot be overstated. Backing up the System State on a Windows Server 2003 includes backing up the following critical operating system components:

➤ Active Directory

➤ Boot-up operating system file

➤ COM+ class registration database files

➤ Registry

➤ SYSVOL, which contains domain policies and scripts

 When you choose to back up or restore the System State data, all the System State data that's relevant to your computer is backed up or restored. You cannot choose to back up or restore individual components of the System State data.

To perform a manual backup of the System State, perform the following steps:

1. Click Start, All Programs, Accessories, System Tools, Backup.

2. Click the Advanced Mode hyperlink to set up the System State backup manually.

3. Click the Backup tab and check the System State check box.

4. Click the Browse button to select the backup media or file location as shown in Figure 5.7.

To perform a manual restore of the System State, perform the following steps:

1. Click Start, All Programs, Accessories, System Tools, Backup.

2. Click the Advanced Mode hyperlink to set up the System State backup manually.

3. Click the Restore and Manage Media tab and navigate to and check the last System State check boxes as shown in Figure 5.8.

4. Click the Start Restore button to restore the System State to its original location.

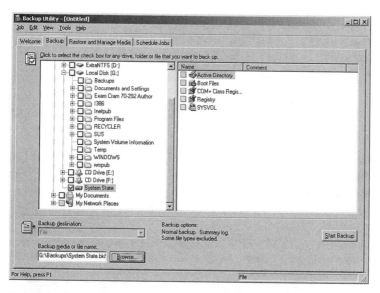

Figure 5.7 Backup showing System State selected; click the Start Backup Button to back up the System State.

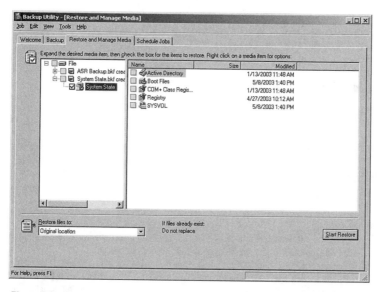

Figure 5.8 Restore and Manage Media tab showing System State selected.

One additional point worth mentioning is the difference between authoritative and nonauthoritative restores. During a normal file restore operation, Windows Backup operates in nonauthoritative restore mode. In this mode, Windows Backup restores all files, including Active Directory objects.

All data restored nonauthoritatively appears to the Active Directory replication system as old data. Old data is never replicated to other domain controllers. The Active Directory replication system updates the restored data with newer data from other domain controllers.

A nonauthoritative restore won't restore accidental deletion of Active Directory objects when the information that the restored domain controller brings back needs to be replicated to all domain controllers.

For example, if one of your administrative assistants accidentally deletes an organizational unit (OU) from your domain, you would have to perform an authoritative restore to recover the OU and replicate the recovered OU to other Domain controllers.

 An authoritative restore should be performed with caution due to the impact it could have on the Active Directory. An authoritative restore must be performed immediately after the computer has been restored from a previous backup, but prior to restarting the domain controller. An authoritative restore replicates all objects that are marked authoritative to every domain controller. To perform an authoritative restore on the computer, you must use the **ntdsutil.exe** tool to make USN (update sequence number) changes to the Active Directory database.

To perform an authoritative restore, perform the following steps:

1. Type ntdsutil at a command prompt and then press Enter.

2. Type authoritative restore and press Enter.

3. Type restore database, press Enter, click OK, and click Yes.

 You must be a member of the local Administrators group or the Backup Operators group to perform backups and restores, or you must be delegated the appropriate authority.

 Before you can schedule a backup, the Task Scheduling service must be running. To start the Task Scheduling service, open the Services applet, scroll down, right-click Task Scheduler, and choose Start. To configure the Task Scheduler to start automatically, right-click the Task Scheduler service and select Properties from the context menu. In the Startup Type section of the Task Scheduler Properties page, select Automatic from the drop-down menu and click the OK button to complete the configuration.

Configuring Security for Backup and Restore Operations

As mentioned previously, you must be a local administrator or backup operator to perform backups and restores on local computers. Likewise, if you're an administrator or backup operator on a domain controller, you can back up any file and folder locally on any computer in the domain. However, if you aren't an administrator or backup operator, you must be the owner of the files and folders that you want to back up, or you must have NTFS permissions for the files and folders you want to back up. One last method worth mentioning is to grant the person who performs backups or restores the Backup Files and Directories right.

Tape Security and Access

By default, the Windows Server 2003 Backup application provides no restrictions to the backup sets or files. You can restrict access to a backup file by selecting Allow Only the Owner and the Administrator Access to the Backup Data in the Backup Job Information dialog box. If you select this option, only an administrator or the person who created the backup file will be able to restore the files and folders.

NTFS File Permissions

NTFS file permissions are written to tape along with the files. They're primarily used for restoring and do not restrict access to the files on the tape. The computer name and username information are stored in the tape header. If you enable the Allow Only the Owner and the Administrator Access to the Backup Data check box, the tape is designated as a secure tape. Only the creator, owner, backup operator, administrator, and users with the Backup Files and Directories right are allowed to read, write, and access the tape.

If you do not use data encryption, the tapes are not truly secure and should be physically secured in an offsite location if you need to protect sensitive data.

Configuring Advanced Restore Options

To configure advanced restore options, perform the following steps:

1. Run Backup.

2. Click the Advanced Mode link.

3. Click the Restore and Manage Media tab.

4. Click the Start Restore button.

5. On the Confirm Restore dialog box, click Advanced.

6. Set the advanced restore option you want and then click the OK button as shown in Figure 5.9.

Figure 5.9 Advanced Restore Options dialog box.

The Advanced Restore options are listed along with a brief description of what each option does in Table 5.1.

Table 5.1 Advanced Restore Options	
Item	Description
Restore Security	Available only on NTFS volumes, this option restores files and folders security settings including permissions, audit entries, and ownership.
Restore Junction Points	Restores junction points and their data on your hard drive. If you're restoring mounted drive data, you much must check the restore points check box in order for your mounted data to be backed up.
Preserve Existing Mount Points	Prevents the restored data from overwriting mount points on the volume you're restoring data to.

Troubleshooting Problems with Restoring Data

The majority of the problems associated with backing up and restoring data are attributed to incorrect, insufficient, or lack of proper permissions and rights. Review the "Configuring Security for Backup and Restore Operations" section earlier in this chapter for details about permissions and rights.

You can use Backup only locally. You cannot back up a remote computer using Backup. You can back up and restore System State data only on a local computer. You cannot back up and restore System State data on a remote computer even if you are an administrator on the remote computer.

Restore problems include the following two major troubleshooting issues using ASR and System State restore:

➤ **After you restore the System State, your computer does not start or your computer enters a continuous restart loop**—This issue can occur when you create the System State backup from the c:\Winnt folder on a Windows 2000 Server and then perform an upgrade to Windows Server 2003, which uses the c:\Windows folder to store its system files. The workaround is to install Windows Server 2003 a second time. Windows 2003 will discover the existing installation in the c:\Windows folder and you'll be prompted to specify a different location. Type c:\Winnt and then complete the installation. When you finish, make sure to delete the old c:\Windows directory.

➤ **When you replace a defective hard drive with one of identical size, ASR cannot restore**—You'll get an error stating that your hard disk capacity is insufficient and cannot be used to recover the partition on the original system drive. Even though the hard disks' sizes appear the same size, the hard drives do not have exactly the same number of sectors. The solution is to purchase a hard disk drive of identical size and geometry. In other worlds, buy the same identical size, make, and model number from the same manufacturer and you can't go wrong.

Troubleshooting Startup Boot Process Issues

Implementing disaster recovery would not be complete without a thorough discussion of Windows Server 2003 startup problems and issues. A successful startup includes the following segments:

➤ The Initial segment

➤ The Boot Loader segment

➤ The Kernel Processing segment

➤ The Logon segment

Startup problems that occur after you select the operating system from the boot loader menu (`boot.ini` file), or after you see the `Please select the oper-ating system to start` message are usually the result of missing or corrupt startup files. You can use Safe Mode, the Recovery Console, or the Windows Server 2003 Repair feature to replace missing or corrupt files.

Windows Server 2003 comes with a variety of startup troubleshooting tools and utilities. In the sections that follow, you'll learn the purpose of each utility and how to use each tool for troubleshooting the startup boot process.

Using the System Information Utility

The System Information utility displays a complete list of your computer's hardware resources, system hardware components, and software environment.

To open and use the System Information utility, perform the following steps:

1. Click, Start, All Programs, Accessories, System Tools, System Information.

2. In the left pane, under System Summary, expand Hardware Resources.

3. Select Forced Hardware and verify in the right pane that your system contains no forced hardware.

4. In the left pane, under Hardware Resources, select Conflicts/Sharing. The right pane displays I/O, IRQ, and memory devices that your computer shares. Most computers list several shared hardware devices. This usually isn't a concern because your computer's Plug and Play bus enumerator allocates and shares these devices efficiently.

5. Expand Components in the left pane and then select Problem Devices. Normally, there are none. If you have a problem device, make note of it.

6. If you have no device conflicts, expand Software Environment in the left pane and select Startup Programs. The right pane lists programs that run automatically when Windows Server 2003 starts. If you suspect that a startup program is causing your computer to malfunction, begin by disabling all startup programs and rebooting. Next, enable one startup program at a time, reboot, and note any unusual startup problems.

If you have forced hardware, conflict/sharing, problem device, or startup conflicts, use Device Manager to uninstall or disable the device. Device Manager is discussed next.

Using Device Manager

You can use Device Manager along with the System Information utility to identify and resolve device conflicts and incompatibilities related to startup problems. Device Manager provides a graphical view of all the hardware installed on your computer. To open and use Device Manager, perform the following steps:

1. Click Start, right-click My Computer, choose Properties, click the Hardware tab, and then click the Device Manager button. Problem devices display a yellow question mark or a red exclamation point next to the device.

2. You can investigate possible device conflicts by double-clicking the device in question, and then clicking the Resource tab. Device conflicts are listed in the Conflicting Device list.

3. Right-click the problem device and choose either Uninstall to remove it or Disable to temporarily disable it.

Using Event Viewer

You should always be using Event Viewer to check, troubleshoot, and diagnose server startup problems. The System and Application event logs types depict general information with a blue I icon, warnings with a yellow icon containing an exclamation point, and errors with a red circle icon with an X inside. System events display Windows Server 2003 startup processes and services. Application events display startup network-related application events such as Backup and Exchange Server services. Double-clicking a warning or error displays the source, category, event ID, and description of the error or warning. Most error and warning events can be researched using Microsoft's Knowledge Base and searching for the event ID number.

An easy way to troubleshoot system and application event errors is by using Microsoft's Knowledge Base to search for the errors by typing in the event ID number in the search for text box.

Using Safe Mode

Starting Windows Server 2003 in safe mode loads generic and basic drivers. You use safe mode to identify, troubleshoot, and resolve problems caused by corrupt or faulty drivers, programs, or services that automatically load at startup. If your computer does not successfully start in normal mode but does start in safe mode, hardware resource incompatibilities with programs, services, device drivers, or the Registry exist.

To disable or uninstall the offending device, use Device Manager. To stop an errant service, open the Services utility, double-click the offending service, and choose Stop. To repair the Registry, use the Registry editor, Regedit. To remove a program, use the System Information tool that was just discussed.

To troubleshoot startup problems using safe mode, perform the following steps:

1. Start your computer and press the F8 function key when you see the startup progress display bar.

2. In the Windows Advanced Options menu, select Safe Mode and then press Enter.

If your computer does not start in safe mode, try using the Recovery Console. If you cannot use the Recovery Console, look for hardware problems such as faulty or defective drivers. If you recently installed a new hardware device, remove it and then restart your computer to see whether that resolves the problem.

You can also use the boot log file, Ntbtlog.txt, as a tool for troubleshooting drivers and services that did not load when you started your computer in safe mode. The log file is located in the %SystemRoot% folder and is viewed by using Notepad.

Some startup problems that occur early in the startup boot process are not written to the log file.

Using Last Known Good Configuration

If you make a change to your Windows Server 2003, such as installing a device driver, and the problem occurs immediately, you should try to start your server using the Last Known Good Configuration option in the Advanced Option menu. Using the Last Known Good Configuration feature restores the previous settings in the Registry key \HKLM\system\ CurrentControlSet. If using the Last Known Good Configuration option solves your problem, you should either remove or update the offending driver.

To troubleshoot startup problems using the last known good configuration, perform the following steps:

1. Start your computer and press the F8 function key when you see the startup progress display bar.

2. In the Windows Advanced Option Menu, select Last Known Good Configuration and then press Enter.

Using the Recovery Console

The Recovery Console is a command-line tool that you can use to fix start-up problems. Using the Recovery Console, you can access drives and directories, enable or disable errant drivers and services, copy files from a Windows 2003 installation disk or a manufacturer's disk, and create a new boot sector or a master boot record (MBR). Use the Recovery Console after you've unsuccessfully tried using the last known good configuration and safe mode recovery tools. To use the Recovery Console, perform the following steps:

1. Check or change CMOS settings and set the boot up sequence to boot from the CD-ROM first. Insert the Windows Server 2003 installation CD-ROM in the drive. Save the CMOS settings and reboot.

2. Text-mode setup begins. When prompted, press R to start the Recovery Console.

 You can also install the Recovery Console on your server's hard drive. Insert the Windows Server 2003 CD-ROM in your CD-ROM drive. Click Start, Run and type *drive letter*\i386\winnt32.exe /cmdcons in the Run text box, where *drive letter* is your CD-ROM.

The Recovery Console is also very useful for detecting and repairing hard drive problems. Use the command-line utility chkdsk with the f (fix) parameter switch to check or repair hard drives.

If **chkdsk** cannot access your hard drive, you might have a hardware failure. Double-check all power, jumper, and cable connections on your hard drive.

If **chkdsk** reports that it cannot fix all problems, your hard drive's boot sector or MBR might be damaged. At a command prompt, run **Fixboot** to repair the boot sector; run **Fixmbr** to repair the master boot record.

Using Automated System Recovery

Using Automated System Recovery (ASR) for restoring failed Windows Server 2003 was discussed in detail at the beginning of this chapter. Remember, when all other recovery methods fail, ASR is your last choice.

Remember, ASR does not restore your data files. Always back up your data files separately. To use ASR, you must be a member of the local Administrators or Backup Operators group.

Using the Repair Option

Damaged, corrupt, or missing installation files can sometimes be repaired using the Windows 2003 Repair feature. To utilize this feature, perform the following steps:

1. Check or change CMOS settings and set the boot up sequence to boot from the CD-ROM drive first. Insert your Windows Server 2003 installation CD-ROM in the drive. Save CMOS settings and reboot.

2. When prompted to start your computer from the CD-ROM, press any key to continue.

3. After Setup starts, press Enter to continue Setup's text-based mode.

4. At the Welcome to Windows screen, select Set Up Windows Now and press Enter to continue.

5. Press the F8 function key to accept the license agreement.

6. Setup searches for previous installations of Windows. When setup finds a previous installation of Windows Server 2003, you should get the following message: If one of the following Windows Server 2003 installations is damaged, setup can try to repair it. Select your previous installation and press R to repair it.

7. Setup next removes your previous installations files and copies new installation files from your CD-ROM.

If Setup does not find your previous installation of Windows Server 2003, you probably have a hardware failure. The Emergency Repair Disk (ERD) feature in Windows 2000 that seldom worked correctly has been removed and is not available in Windows Server 2003. The ASR feature in Windows Server 2003 is the new improved ERD disk feature from Windows 2000 Server.

 Learn each troubleshooting startup boot process utility well. Know when and how to use each one. Troubleshooting startup process issues fits nicely into scenario-type exam questions.

Exam Prep Questions

Question 1

Ann administers a Windows Server 2003 and experiences a major hardware failure in the server due to malicious vandalism. What must Ann do to completely
restore her Windows Server 2003 on a network? Each answer is part of the
solution. (Select two.)

❑ A. Use Shadow Copies to restore the network's user data files.

❑ B. Run Backup.

❑ C. Create an Emergency Repair Disk (ERD).

❑ D. Use ASR to restore the server.

❑ E. Manually configure storage hardware to match pre-disaster hardware.

Answers B and D are correct. Ann needs use Automated System Recovery
(ASR) to restores the server's operating system and all applications. Ann next
needs to run Backup to restore the network's user data. Windows Server
2003 does not have the ERD feature. ASR automatically configures storage
hardware to match pre-disaster hardware.

Question 2

You complete an upgrade of Windows 2000 Server to Windows Server 2003
and create an ASR recovery disk and file. Your Windows Server 2003 has a
major hardware failure. You repair the hardware and run ASR recovery, but
Windows Server 2003 enters a continuous restart loop. How do you fix this
problem? Select the best answer.

○ A. Use Windows 2003 Repair feature.

○ B. Install Windows Server 2003 a second time.

○ C. Use the Driver Rollback feature.

○ D. Use safe mode and reinstall Windows Server 2003.

Answer B is correct. Install Windows Server 2003 a second time. Windows
2003 will discover an existing installation and prompt you to specify a different location for its files. Point to the c:\WINNT folder. The server failed. You
cannot use safe mode. The Repair feature will not fix the problem. Driver
Rollback is used to fix bad device drivers.

Question 3

Shadow Copies for Shared Folders has several benefits. Select two important benefits of shadow copy.

❑ A. Open files are not omitted during backup.

❑ B. Backups can be performed at any time.

❑ C. Backups and restores are lightning fast.

❑ D. Users cannot restore their own previous file versions.

❑ E. Applications cannot continue to write data.

Answers A and B are correct. Open files are not omitted during backup and backups can be performed at any time are two benefits of Shadow Copies. Shadow Copies is not lightning fast. Applications can continue to write data. Users can restore their own previous file versions.

Question 4

Shadow Copies for Shared Folders is installed on a Windows Server 2003. User Amy has accidentally deleted her 55-page Word 2000 document. How does Amy recover this file? Select the two best answers.

❑ A. Right-click the folder containing the deleted file, choose Properties, and select the Previous Versions tab. Select Restore.

❑ B. Right-click the folder containing the deleted file, choose Properties, and select the Previous Versions tab. Select Copy.

❑ C. Right-click the folder containing the deleted file, choose Properties, and select the Previous Versions tab. Select View.

❑ D. Drag-and-drop the Shadow Copies document file to a folder.

❑ E. Right-click the folder containing the deleted file, choose Properties, and select the Customize tab.

Answers A and D are correct. Amy can right-click the folder containing the deleted file, choose Properties, select the Previous Versions tab, and select Restore. Amy can also drag and drop the Shadow Copies document file to a folder. Viewing or restoring will not recover Amy's document. The Customize tab does not contain settings to recover Amy's file.

Question 5

Mike administers a Windows Server 2003. Shadow Copies for Shared Folders is installed. Mike is studying for his MCSE certification and needs to learn more about Shadow Copies for Shared Folders. Help Mike out and select one best practice (select the best answer).

○ A. Perform weekly backups of data.

○ B. Select the same volume for storing data.

○ C. Schedule Shadow Copies to occur every 30 minutes.

○ D. Schedule Shadow Copies to occur once every hour.

Answer D is correct. Mike should not schedule Shadow Copies to occur more than once every hour. Mike needs to perform daily backups and select a different volume on another disk for the storage area.

Question 6

Max has accidentally deleted a printer driver on a Windows Server 2003. Max tries to use the Driver Rollback feature to restore a printer driver. How does Max do this? Select the best answer.

○ A. Using Device Manager, right-click the printer device and choose Properties. Click the Drivers tab and then click Roll Back.

○ B. Printer drivers cannot use Driver Rollback.

○ C. In the Printer panel, right-click the printer device and choose Properties. Click the Drivers tab and then click Roll Back.

○ D. In the Printer panel, right-click the printer device and choose Properties. Click the Resource tab and then click Roll Back.

Answer B is correct. Printer drivers cannot use the Driver Rollback feature. All other answers will not work.

Question 7

Max has accidentally deleted a video driver on a Windows Server 2003. Max tries to use the Driver Rollback feature to restore a video driver. How does Max do this? Select the best answer.

○ A. Using Device Manager, right-click the video device and choose Properties. Click the Drivers tab and then click Roll Back.

○ B. Video drivers cannot use Driver Rollback.

○ C. In the Video panel, right-click the video device and choose Properties. Click the General tab and then click Roll Back.

○ D. In Device Manager, right-click the video device and choose Properties. Click the Resource tab and then click Roll Back.

Answer A is correct. Max should use Device Manager, right-click the video device, and choose Properties. Click the Drivers tab and then click Roll Back. You can use Driver Rollback feature for video cards. The General tab and Resource tab do not have a Roll Back button.

Question 8

Amanda is an assistant administrator for a small company and needs to learn more about the System State backup features for her MCP Windows Server 20003 exam. Backing up the Windows Server 2003 System State files does not include one of the following. Select the best answer.

○ A. Active Directory

○ B. The Registry

○ C. The Windows System32 directory

○ D. COM+ files

Answer C is correct. Backing up the Windows Server 2003 System State files includes Active Directory, the Registry, COM+ files, and the boot up files. It does not include the Windows System32 directory.

Question 9

AdepTek operates a Windows 2003 AD domain. Jack accidentally deletes the AdepTek organizational unit (OU). Users can no longer log on and use company-shared folders. How can the network administrator recover AdepTek's OU? Select the best answer.

○ A. Perform an authoritative restore.

○ B. Use ASR restore.

○ C. Perform a full restore using Backup.

○ D. Perform a nonauthoritative restore.

Answer A is correct. Perform an authoritative restore to recover the OU and replicate it to other domain controllers. Performing a nonauthoritative restore would not restore AdepTek's OU. Using ASR or performing a full backup cannot be done until the authoritative restore process has completed.

Question 10

Amy is a member of the Power Users group and needs to do a full backup on Windows Server 2003, but cannot do so. How can Amy perform a full backup? Select the best answer.

○ A. Make Amy a member of the System Operators group.

○ B. Make Amy a member of the local Administrators group.

○ C. Perform a full backup using Backup.

○ D. Perform a nonauthoritative backup.

Answer B is correct. Amy needs to be a member of the local Administrators group or Backup Operators group. Amy cannot do a backup as a Power User. There is no nonauthoritative backup function.

Need to Know More?

 Technical Overview of Windows Server 2003 File Services: `http://www.microsoft.com/windowsserver2003/techinfo/overview/file.mspx`

 Technical Overview of Windows 2003 Security Services: `http://www.microsoft.com/windowsserver2003/techinfo/overview/security.mspx`

 Technical Overview of Windows 2003 Storage Management: `http://www.microsoft.com/windowsserver2003/techinfo/overview/storage.mspx`

 Introduction to Shadow Copies of Shared Folders: `http://www.microsoft.com/windowsserver2003/techinfo/overview/scr.mspx`

 Shadow Copies of Shared Folders Demo: `http://www.microsoft.com/windowsserver2003/docs/ShadowCopiesSharedFolders.swf`

 Introducing the Windows Server 2003 Family—Core Technologies: `http://www.microsoft.com/windowsserver2003/evaluation/overview/family.mspx`

Managing Name Resolution

Terms you need to understand:

✓ DNS
✓ Forward lookup zones
✓ Reverse lookup zones
✓ Conditional forwarding
✓ Secure dynamic updates
✓ AD-integrated zone
✓ Stub zone
✓ Round robin

Techniques you need to master:

✓ Installing DNS
✓ Creating forward lookup zones
✓ Creating reverse lookup zones
✓ Configuring DNS conditional forwarding
✓ Configuring DNS zones
✓ Creating DNS stub zones
✓ Managing a DNS server

Windows Server 2003 makes a major leap forward using Domain Name System (DNS) for name resolution! Windows 2000 and Windows 2003 domain controller (DC) servers use DNS to dynamically register their information in Active Directory (AD). Active Directory doesn't work without DNS. Network clients including Windows 2000 Server, Windows 2000 Professional clients, Windows XP Professional clients, and other machines running Windows Server 2003 that are part of the domain query Windows 2003 AD-integrated servers to find AD information.

Windows NT Server previously relied on the Windows Internet Name Service (WINS) to resolve computer or NetBIOS names into IP addresses. DNS resolves Internet domain names into IP addresses. The Internet uses DNS servers exclusively for name resolution.

Windows Server 2003, like Windows 2000 Server, supports four types of DNS servers: primary, secondary, AD-integrated, and caching-only. One primary DNS server is designated for each zone and is authoritative for that zone. Creating your first zone installs a primary DNS server. The primary server hosts the DNS resource record database and is the contact for all secondary DNS servers in the subnet on your network. Secondary DNS servers contain a read-only copy of the primary server's database. The Refresh interval sets the interval at which the secondary servers query the primary server. If the primary server has a higher serial number, the secondary servers will pull a copy of the changes to the database based on the "up-to-datedness" vectors. You can set the primary to send changes immediately by using the Notify feature on the Zone Transfers tab.

You should always install a secondary DNS server for load-balancing. If the primary server fails, it's only a matter of time (default to 1 day) before the secondary will fail as well. On the other hand, Active Directory–integrated zones do provide for fault tolerance because all AD zones are primary. The only way to add more primary servers is to convert them into Active Directory–integrated servers.

Caching-only DNS servers do not host zones and are not authoritative for the domain. They build and maintain a list of domain names and IP addresses learned from DNS forwarders. These are set on the server Properties tabs and can be made conditional forwarders in Windows Server 2003. Caching-only DNS servers are well suited for branch or remote office locations where creating a new domain or subnet isn't feasible.

Active Directory–integrated DNS servers are primary servers in a sense. Each AD domain DNS server uses AD replication and maintains a database that is part of Active Directory's database information.

To increase fault tolerance on your AD domain, install a second AD-integrated server. If one AD-integrated DNS server fails, the remaining AD-integrated DNS server takes over.

This chapter shows you how to install DNS by using the Manage Your Server tool. You also learn how to configure DNS server options and DNS forwarding, as well as create and configure forward and reverse lookup zones. Configuring zone options, zones for secure dynamic update, and Active Directory–integrated zones are discussed.

Two new DNS features added to Windows Server 2003, conditional forwarding and stub zones, are analyzed in detail. Finally, managing a DNS server, including zone settings, record settings, and server options are examined in this chapter.

Installing a DNS Server

Several methods are used to install DNS servers, including the following:

➤ You can add DNS during the installation of Windows Server 2003.

➤ You can install DNS manually using the Add or Remove Programs applet, Add/Remove Windows Components in the Control Panel.

➤ If you're setting up a domain controller (DC), another method is to install the Active Directory service. Because AD depends on DNS to operate, the AD Wizard searches for a DNS server. If the wizard doesn't find a DNS server, it installs DNS for you.

➤ The Configure Your Server Wizard can be selected separately from the Administrative Tools menu. The Configure Your Server Wizard sets up various server roles, such as WINS, DHCP, or DNS for your server. You select the role; the wizard guides you through the rest of the installation.

➤ You can also use the Manage Your Server Wizard interface that uses the Configure Your Server Wizard to set up server roles. Installing a DNS server using the Manage Your Server interface is straightforward.

To install a DNS server using the Manage Your Server Wizard:

1. Click Start, All Programs, Administrative Tools, Manage Your Server. The Manage Your Server window opens.

2. Also using the Configure Your Server Wizard, the Manage Your Server window component is all about managing various server roles. Server roles already defined are displayed in the left column, as shown in Figure 6.1.

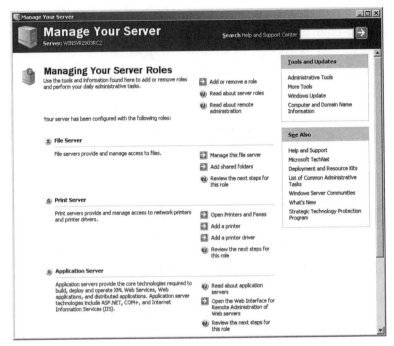

Figure 6.1 The Manage Your Server window showing File Server, Print Server, and Application Server roles.

3. In the middle column, click the Add or Remove a Role button to start the Configure Your Server Wizard.

4. The Configure Your Server Wizard, Preliminary Steps dialog box opens and displays a list of reminders, such as making sure to attach all cables. Click the Next button to continue.

5. The wizard analyzes your server and displays a list of server roles with a Configured Yes or No status as shown in Figure 6.2.

6. Select the DNS Server role and click the Next button.

7. The Summary of Selections dialog box appears. Install DNS Server and run the Configure a DNS Server Wizard to configure DNS as listed in the Summary text box. Click the Next button to begin the installation process.

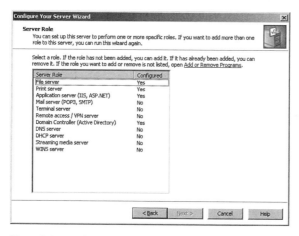

Figure 6.2   The Configure Your Server Wizard, Server Roles dialog box.

8. Setup begins. Note: You might be prompted for the Windows Server 2003 Installation CD-ROM. Click the OK button and insert your CD-ROM, and type in or browse to the location of the i386 folder installation files. Click the OK button to continue.

You might also receive the following prompt during the DNS installation: `Internet Information Services (IIS) must be configured to enable Phone Book Service (PBS) requests. Click Yes to enable PBS requests. Click No to install PBS and IIS without enabling PBS.` If you click No, you must manually configure IIS to accept PBS requests by using the IIS Security Wizard.

9. The Applying Selections dialog box displays in the background while the Configure a DNS Server Wizard Welcome screen displays in the foreground, as shown in Figure 6.3.

10. Notice the DNS Wizard configures both forward and reverse lookup zones along with specifying root hints and forwarders. You can also click the DNS Checklists button to review a checklist sorted by company size. Click the Next button to continue.

11. In the Select Configuration Action dialog box, you select the appropriate lookup zone types for your network as shown in Figure 6.4. For small networks, select the Create a Forward Lookup Zone radio button. For medium- and large-sized networks, select Create Forward and Reverse Lookup Zones. Select Configure Root Hints to configure just root hints. Choose an appropriate action and click the Next button to continue.

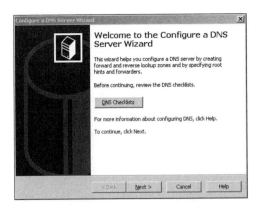

Figure 6.3 The Configure a DNS Server Wizard Welcome screen.

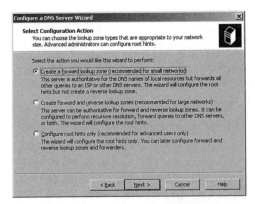

Figure 6.4 Select Configuration Action dialog box showing Create a Forward Lookup Zone selected.

12. If you choose the Create a Forward Lookup Zone option on the Primary Server Location screen, you can choose which DNS server will maintain your primary forward lookup zone. Your choices include either the server you're currently configuring or to have an ISP maintain the zone, with a read-only secondary copy residing on your server. Click the Next button to maintain the zone on the server that you're currently configuring.

13. At the Zone Name screen, you must provide a name for the zone for which the server will be authoritative. Type the name in the Zone Name field and click the Next button to continue.

14. At the Zone File screen, accept the default entry in the Create a New File with This File Name field to create the new zone file and click the Next button to continue.

15. At the Dynamic Updates screen, you can specify whether the new zone should accept zone updates and which types. Click the Next button to accept the default setting of Do Not Allow Dynamic Updates and continue with the DNS installation.

16. At the Forwarders screen, enter the IP address of another DNS server on your network that can be used to resolve DNS inquiries if this DNS server cannot provide an immediate answer to a client inquiry. Click the Next button to continue.

17. The Completing the Configure a DNS Server Wizard dialog box displays your settings for review. Click the Finish button. The Server Is Now a DNS Server dialog box appears. Click the Finish button. The Manage Your Server window now contains DNS as an added role. Close the Manage Your Server window.

Installing and Creating Forward and Reverse Lookup Zones

Your DNS forward and reverse lookup zones might already be installed, depending on the action you selected in step 12 in the preceding task. Using DNS enables you to divide your namespace into zones that store name information in a database. Zones are primarily used for administration. DNS zones are represented by zone database files. Each DNS zone contains a primary zone database file and a secondary zone database file. Only the primary zone database file can be directly written to. Zones can be set up for a subnet, single domain, or multiple domains.

Each zone contains a forward lookup zone and optionally a reverse lookup zone. When a client requests an IP address for a hostname, the forward lookup zone resolves the hostname into an IP address. Reverse lookup zones resolve IP addresses into hostnames. Small companies need only a forward lookup zone. The only real difference between forward and reverse lookup zones is the way in which they are sorted. Reverse lookup zone database files are in numerical order by IP addresses, thereby speeding up queries of IP address to domain name. Larger companies that have custom applications and multiple domains should install both forward and reverse lookup zones.

 If you plan on using the command-line DNS troubleshooting tool, **NSLookup**, you must have a reverse lookup zone installed and configured. **NSLookup** will not function unless a reverse lookup zone is installed.

Installing forward and reverse lookup zones is clear-cut. To install and create a forward lookup zone, perform the following steps:

1. Open the DNS MMC console.

2. In the console tree, right-click your DNS server and choose New Zone. The New Zone Wizard appears. Click Next.

3. Select Primary Zone. If your Windows Server 2003 is AD-integrated, make sure that the Store Zone Information in Active Directory check box is checked. Click Next to continue.

4. In the Active Directory Zone Replication Scope dialog box, select how you want DNS zone data replicated. If you have just one domain, accept the default selection as shown in Figure 6.5 and click the Next button to continue.

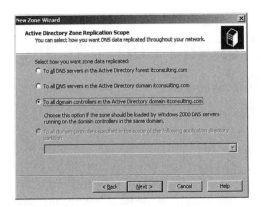

Figure 6.5   New Zone Wizard, Active Directory Zone Replication Scope dialog box.

5. Select Forward Lookup Zone and click Next to continue.

6. In the Zone Name text box, type a zone name. Normally it's your domain name or a portion of your domain name. It is not your DNS server computer name. Click Next to continue.

7. In the Dynamic Name dialog box, you can select secure, nonsecure, or no dynamic updates for your DNS zone updates. Domains using AD-integrated zones should accept the default: Allow Only Secure Dynamic Updates. Make a selection and click the Next button.

8. The Completing the Zone Wizard dialog box displays, listing a summary of your selections. Click the Finish button to install a forward lookup zone.

To install and create a reverse lookup zone, perform the following steps:

1. Open the DNS MMC console.

2. In the console tree, right-click your DNS server and choose New Zone. The New Zone Wizard appears. Click Next.

3. Using the New Zone Wizard, follow the preceding instructions to create a reverse lookup zone. One difference in creating a reverse lookup zone is to specify your network IP address. Figure 6.6 shows the network ID for a class C private network address. Notice the reverse lookup zone name `0.168.192.in-addr.arpa` appears in the lower grayed-out text box.

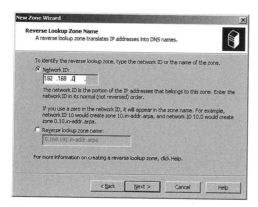

Figure 6.6   Reverse Lookup Zone Name dialog box showing Network ID: 192.168.0.

Configuring and Managing DNS Zones

Configuring DNS zones includes configuring zone options, secure dynamic updates, and configuring AD-integrated zones.

Now that you have forward and reverse lookup zones created on your Windows 2003 DNS server, let's explore DNS zone options next.

Configuring Zone Options

In the DNS Console, right-click the forward or reverse lookup zone and choose Properties. Your zone's General tab displays as shown in Figure 6.7.

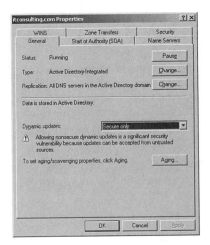

Figure 6.7 Forward Lookup Zone Properties, General tab.

The zone properties dialog box on Windows Server 2003 is very similar to the zone properties dialog box on Windows 2000 Server. One difference is the General tab on Windows 2003 DNS Server. Added beneath Status and Type is Replication along with a Change button. Click the Change button to change the replication scope for an AD zone. The Active Directory Zone Replication Scope dialog box opens. This dialog box previously appeared under the heading Create a Forward Lookup Zone (step 5 in the list that described how to install forward and reverse lookup zones).

If you have installed AD on your Windows Server 2003, your zone type by default is Active Directory (AD) Integrated. AD-integrated zones store their zone information in Active Directory's database. To change the zone type to primary, secondary, or stub zone (discussed later), click the Change button. You can also change zone types using the dnscmd command-line tool.

If you select the secondary or stub zone type, you must specify the source or primary DNS server IP address that is used for obtaining updated zone information.

The zone property tabs and their descriptions are listed in Table 6.1.

Table 6.1 Zone Property Tabs	
Item	**Description**
General	View status; view or change zone type; view or change replication; view or change dynamic updates; set/aging scavenging properties.
Start of Authority (SOA)	Information on primary server; refresh and retry intervals; expire and TTL settings.
Name Servers	The fully qualified domain name (FQDN) of the name server with options to add, edit, and remove name servers.
WINS	Option to enable WINS forward lookup servers for down-level clients.
Zone Transfers	Configures secondary servers to query for zone transfers to any server, only the servers listed in the Names tab, or specific servers. Click the Notify button to configure secondary servers to notify for changes.
Security	Configure permissions for AD-integrated zones.

Active Directory–Integrated Zones and Secure Dynamic Updates

AD-integrated zones store and replicate DNS information as part of the AD database replication. AD-integrated zones are created on domain controllers hosting DNS. Each DC contains a read-write copy of the zone information stored in AD. In the Dynamic Updates section on the General properties tab, Secure Only is selected by default. Secure dynamic updates are supported only for AD-integrated zones. Clients using secure dynamic updates automatically register and update their own resource records with the DNS server.

Using secure dynamic updates eases DNS administration and reduces the need to manually add and update resource records. Properly configured DHCP servers can dynamically register records for down-level clients such as Windows NT and Windows 98 computers. For good security practices, you should not change the default dynamic updates unless you have a valid reason. For example, a Unix DNS server not supporting the latest version of BIND on your network is a good reason to choose the medium-level security dynamic update option, nonsecure and secure.

In an AD domain, you should always try use the secure dynamic updates for maximum security. Larger companies with mixed Windows clients, such as NT workstations and Windows 98 clients, should deploy a DHCP server and configure the DNS tab of the DHCP server options to Always Update DNS and check Enable Updates for DNS Clients That Do Not Support Dynamic Update. Down-level, non–DNS-aware clients then use DHCP to dynamically register their DNS records.

Zone Transfers and Security

Secondary DNS servers receive their zone information from the master name DNS server. The Zone Transfers tab has options to Send Zone Transfers to Any Server, Only Servers Listed in the Name Servers Tab, or Only to the Following Servers. You add DNS servers by typing their IP addresses and clicking the Add button.

Windows 2000 and Windows Server 2003 both support incremental zone transfers. Early implementations of DNS supported only full zone transfers. When you use incremental zone transfers, only the zone changes that occur on the primary DNS server are transferred and synchronized with the secondary DNS server, thus reducing DNS network traffic. Primary servers have the Notify button and can be configured to notify selected secondary servers as soon as a change is made. Otherwise, the secondary servers will query the primary at each Refresh Interval. Secondary DNS servers have a Notify button located on the Zone Transfer tab of the Zone Properties page. After clicking the Notify button, you can use this property page to specify the secondary servers to be automatically notified when the zone changes. You use this to restrict or limit zone transfer access to specific servers in the list.

 To perform these procedures, you must be a member of the Domain Admins or DnsAdmins group in AD, or you must be delegated the appropriate authority. Microsoft likes to test your knowledge of group memberships for various activities.

Another method used for assigning DNS administration tasks is to delegate control. Delegations are used to separate servers in the same domain so that certain individuals or groups can manage one server and others can manage other servers. To create a zone delegation, right-click the domain to which you want to delegate control and choose New Delegation. The New Delegation Wizard guides you through the process.

Configuring and Managing a Stub Zone

A *stub zone* is a copy of the zone containing only resource records to identify the authoritative DNS server for the zone. Stub zones improve name resolution efficiency and keep delegated zone information current by providing the DNS server in the parent zone with its resource records list of name servers for its child zone. The master DNS server for the stub zone usually hosts the primary zone and is authoritative for the child zone. Stub zones can simplify DNS administration by distributing their resource lists to authoritative DNS servers for the zone without adding, maintaining, or using secondary zones. Companies with multiple domains can use stub zones to simplify DNS administration.

On a DNS server configured as a DC, stub zones store their resource records in Active Directory. Active Directory–integrated stub zones contain the stub zone name, zone type, and the list of master servers.

A stub zone consists of the following:

➤ A Start of Authority (SOA) resource record.

➤ Name server (NS) resource records.

➤ Glue A resource records (a new DNS resource record added in Windows Server 2003). A Glue A resource record is a delegation record used for finding authoritative DNS servers for the delegated zone.

➤ One or more master DNS servers IP addresses used to update the stub zone.

To add a stub zone, perform the following steps:

1. Open your DNS MMC console.

2. In the console tree, right-click your DNS server and choose New Zone. The New Zone Wizard opens.

3. Click Next and select Stub Zone as shown in Figure 6.8.

4. In the Active Directory Zone Replication Scope dialog box, select how you want DNS zone data replicated. If you have just one domain, accept the default selection and click Next.

5. Select Forward Lookup Zone and click Next. Type in your zone name and click Next.

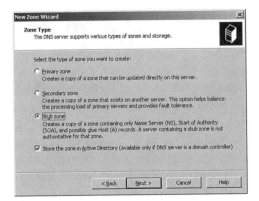

Figure 6.8 Zone Type dialog box showing Stub Zone selected.

6. To configure master DNS servers for your stub zone, type the IP address of the DNS master server in the Master DNS Servers dialog box and click Next as shown in Figure 6.9.

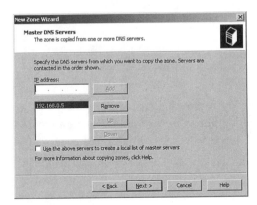

Figure 6.9 Master DNS Server IP address.

7. Click the Finish button.

8. Add records to the stub zone manually or dynamically update the stub zone from the master DNS server.

Configuring Conditional Forwarding

Another new feature added to Windows 2003 DNS server is conditional forwarding. *Conditional forwarding* forwards DNS queries to the DNS name server specified in the query. Both stub zones and conditional forwarding provide the ability to control routing DNS traffic on your network.

Windows 2000 Servers forward all requests to the same set of servers listed as forwarders. This can be inefficient because not all servers have information about the query. Conditional forwarding improves granularity with name-specific forwarding.

 When do you use conditional forwarding instead of stub zones? Both allow a DNS server to respond to a query with a referral or forwarding to another DNS server. A conditional forwarder configures the DNS server to forward the query it receives to a DNS server listed in the header of the query. A stub zone keeps the DNS server hosting the parent zone aware of all authoritative servers for the child zone.

Managing Your DNS Server

Managing your DNS server is performed in the DNS console by right-clicking your server and choosing an action from the shortcut menu. Actions not discussed previously include the following:

➤ Create Default Application Directory Partitions—Partitioning in Active Directory is used to differentiate data for different replication purposes.

➤ Set Aging/Scavenging for All Zones—Configure refresh intervals for resource records.

➤ Scavenge Stale Resource Records—Use this option to manually remove old outdated resource records.

➤ Update Server Data Files—Writes all zone file changes in AD.

➤ Clear Cache—Flushes the name server's cache.

➤ Launch nslookup—Runs the `nslookup` utility for troubleshooting DNS problems.

Additional server options are available on the DNS Server Properties tab as shown in Figure 6.10.

➤ Interfaces—Configure the Interfaces tab to listen for DNS server requests on all IP addresses or only the following IP address.

➤ Forwarders—Configure forwarder DNS server IP addresses to resolve DNS queries not answered by this server. Commonly used to add ISP DNS primary and secondary DNS servers IP addresses, which improves DNS query response time and efficiency on the Internet.

➤ Advanced—Advanced configuration options include Disable Recursion and Forwarding, BIND secondaries (enable if you have Unix DNS servers using BIND), Fail on Load If Bad Zone Data, Enable Round

Robin (a feature used for load balancing of resource records), Enable Netmask Ordering, and Secure Cache Against Pollution.

➤ Root hints—Root hints are used to learn and discover authoritative servers in the upper hierarchy of the DNS domain namespace.

➤ Debug Logging and Event Logging—Use for diagnostic trouble-shooting.

➤ Monitoring—Verifies DNS configuration using manual or automatic testing. A simple query tests your internal zone or subnet. A recursive query tests DNS servers outside your zone, such as your ISP's DNS servers.

➤ Security—Use to view, add, and remove user and groups and their associated permissions.

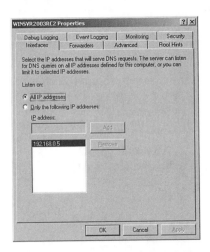

Figure 6.10 DNS Server Properties dialog box showing the Interfaces tab.

Best DNS Practices

The following are some guidelines for receiving the full benefit from utilizing DNS:

➤ Use preferred practices and standard guidelines for managing your DNS infrastructure.

➤ For AD domains, always use Active Directory–integrated zones for increased security and fault tolerance and easier management and deployment.

➤ If your DC is also a DNS server, make sure that your domain controller is pointing to itself for all DNS resolution. Otherwise, just make sure that it is pointing to an internal DNS server. Pointing to an ISP DNS server, for example, would result in inaccurate registered records in the Netlogon service. Your TCP/IP network properties dialog box, in other words, should list only your DNS server as the preferred DNS server.

➤ For each additional server running DNS added to your domain, the preferred DNS IP address is the parent DNS IP address. The IP address of the added server running DNS is placed in the Alternate IP Address text box.

➤ During AD installation and setup, if you created a domain name with a (domain name).local extension, delete the ".(zone)" listed under Forward Lookup Zones. Otherwise, clients might have external name resolution problems on the Internet.

➤ If your internal and registered external domain names are the same, make sure to add a Host (A) record and an Mail Exchange (MX) record to your DNS server forward lookup zone. Otherwise, users will not be able to browse your company's Internet Web site home page and related links.

➤ For each person in charge of managing a zone, add an email address (MX) record to your DNS server database, replacing the @ sign with a period.

➤ If your DNS server is behind a proxy server or firewall, make sure to open UDP and TCP port 53 on the proxy server or firewall.

➤ Add only necessary alias records to a zone.

➤ Consider using secondary zones for load balancing when DNS query traffic is heavy.

➤ If you need to add child domains, create a delegation record on the parent DNS server for the child DNS server. Create a secondary zone for the child server and specify the name server or parent DNS server for zone transfers.

➤ For large and complex DNS planning and designing, always review the DNS-related Request for Comments (RFC) documents from the RFC Editor Web site.

Exam Prep Questions

Question 1

> Tom finishes installing Windows Server 2003 on his computer. He wants to make his computer a domain controller (DC) for a new domain. What two components does Tom need to install to make his computer a DC? (Select two choices.)
>
> ❏ A. A second NIC card
> ❏ B. Active Directory services
> ❏ C. DHCP
> ❏ D. DNS
> ❏ E. WINS

Answers B and D are correct. Tom needs to install Active Directory and DNS to make his computer a domain controller. WINS is an optional component that uses NetBIOS resolution for down-level clients. DHCP is another optional component that provides automatic assignment of TCP/IP addresses. You do not need to install a second NIC card to make a computer a DC.

Question 2

> Sara administers a Windows Server 2003. Sara installs and creates a primary DNS for a subnet. Sara is concerned about DNS fault tolerance for the Primary DNS zone. What can Sara do to provide load balancing and fault tolerance for the primary DNS server?
>
> ○ A. Install a second NIC card
> ○ B. Install an AD-integrated DNS server
> ○ C. Install DHCP
> ○ D. Install a secondary DNS server

Answer D is correct. Sara needs to install a secondary DNS server to provide load balancing and fault tolerance. If the primary DNS server fails, the secondary DNS server can continue resolving client queries with its read-only copy of the database. DHCP provides automatic assignment of TCP/IP addresses, not fault tolerance. Installing a second NIC card does not increase fault tolerance. Although installing an AD-integrated DNS server provides fault tolerance, there is no mention of an AD domain.

Question 3

Sara administers a Windows 2003 domain server. Sara installs Active Directory and creates an AD-integrated DNS server for her domain. Sara is concerned about DNS fault tolerance. What can Sara do to provide fault tolerance for her AD domain?

- ○ A. Install a primary DNS server
- ○ B. Install another AD-integrated DNS server
- ○ C. Install a caching-only DNS server
- ○ D. Install a secondary DNS Server

Answer B is correct. Sara needs to install another AD-integrated DNS server to provide fault tolerance. If one AD-integrated DNS server fails, the other AD-integrated DNS server continues to resolve client DNS queries. Adding a second AD-integrated DNS server also creates a second domain controller that also increases fault tolerance for the domain. Installing a primary DNS server cannot be done. The AD-integrated DNS server is a primary DNS server for an AD domain. Secondary DNS servers provide load balancing for primary DNS servers, not AD-integrated DNS servers. A caching-only DNS server does not contain a read-write resource records database, and thus provides no fault tolerance.

Question 4

Max administers a Windows Server 2003 AD domain for AdepTek's corporate headquarters. AdepTek also has a small branch office that uses a demand dial connection to connect to headquarters and the Internet. Branch office users are complaining that Internet access and browsing is slow. Tom needs to install a DNS server at the branch office to improve Internet access and response times. What type of DNS server is best suited for the branch office?

- ○ A. Install a primary DNS server
- ○ B. Install another AD-integrated DNS server
- ○ C. Install a caching-only DNS server
- ○ D. Install a secondary DNS server

Answer C is correct. Max needs to install a caching-only DNS server at the branch office. Caching-only DNS servers build and maintain a list of domain names and IP addresses learned from clients performing recursive queries. Caching-only DNS servers are well suited for branch or remote office locations where creating a new domain or subnet isn't feasible. An

AD-integrated DNS server, primary DNS server, or secondary DNS server would not function well at the branch office, due to the demand dial connection.

Question 5

> Amy finishes installing Windows Server 2003 on her computer. Amy also needs to install DNS to provide name resolution for users. Using the least amount of administrative effort, select two methods for Amy to use and install the DNS service. (Select the best two answers.)
>
> ❏ A. Reinstall Windows Server 2003
>
> ❏ B. Install Active Directory
>
> ❏ C. Install the Recovery Console
>
> ❏ D. Use the Manage Your Server Wizard
>
> ❏ E. Use ASR

Answers B and D are correct. If Amy needs to set up an AD domain, installing Active Directory will also install an AD-integrated DNS server. Amy could also use the Manage Your Server Wizard to install DNS. Although Amy could reinstall Windows Server 2003 and select DNS as an additional component to install, doing so involves too much administrative effort. The Recovery Console and ASR are used for disaster recovery.

Question 6

> John administers a Windows Server 2003 AD domain for AdepTek's corporate headquarters. AdepTek's domain contains five subnets. John needs to maximize DNS efficiency and reduce administration. How can John set up the five subnets for DNS resolution and administration?
>
> ○ A. Create and set up one DNS zone with four delegations
>
> ○ B. Create five domains and install Active Directory in each
>
> ○ C. Install five caching-only DNS servers
>
> ○ D. Create a master domain and four child domains

Answer A is correct. John should create and set up one DNS zone with four delegations. Zones are used for administration. Each DNS zone is authoritative for its zone and contains the domain information for that zone. Using four delegations divides the administrative duties for the zone. Zones can be set up for a subnet, single domain, or multiple domains. Creating five domains and installing Active Directory in each would increase administration. Installing five caching-only DNS servers, one for each subnet, would not maximize DNS efficiency and reduce administration. Furthermore, caching-only DNS servers are not authoritative and would do little in terms of maximizing DNS efficiency. Creating a master domain and four child domains would increase administration and decrease DNS efficiency.

Question 7

Sara administers a Windows Server 2003 AD domain for AdepTek's corporate headquarters. AdepTek's domain contains one subnet. Sara creates a forward lookup zone for the subnet but encounters problems. Sara needs to troubleshoot her DNS resolution problems. She tries to use the NSLookup command-line tool for troubleshooting, but receives an error and cannot do so. What must Sara do to use the NSLookup DNS troubleshooting tool?

○ A. Install another forward lookup zone

○ B. Install a reverse lookup zone

○ C. Install a caching-only DNS server

○ D. Install an AD-integrated zone

Answer B is correct. To use the NSLookup DNS troubleshooting tool, Sara needs to install a reverse lookup zone. The NSLookup tool is not available until you install a reverse lookup zone. AdepTek already has an AD-integrated zone. One subnet can only contain one forward lookup zone or AD-integrated zone. A caching-only DNS would not help Sara troubleshoot using the NSLookup tool.

Question 8

Max administers Windows Server 2003 AD domains for InnoTek Solutions. InnoTek has three domains. Max creates a forward lookup zone for each domain. Each domain contains 200 Windows XP Professional client computers and three additional servers running Windows Server 2003. InnoTek also runs two custom company applications in each domain. To maximize DNS efficiency, what else should Max set up for each domain?

○ A. Install another forward lookup zone

○ B. Install a reverse lookup zone

○ C. Install a caching-only DNS server

○ D. Install an AD-integrated zone

Answer B is correct. To maximize DNS efficiency, Max should install and set up a reverse lookup zone for each domain. Larger companies that have custom applications and multiple domains should install both forward and reverse lookup zones because of the way the zone database file is sorted. InnoTek already has AD-integrated zones. Each domain can only contain one forward lookup zone or AD-integrated zone. Because each domain contains 200 clients, caching-only DNS servers would not help for providing dynamic registration and internal name resolution.

Question 9

> Sara administers a Windows Server 2003 for InnoTek Solutions. InnoTek has one domain. Sara creates a primary DNS server and a forward lookup zone for the domain. The domain contains 100 Windows 98 client computers, 100 Windows XP Professional computers, and one additional Windows Server 2003. Sara starts to manually add resource records for the Windows 98 computers. Sara needs an automated method for Windows 98 clients to automatically register and update resource records. She would also like her clients to use secure dynamic updates during the registration process. What method can Sara use to have clients automatically register and update resource records using secure dynamic updates? Each answer is part of the solution. (Select the two best answers.)
>
> ❏ A. Install Active Directory
> ❏ B. Install a secondary DNS server
> ❏ C. Install a caching-only DNS server
> ❏ D. Install a DHCP server
> ❏ E. Install a second domain controller

Answers A and D are correct. To have clients automatically register and update resource records using secure dynamic updates, Sara needs to first install Active Directory. Installing AD creates a DC and an AD-integrated DNS server with secure dynamic updates enabled by default. Windows XP Professional clients will automatically register and update their own resource records using secure dynamic updates. Sara also needs to install a DHCP server and set appropriate options so that the DHCP server can dynamically register Windows 98 clients hostnames with the DNS server. Installing a secondary DNS server or caching-only DNS server will not help clients to automatically register and update their own resource records using secure dynamic updates. Adding a second DC cannot be done until AD is first installed.

Question 10

John, a member of the local Administrators group, administers a Windows Server 2003 AD domain for InnoTek Solutions. InnoTek has one AD domain. John uses an AD-integrated DNS server for resolving client queries. He needs to check and reset several security permissions on the AD-integrated DNS server, but finds the Security tab dimmed and not available. What must John do to use the Security tab on his AD-integrated DNS server? (Select the two best answers.)

❑ A. Become a member of the Power Users group

❑ B. Become a member of the WINS Proxy group

❑ C. Become a member of the Domain Admins group

❑ D. Install a DHCP server

❑ E. Become a member of the DnsAdmins group

Answers C and E are correct. For John to view or modify security permission on an AD-integrated DNS server, John must be a member of either the Domain Admins or DnsAdmins groups. Neither the Power Users nor the WINS Proxy group has proper permissions. Installing a DHCP server eases John's administration tasks, but won't help John view or modify the securities properties tab on his AD-integrated DNS server.

Need to Know More?

 New features for DNS: http://www.microsoft.com/technet/treeview/default.asp?url=/technet/prodtechnol/windowsserver2003/proddocs/standard/sag_DNS_ovr_NewFeatures.asp

 Security information for DNS: http://www.microsoft.com/technet/treeview/default.asp?url=/technet/prodtechnol/windowsserver2003/proddocs/standard/sag_DNS_ovr_topnode.asp

 Managing Servers: http://www.microsoft.com/technet/treeview/default.asp?url=/technet/prodtechnol/windowsserver2003/proddocs/standard/sag_DNS_imp_ManagingServers.asp

 DNS defined: http://www.microsoft.com/technet/treeview/default.asp?url=/technet/prodtechnol/windowsserver2003/proddocs/standard/sag_DNS_imp_ManagingZones.asp

 Minasi, Mark et al. *Mastering Windows Server 2003*. Sybex, 2003.

Maintaining Network Security

Terms you'll need to understand:

✓ Security Configuration and Analysis
✓ **setup security.inf**
✓ **DC Security.inf**
✓ **Compatws.inf**
✓ **secure*.inf**
✓ **hisec*.inf**
✓ **rootsec.inf**
✓ **notssid.inf**
✓ **Secedit**
✓ Server Message Blocks (SMB)
✓ Software Update Service (SUS)
✓ Automatic Updates
✓ **WUAU.ADM**

Techniques you'll need to master:

✓ Using security templates to implement security baseline settings
✓ Using, applying, and analyzing security templates
✓ Using security templates to audit and implement security settings
✓ Implementing the Principle of Least Privilege
✓ Installing and configuring software update services
✓ Installing and configuring automatic client update settings
✓ Configuring software updates on earlier operating systems

System administrators are overtaxed administering and maintaining network security. Temporary changes in security settings to resolve administration and network problems often result in unforeseen permanent changes that no longer meet security requirements.

Implementing security analysis enables administrators to track and ensure that adequate levels of security are maintained throughout the enterprise. Regular security analysis not only tunes security levels, but also detects any security flaws that might occur over time. Administrators need an easy-to-use security analysis tool that can track, detect, compare, fix, adjust, reset, and remove security settings.

In earlier chapters, you learned that user and group security permissions could be applied on one or many computers to control password policies, account lockout policies, Kerberos policies, auditing policies, user rights, and other policies. You learned that applying policies to many computers in a domain is best accomplished by using a Group Policy Object (GPO). GPOs are applied at the site, domain, organizational unit (OU), or local level.

In this chapter, you'll learn about another method used to apply security policies systemwide by using the Security Configuration and Analysis tool. Using the Security Configuration and Analysis component built in to Windows Server 2003, you can track, detect, compare, edit, adjust, reset, apply, and remove security policy settings. The Security Configuration and Analysis tool analyzes and configures system security at the local, domain, OU, or site level.

The Security Templates component is used to create, view, and modify security policy templates settings. With one of the predefined, built-in templates as a starting point, you'll learn how to integrate domainwide company security policies. Using Security Templates along with the Security Configuration and Analysis tool, you'll become skilled at how to implement security baseline settings and audit security policy settings.

You'll review the Principle of Least Privilege as it applies to administrators using the Runas command. This chapter also takes an in-depth look, from a security perspective, at installing and configuring Microsoft's Software Update Service along with configuring and deploying Windows clients to use Automatic Updates services.

Installing and Implementing Security

The Security Configuration and Analysis MMC snap-in component, which is built in to Windows Server 2003, enables you to quickly review security analysis results. Using a personal database to store the security analysis results, the Security Configuration and Analysis tool compares your present security settings with custom or built-in security templates settings. Recommendations are presented alongside your current system baseline settings along with visual flags and remarks highlighting areas that do not match your proposed level of security. The Security Configuration and Analysis utility can also resolve or fix any security policy discrepancies.

 You might be tempted to use the Security Templates' MMC snap-in module for applying templates. However, the Security Templates Console is used to view and create security templates. The Security Configuration and Analysis tool is the preferred tool to use for applying the security template you created. Note that you could also use Active Directory Users and Computers to apply a security template to a policy linked to the appropriate container.

The components of the Security Configuration and Analysis tool and a brief description of each are listed in Table 7.1.

Table 7.1 Security Configuration and Analysis Components	
Components	**Description**
Security Templates	Predefined, built-in security policies. Templates can be applied to your local computer or to Group Policy Objects.
Security Settings Extensions to Group Policy	Used for editing security settings on a domain, site, or organizational unit.
Local Security Policy	Used for editing security settings on you local computer.
secedit commands	Command-line tool used to automate security settings.

All security policies are computer-based policies. The built-in predefined security templates are provided to get you started building you own custom security template for your company's security policies. Using the Security Templates tool, select the template that comes closest to meeting your company's policy objectives, copy and save it with a different name, and then customize it to meet your company's security needs. The custom template can serve as a security baseline for analyzing future security discrepancies or policy violations. The original template you copied is still available for future use, if needed.

To install the Security Templates and the Security Configuration and Analysis MMC snap-in, follow these steps:

1. Click Start, Run and type mmc in the Run text box. An empty console and console window open.

2. From the File menu, select Add/Remove Snap-in.

3. In the Add/Remove Snap-in dialog box, select Security Templates and then click the Add button.

4. In the Add/Remove Snap-in dialog box, select Security Configuration and Analysis, click Add, and click Close.

5. Click the OK button again to return to Console1. Notice that both Security Templates and Security Configuration and Analysis are displayed in the left pane.

6. From the menu, choose File, Save As, and type a meaningful name, such as *Security*, to save the file. Figure 7.1 shows the Security Templates and Security Configuration and Analysis snap-ins.

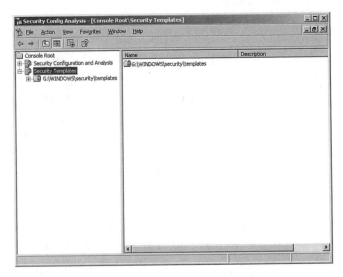

Figure 7.1 Security console showing Security Templates and Security Configuration and Analysis snap-ins.

Using Security Templates

Before beginning to create and import your security template, you need some knowledge of what each predefined security template contains and what its primary security use is. By default, the built-in security templates are located in the systemroot\Security\Templates directory on your Windows Server 2003.

Table 7.2 lists Windows Server 2003's built-in security templates along with a brief description of each.

Table 7.2 Built-in Security Templates and Descriptions	
Security Template	**Description**
Default Security **setup security.inf**	Default computer security settings that were applied during the installation, including file permissions for the root directory. Member servers and clients can use this template, but not domain controllers (DCs).
DC Default Security **DC Security.inf**	Created during the installation of Active Directory (AD), when the server is promoted to a DC. It contains the DC's Registry, file, and system service default security settings.
Compatible **Compatws.inf**	Relaxes default file and Registry permissions for users so that users can run applications that lack the Windows Logo Program for Software Approval.
Secure **secure*.inf** ***ws-workstations** ***dc-domain controllers**	Medium-level security settings with minimal impact to application compatibility. Also used to limit the use of LAN Manager (NTLM) authentication protocols and for enabling Server Message Block (SMB) packet signing. Packet signing will be negotiated between client computers and servers at a secure level. Best used in pristine computer environments (no down-level clients).
Highly Secure **hisec*.inf** ***ws-workstations** ***dc-domain controllers**	Highly secure templates require strong encryption and signing for a secure channel. To use highly secure settings, domain controllers must use Windows 2000 or Windows Server 2003. Users can use only Windows Logo–approved application software. Use of logon cache data is limited. The Power Users group is removed and only domain admins and the local Administrator account are members of the local Administrators group.
System Root Security **rootsec.inf**	Specifies root-level permissions. Use this template to reapply and restore default root directory settings or to apply setting to other disk volumes.
No Terminal Server User SID **notssid.inf**	Removes Windows Terminal Server security identifiers (SIDs) from Registry and file locations when Terminal Server is idle.

The default security template, **setup security.inf**, should not be applied using Group Policy because it contains a large amount of data that can degrade network performance due to periodic refreshing of the policy. The Setup Security template should not be applied through Group Policy.

The Compatible template, **compatws.inf**, should not be applied to domain controllers. In other words, do not import the Compatible template into the default domain policy or the default domain controller policy.

To create a new security template based on a predefined template:

➤ In the Security console tree, right-click the predefined template that comes closest to meeting your company's security policy needs, and choose Save As.

➤ Type a name for the template in the Name text box and then click the Save button. In the left pane listed under Security Templates, Figure 7.2 displays the securedc template, saved as test securedc.

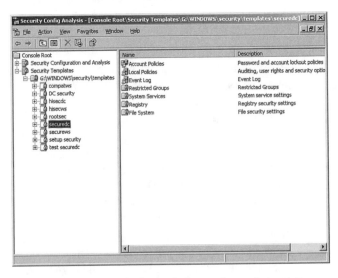

Figure 7.2   Security console showing **test securedc** security template.

Applying Security Templates

To configure your company's computers for domainwide security, begin by importing the custom security template that you created into the Security Configuration and Analysis MMC snap-in and saving this template as a new database file. Choose Analyze Now from the menu to analyze the imported security templates settings with your local Windows Server 2003. Columns are displayed in the right pane after analysis is completed. Compare your server's present security settings with the imported security template and make adjustments, as necessary, to conform to your company's security policies. When completed, choose Configure Computer Now to complete the operation and apply the security policy settings. Use the View Log File menu action to review any errors or problems. Make changes as necessary.

To import your custom security template and create a security database file:

1. Open your security console containing the Security Templates and the Security Configuration and Analysis snap-ins.

2. Right-click Security Configuration and Analysis and choose Open Database.

3. Type a meaningful name for your database file in the File Name text box, and then click Open.

4. Click the custom company security template you created earlier and then click Open to import your company's custom security template entries into the database file.

5. Leave the security console open for the next section.

Analyzing Security Templates

To analyze your system security settings:

1. In the security console, right-click Security Configuration and Analysis and choose Analyze Computer Now.

2. In the Perform Analysis dialog box, accept the default location for the error log file path and click the OK button to continue.

3. When the analysis completes, expand all nodes in the left pane under Security Configuration and Analysis. Make sure to expand the Registry and file system last because they contain complex hierarchies. In the right pane, view and compare your security database policy settings with the current settings on your local Windows Server 2003.

When you analyze security settings, no changes are made to your system. The results of the security analysis show the differences in your custom security template as compared to your actual computer system settings. Figure 7.3 depicts the Local Policies, Security Options Policies analysis, in the right pane, using the `test securedc` template default settings.

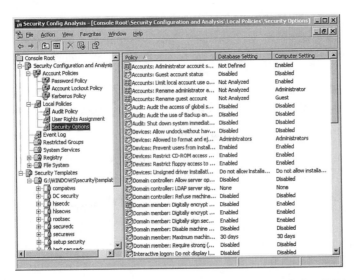

Figure 7.3 Security console showing the Local Policies, Security Options Policies analysis in the right pane.

Notice that entries in the right pane have various icons indicating their status. These icon symbols are defined as follows:

➤ **Red X**—Security values in the analysis database do not match computer system settings.

➤ **Green check mark**—Security values in analysis database match computer system settings.

➤ **Question mark**—Security value in analysis database is not defined and was not analyzed.

➤ **Exclamation point**—Security value in analysis database is defined but does not exist in computer system settings.

➤ **No symbol**—Security value in analysis database is not defined.

If a setting is not defined in your database, you can add it. To add a setting to your database:

1. Right-click the nondefined entry and choose Properties.

2. Click the Define This Policy in a Database check box, and then click other appropriate check boxes and then OK.

3. To apply your new settings, right-click Security Configuration and Analysis in the left pane and choose Save.

The red flag icon displays differences in your security settings database when compared to your local computer settings. If security policy settings need changing in your database file, you can modify them. To edit a setting in your security policy database file:

1. Right-click the entry to be edited and choose Properties.

2. Make sure that the Define This Policy in a Database check box is checked, and then click the appropriate attribute you want to change and then OK. Figure 7.4 shows the Digitally Encrypt or Sign Secure Data Channel enabled on the local system computer. Select the Enabled radio button to define the policy in your database.

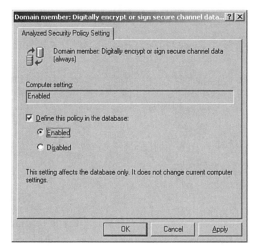

Figure 7.4 The Analyzed Security Policy Setting tab showing the Digitally Encrypt or Sign Secure Data Channel enabled on the local system computer.

3. To apply your settings, right-click Security Configuration and Analysis in the left pane and choose Save.

 If you make mistakes and need to revert to your original default security settings on your Windows Server 2003 domain controller, right-click Security Configuration and Analysis in the left pane, choose Import Template, and then click DC Security. Select the Clear This Database Before Importing check box and click Open. Right-click Security Configuration and Analysis in the left pane and choose configure Computer Now. Accept the default error log file path. When the analysis completes, right-click Security Configuration and Analysis in the left pane and choose View Log File. Review any errors or problems you find.

You must be a member of Domain Admins or Enterprise Admins or have been delegated appropriate authority to use the Security Configuration and Analysis console on
a domain controller.

For creating, modifying, or viewing security settings using the Security Templates
console, you must be a member of the local Administrators group or have been
delegated appropriate authority.

Changes you make to the analysis database are made to the stored template
security settings in the database file, not to the security template file itself.
You need to use the Security Templates snap-in component to make changes
to your security policy templates.

The Configure Computer Now option and the Save option accessed by right-clicking
Security Configuration and Analysis in the left pane perform the same actions. They
both write changes to your database file. When using the Configure Computer Now
option, make sure to modify only areas not affected by Group Policy settings because
Group Policy settings take precedence over local computer settings.

If you analyze large numbers of computers in your domain infrastructure, use the
secedit command-line tool instead of the Security Templates console. Then view your
results using the Security Configuration and Analysis snap-in console.

Auditing and Implementing Security Settings

The Security Templates console can also be used to audit and track potential
security problems, create an audit baseline of computer and network performance, ensure user accountability, and to provide evidence in the event of
a security breach. Effective audits can detect attacks and threats, and determine as well as prevent future damage. To audit events effectively, you have
to establish an audit policy based on the security needs of your company.

Auditing tracks user and network activities and records events in your server's Event Viewer security log. Figure 7.5 shows the Event Properties dialog
(left side) of a logon/logoff failure audit in Event Viewer security (right side).
The Event Properties dialog box results show the reason for the failure (bad
username or password), who the user was, and the date and time the logon
failure occurred. The end result, logon failure, is displayed in the Event
Viewer security log.

Be careful what you audit because auditing events can quickly build up in Event Viewer.
For example, auditing user logon success events for large companies would create
hundreds or even thousands of success log entries in the security log of Event Viewer.

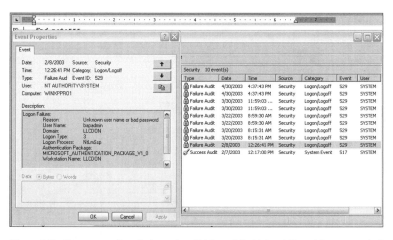

Figure 7.5 Event properties of a logon/logoff failure (left side) and Event Viewer security log, audit failure (right side).

If you need to change only a few security audit settings on one or several computers, use the Local Security Policy utility. Use Group Policy and the Security Configuration and Analysis snap-in to implement an audit policy for your domain. Figure 7.6 shows the securedc-defined audit policies listed under Security Templates. You need to create, modify, and save audit policy settings using the Security Templates snap-in. Then import them and apply the settings to a Group Policy Object (GPO) using the Security Configuration and Analysis snap-in.

Remember, you need to modify and save the audit policy settings using the Security Templates snap-in and then import them and apply the settings to a Group Policy Object (GPO) using the Security Configuration and Analysis snap-in.

The account policy must be defined in either the Default or new Domain GPO. There is only one account policy per domain. If other account policies are defined elsewhere, the default domain policy overwrites them.

Common events to audit include the following:

➤ Account logon events—User logon and logoff events, which when enabled, records results in the Event Viewer security log.

➤ Account management—Computer account events such as creating, modifying, and deleting user accounts and setting and changing passwords.

➤ Object access—Any object that contains an access control list (ACL) that users access, such as files, folders, and printers.

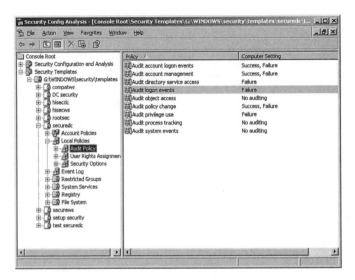

Figure 7.6   Security Templates showing **securedc** audit policies.

For multiple security policy settings defined by several policies, the order of precedence, from highest to lowest, is

➤ Organization unit policy
➤ Domain policy
➤ Site policy
➤ Local computer policy

Implementing the Principle of Least Privilege

Companies need to balance securing their network environments with maintaining maximum user functionality. The Principle of Least Privilege stipulates that users should have only the permissions and privileges necessary to perform their daily functions and tasks. Administrators, likewise, should perform routine, nonadministrative tasks using a restrictive account with the minimum level of permissions and privileges. In other words, administrators should perform routine, daily tasks with an account that has just the necessary permissions to perform those tasks. When administrators need to perform specific tasks that require extensive permissions, they can use either an administrative account containing the elevated permissions and privileges or they can use the Runas command to access administrative applications, tools, and utilities that require the broader permissions.

Using the Runas command or an account with minimum permissions ensures that if security is compromised, the impact of the security violation is minimized by the limited privileges of the user or administrator account. Using the Runas command is also efficient; you save time by not having to log off and then log back on again. Remote computer management using the Active Directory Users and Computers console with administrative credentials can also be accomplished using the Runas tool. For example, to use AD Users and Computers with domain admin credentials, type the following:

```
Runas /user:<YourComputerName>\administrator "mmc%windir%\system32\dsa.msc"
```

Installing and Configuring Software Update Infrastructure

System administrators need to check the Windows Update Web site frequently to obtain the latest security patches and operating system stability fixes. Microsoft's Windows Update Web site automates the process by scanning your hard drive for previous installed patches before displaying a list of the latest recommended patches. Administrators, however, must still download and test the latest patches before manually distributing and applying them to client computers.

 Traditional enterprise software tools, such as Microsoft's Systems Management Server (SMS), are also used to update clients' computers. If you're using electronic software distribution solutions for complete software management, Microsoft recommends that you continue to do so. SUS is not a replacement for SMS or Microsoft Group Policy–based software.

Many companies implement policies to prevent users from browsing the Internet for software updates. The Software Update Service (SUS) provides a solution to the problem of managing and deploying Windows patches by dynamic notification of critical updates, at scheduled times, to Windows client computers. Updates can be tested by the administrator and then scheduled to automatically update selected client computers. Large companies can use a centralized distribution point SUS server to deploy updates to other servers. Updates include security fixes, critical updates, and critical driver updates.

SUS is installed on a Windows 2000 (SP2 or later) or Windows Server 2003 inside the company's firewall. After it's installed, the SUS server downloads all critical updates and security roll-ups when they're posted to the Windows Update Web site. After the download completes, a blue globe icon appears in the taskbar tray with a message informing you that the updates are ready to be installed. The administrator also has the option of receiving email notification when new updates are posted.

SUS contains the following features:

➤ Software Update Services server—The SUS server on your internal intranet synchronizes with the Windows Update Web site whenever new critical updates for Windows 2000, Windows 2003, or Windows XP computers are available. Administrators can perform the synchronization manually or automatically. After all updates are downloaded to your SUS server, you can test and decide which updates you want to publish to the client computers. SUS server is supported for Windows 2000 Server (SP2 or later) and the Windows Server 2003 family.

➤ Automatic Updates client—This client component is usually configured to connect to your SUS server for updates. Administrators can control which clients connect and can also schedule when to deploy the critical updates, either manually or by using Active Directory Service Group Policy. The Automatic Updates client software is automatically installed when you install Windows Server 2003, Windows 2000 Server (SP3 or later), Windows 2000 Professional (SP3 or later), or Windows XP Professional and Home Editions (SP1 or later).

The Automatic Updates client software is supported and available for the following:

➤ Windows 2000 Professional with Service Pack 2

➤ Windows 2000 Server with Service Pack 2

➤ Windows 2000 Advanced Server with Service Pack 2

➤ Windows XP Professional

Clients can obtain the Automatic Updates client at

http://www.microsoft.com/windows2000/downloads/recommended/susclient/default.asp

Installing and Configuring SUS on a Server

The minimum configuration requirements are as follows:

➤ Pentium III 700MHz or higher processor

➤ 512MB of RAM

➤ 6GB of free hard disk space

➤ Internet Explorer (IE), version 5.5 or higher

➤ Internet Information Server (IIS) installed

Perform the following steps to install SUS with default settings:

1. Download the SUS package. Using IE version 5.5 or higher, browse to the following Web site and download the Software Update Services setup package from the SUS page: `http://www.microsoft.com/downloads/` `details.aspx?FamilyId=A7AA96E4-6E41-4F54-972C-AE66A4E4BF6C&displaylang=en`.

2. To install SUS SP1, double-click the `sus10sp1.exe` file and click Next on the Welcome screen of the SUS Setup Wizard. Read and accept the End User License Agreement and click Next.

3. Select Typical if you want to have all the defaults applied or select Custom to configure the SUS options now. Select Custom and click the Next button.

4. You can store the updates locally or have clients update their files from a Microsoft Windows Update server. In the Update Storage section, select the Save the Updates to This Local Folder (by default, `c:\SUS\content`) radio button and then click Next.

5. By default, the All Available Languages radio button is selected, which results in more than 600MB of updates. If you don't need additional languages, select the English Only (about 150MB of updates) button. Select the Specific Languages radio button if you need to add additional languages. Select the English Only button and click Next (see Figure 7.7).

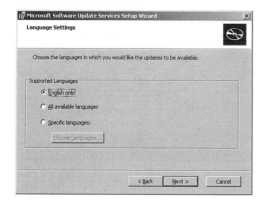

Figure 7.7   You can conserve disk space by specifying a language on the Language Settings screen.

6. You can manually or automatically approve new versions. Select the Automatically Approve New Versions of Previously Approved Updates radio button and click Next to continue.

7. The Ready to Install property page is displayed. Click the Install button to proceed. On the Installing Microsoft Software Update Service

property page, SUS installs and applies the IIS lockdown tool to Windows 2000 SP2 Server, Advanced Server and earlier versions. Note the IIS lockdown tool is included with Windows 2000 Server (SP3 and later) and the Windows Server 2003 family.

8. Click the Finish button to complete the installation. SUS setup adds a Start menu shortcut in the Administrative Tools folder and opens the SUS administration Web site in Internet Explorer at `http://` `<yourservername>/SUSAdmin`.

 You must be a local administrator on the SUS Server to install and view the Administration Web page.

If you try to connect to the Administration Web site with a version of IE older than version 5.5, you'll see an error page reminding you to upgrade to IE 5.5 or later.

If your network uses a proxy server to connect to the Internet, configure your proxy server settings on the SUS Administration Web page under the Select a Proxy Server configuration section.

Configuring Client Automatic Updates

To use the SUS server for updates, client computers must be running the updated Automatic Updates client. Windows 2000 Professional and Server (SP2 or earlier), and Windows XP Home and Windows XP Professional clients must update their operating system to use SUS. The update is available at `http://www.microsoft.com/windows2000/downloads/recommended/susclient/` `default.asp`.

The administrator can configure Windows XP or Windows 2000 automatic client updates either by using the Automatic Updates tab in the System Properties dialog box of the System applet in the Control Panel or by connecting to a wizard after waiting at least 24 hours after connectivity to the update service has been established. The System Properties Automatic Updates tab configuration options are shown in Figure 7.8.

The following options are used to control how updates are applied:

➤ Notify before updates are downloaded and notify again before the updates are installed.

➤ Download the updates automatically and notify before the updates are installed.

➤ Download the updates automatically and install the updates based on a specified schedule.

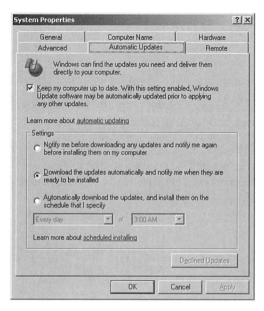

Figure 7.8   You configure the Automatic Updates options in the System applet from the Control Panel.

   Know the difference between Windows Update and Automatic Updates. All Windows client computers and users can use Windows Update. The Automatic Updates service uses Windows Update to automatically obtain critical updates.

Using Group Policy to Configure SUS Clients

In a domain environment, using Group Policy is the preferred way of applying updates to your clients. Policies can also be configured using Windows NT 4 System Policy or by manually setting Registry keys.

   Remember that Active Directory Group Policy settings always take precedence over local group policies and user-defined options.

To set up a group policy using Active Directory installed on Windows 2000 or Windows Server 2003, perform the following steps:

1. Click Start, All Programs, Administrative Tools, Active Directory Users and Computers to open the Active Directory Users and Computers MMC interface.

2. Right-click the OU or domain where you want to create the policy, and then click Properties.

3. Click the Group Policy tab, and then click New. Type a name for your policy, and then click the Edit button. The Group Policy editor opens.

4. Navigate to and expand the Computer Configuration folder. Right-click Administrative Templates, choose Add/Remove Templates, and then click Add.

5. In the Policy Templates dialog box, select the wuau.adm template and click the Open button. Verify that your template has been added and then close the Add/Remove Templates dialog box. Note that steps 4 and 5 are not necessary on a Windows Server 2003. The wuau.adm is already installed, by default.

6. Under Computer Configuration, expand the Administrative Templates folder, expand the Windows Components folder, and then select the Windows Update folder.

   Four policies that you can configure are displayed in the right pane: Configure Automatic Updates, Specify Intranet Microsoft Update Service Location, Reschedule Automatic Updates Scheduled Installations, and No Auto-Restart for Scheduled Automatic Updates Installations.

7. Double-click Configure Automatic Updates and select the Enabled radio button.

8. In the Configure Automatic Updates section, select one of the following options from the drop-down list box:

   ➤ Notify for Download and Notify for Install

   ➤ Auto Download and Notify for Install (default setting)

   ➤ Auto Download and Schedule the Install

9. When you finish, click the Close button.

10. Next, in the right pane, double-click Specify Your Intranet Microsoft Updates Service Location and select the Enabled radio button as shown in Figure 7.9.

11. To specify a location for the SUS server that your Windows clients will be redirected to, type the URL in the Set the Intranet Update Service for Detecting Updates text box. Click the OK button when complete.

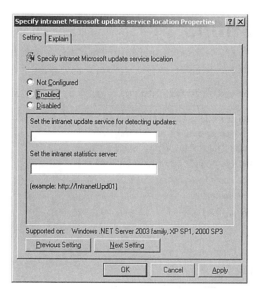

Figure 7.9   You can enable automatic updates via the Specify Intranet Microsoft Updates Service Location Properties screen.

Best Practices for Security Settings

Follow these best practices for security settings to secure your network:

➤ Allow only administrators physical access to domain controllers

➤ Use the Principle of Least Privilege to perform administrative tasks

➤ Always test a new security policy before applying it to your network

➤ Remember the order of precedence when applying multiple security policies

➤ The account policy for your domain is the default domain policy

➤ Apply your security templates correctly

➤ When you configure Local Security Policy, use the proper tools

➤ Properly define groups and group memberships

➤ Properly secure data on computers

➤ Use complex or strong passwords throughout your organization

➤ Never download programs from untrusted sources

➤ Always run antivirus software and keep virus definitions up-to-date

➤ Always keep all software security fixes and patches up-to-date

Exam Prep Questions

Question 1

> Max works for AdepTek. AdepTek has a Windows Server 2003 AD domain. Max
> creates a security template to establish a security baseline for AdepTek's net-
> work. He wants to apply this template, but can't find the correct command in the
> Security Templates utility. What must Max do to apply the security template?
> (Choose two answers.)
>
> ❏ A. Use the Security Templates Save As command
>
> ❏ B. Use the Security Configuration and Analysis tool
>
> ❏ C. Use a GPO
>
> ❏ D. Security Templates cannot be used to apply settings
>
> ❏ E. Apply a GPO to the domain container

Answers B and D are correct. Max needs to use the Security Configuration
and Analysis tool. Security Templates cannot be used to apply settings. Using
the Save As command in Security Templates saves only settings. GPOs are
used for sites, domains, and organizational units.

Question 2

> Sara works for InnoTek. InnoTek has a Windows Server 2003 AD domain. Sara
> wants to create a security template on the Windows 2003 DC to establish a
> security baseline for AdepTek's network. She doesn't know which predefined
> template to select. Which built-in security template should Sara select?
>
> ○ A. Setup security
>
> ○ B. **compatws**
>
> ○ C. **rootsec**
>
> ○ D. DC security

Answer D is correct. Sara needs to use the DC security built-in template to
begin building a security baseline for AdepTek's network. The rootsec security template contains the default settings for the local computer and is commonly used to reapply default settings. The setup security template and the
compatws template should not be used on domain controllers.

Question 3

Amy works for InnoTek Solutions. InnoTek Solutions has a Windows Server 2003 AD domain. Amy creates a security template to establish account policies for the InnoTek Solutions network. She wants to edit security settings, but can't find the correct component in the Security Templates utility. What component must Amy use in Security Templates to edit security settings?

- ○ A. Use the Security Templates Save As command
- ○ B. Use the Local Security Policy
- ○ C. Use the Security Settings Extensions to Group Policy tab
- ○ D. Use the **secedit** command-line tool

Answer C is correct. Amy needs to use the Security Settings Extensions to Group Policy tab to edit domain security settings. Using the Save As command in Security Templates only saves settings. The Local Security Policy tab is only used to edit local settings. The secedit command-line tool is used to automate security settings for large companies.

Question 4

John works for InnoTek. InnoTek has a Windows Server 2003 AD domain. Innotek has 150 Windows XP Professional clients and 50 Windows 2000 Professional clients. John needs to create a security template to enable Server Message Block (SMB) packet signing on his DC with minimal impact to Innotek's custom applications. What built-in security template must John use in Security Templates to enable SMB packet signing?

- ○ A. Default security
- ○ B. DC Default security
- ○ C. Secure
- ○ D. Highly Secure

Answer C is correct. John needs to use the Secure settings template. Secure has medium-level security settings with minimal impact to application compatibility and can be used for enabling SMB packet signing. Secure is best used in pristine computer environment. Default security cannot be used on DCs. DC Default security, created during the installation of AD, is commonly used to restore settings and does not enable SMBs. Highly Secure templates require strong encryption and signing for a secure channel and can use only Windows Logo–approved software.

Question 5

Susan works for AdepTek. AdepTek operates a Windows Server 2003 AD domain. AdepTek has 50 Windows XP Professional clients and 150 Windows Professional 2000 clients. Susan creates a security template to enable Server Message Block (SMB) packet signing on her DC with minimal impact to AdepTek's custom applications. She saves it as **securedc**. What is the next step that Susan should perform?

- ○ A. Import **securedc** into the Security Configuration and Analysis tool
- ○ B. Apply **securedc** using the Security Templates tool
- ○ C. Use the Save As command and save the template as **securedc2**
- ○ D. Apply **securedc** using the Security Configuration and Analysis tool

Answer A is correct. Susan needs to import securedc into the Security Configuration and Analysis utility and then choose Analyze Now to apply the security settings from the securedc template into a database file. Applying securedc using the Security Templates tool cannot be done. Susan has already saved her template and does not need to save it again. Applying securedc using the Security Configuration and Analysis tool is the second step. Susan must first import it into Security Configuration and Analysis.

Question 6

Max works for InnoTek and is using a Windows Server 2003 member server. InnoTek manages a Windows Server 2003 AD domain. InnoTek has 60 Windows XP Professional clients, 10 Windows Professional 2000 clients, and 80 Windows 98 clients. InnoTek also has two custom applications that lack the Windows Logo certification for software approval. What template should Max select to allow users to run InnoTek's custom applications?

- ○ A. Secure
- ○ B. System root security
- ○ C. DC Default security
- ○ D. Compatible

Answer D is correct. Max needs to use the Compatible template that relaxes default file and Registry permissions so that users can run applications that lack the Windows Logo Program for Software approval. The Secure template cannot be used on custom applications that lack the Windows Logo seal of approval. The Default DC security template is only used on DCs. The System root security template is used to reapply security settings on a DC.

Question 7

Amy works for InnoTek Solutions and is using a Windows Server 2003 DC. InnoTek operates a Windows Server 2003 AD domain. InnoTek Solutions has 60 Windows XP Professional clients, 10 Windows Professional 2000 clients, and 80 Windows 98 clients. Amy creates a security template and saves it as **securedc**. She imports it into Security Configuration and Analysis. Next, she chooses Analyze Now, compares and edits security settings, and chooses Configure Computer Now. She needs a way to find out whether there are any errors. How can Amy find out whether there are any errors in the **securedc** template?

○ A. Use the security template

○ B. Use View Log File

○ C. Choose Save and view the errors

○ D. Choose Analyze Now

Answer B is correct. Amy needs to use the View Log File menu command to review any errors or problems. The security template cannot be used to view errors. The Configure Computer Now command saves the files. Therefore, it isn't necessary for Amy to save it again. The Analyze Now command has already been performed.

Question 8

Ralph works for AdepTek and is using a Windows Server 2003 DC. AdepTek manages a Windows Server 2003 AD domain. AdepTek Solutions has 150 Windows XP Professional clients, 40 Windows Professional 2000 clients, and 25 Windows 98 clients. Ralph creates a security template and saves it as **securedc**. He imports it into Security Configuration and Analysis. Next, Ralph chooses Analyze Now, compares and edits security settings, and chooses Configure Computer Now. Ralph uses the View Log File menu command and discovers many errors. He needs to revert to the original settings on the Windows Server 2003 DC. Which template should Ralph use to revert back to the original settings on the Windows Server 2003 computer?

○ A. Secure

○ B. System Root security

○ C. DC Default security

○ D. Default security

Answer B is correct. Ralph needs to use the System Root security template to reapply and restore default root directory settings. The Compatible and the Default security templates cannot be used on a DC. The DC Default security template should not be used to revert back to original settings.

Question 9

Sara works for InnoTek and is using a Windows Server 2003 DC. InnoTek operates a Windows Server 2003 AD domain. InnoTek has 150 Windows XP Professional clients and 40 Windows Professional 2000 clients. Sara is working on a user's Windows Professional 2000 computer and needs to access the Windows Server 2003 DC Computer Management console. Sara's company adheres to the Principle of Least Privilege. What two methods can Sara use at the user's workstation to access the Computer Management tool on the Windows Server 2003 AD DC?

❑ A. Log off the workstation and log back on as Domain Administrator

❑ B. Log off the workstation and log back on as Administrator with restricted privileges

❑ C. Use the **Runas** command

❑ D. Log off the workstation and log back on as a Power User

❑ E. Log off the workstation and log back on as Enterprise Administrator

Answers B and C are correct. Sara needs to either log off the workstation and log back on as Administrator with restricted privileges, or use the Runas command and adhere to the Principle of Least Privilege. Logging off the workstation and logging back on as domain administrator or enterprise administrator gives Sara too much authority. Power Users do not have the authority to run the Computer Management tool on a DC.

Question 10

Max works for AdepTek and is using a Windows DC Server 2003. AdepTek operates a Windows Server 2003 AD domain. AdepTek has 150 Windows XP Professional clients, 40 Windows Professional 2000 clients, and 10 Windows 98 computers. Adeptek wants a security policy that prevents users from browsing the Internet for updates. AdepTek wants its Windows 2003 Server DC to automatically download software updates and deploy updates to users' computers. What should Max install on the Windows Server 2003 DC?

○ A. Secure Security template

○ B. Software Update Services (SUS)

○ C. Highly Secure template

○ D. Windows Update

Answer B is correct. Max needs to install the Software Update Service (SUS) on the Windows 2003 DC Server. Both the Secure and Highly Secure templates cannot be used in mixed computer environments. Windows Update is already installed on Windows Server 2003 and cannot be used to automatically deploy patches to client computers.

Need to Know More?

 Software Update Services components and features: http://www.
microsoft.com/windows2000/windowsupdate/sus/suscomponents.
asp

 Security administration tasks: http://www.microsoft.com/technet/
treeview/default.asp?url=/technet/prodtechnol/
windowsserver2003/proddocs/entserver/comexp/
adsecuretasks_6dkj.asp

 Security—Best Practices for Security Configuration and Analysis
http://www.microsoft.com/technet/treeview/default.asp?url=/
technet/prodtechnol/windowsserver2003/proddocs/standard/
sag_SCMbp.asp

 Security Overview http://www.microsoft.com/technet/treeview/
default.asp?url=/technet/prodtechnol/windowsserver2003/
proddocs/standard/sag_SEconceptsSecModel.asp

 Security Configuration Manager http://www.microsoft.com/
technet/treeview/default.asp?url=/technet/prodtechnol/
windowsserver2003/proddocs/standard/seconcepts_SCM.asp

 White Paper: Windows Server 2003 Security Guide
http://microsoft.com/downloads/details.aspx?FamilyId=8A2643
C1-0685-4D89-B655-521EA6C7B4DB&displaylang=en

 Support Center Windows Server 2003:
http://support.microsoft.com/default.aspx?scid=fh;EN-US;
winsvr2003#faq555

 Stanek, William R., *Windows Server 2003*, Microsoft Press, 2003

Practice Exam 1

Question 1

Jane is the network administrator for Wiggin Enterprises. She needs to change Group Policy settings for the Sales group to give the salespeople access to new specs on their latest product. Jane decides to use the GPMC for this task. Which of the following types of policy settings can she change using this tool? (Select all that apply.)

- ❏ A. Domain
- ❏ B. Organizational unit
- ❏ C. Security
- ❏ D. Site
- ❏ E. User
- ❏ F. Computer
- ❏ G. Forest

Question 2

John is the IT assistant for EDGE Services Group. He has been assigned the task of DNS server management. To which group must John belong to manage and perform administrative tasks on DNS servers?

- ○ A. Local Administrators group
- ○ B. DomainAdmin group
- ○ C. System Operator
- ○ D. Power User

Question 3

Mary is the network administrator for SmallCorp, and is responsible for documentation of the Active Directory domain used by SmallCorp for its information technology needs. As a part of this documentation, Mary has to provide a comma-separated (**.csv**) file that details the attributes for Active Directory accounts. Which utility should Mary use for this purpose?

○ A. **Csvde**

○ B. **Dsget**

○ C. **Dsmod**

○ D. **Dsquery**

○ E. **Ldifde**

Question 4

Dan needs to delegate control to an assistant to manage and perform most administrative tasks using Security Templates on Windows Server 2003. What group membership is required for the assistant assigned to this task?

○ A. Local Administrators group

○ B. Domain Admin group

○ C. System Operator

○ D. Power User

Question 5

Ed has been tasked to set up Kerberos authentication, with a high level of security, for all users on the network. Which of the following options should he select?

○ A. Advanced Digest Authentication

○ B. Digest Authentication

○ C. Integrated Windows Authentication

○ D. .NET Passport Authentication

Question 6

Craig is upgrading his company's network to Windows Server 2003 and needs to provide a report to management on the new features for storage management with a focus on disaster recovery. Which options in the following are new disaster recovery features in Windows Server 2003? (Select two.)

❏ A. Backup

❏ B. Driver Rollback

❏ C. ASR

❏ D. Emergency Repair Disk (ERD)

❏ E. System State

Question 7

You would like to delegate control to certain users to allow them to manage and perform most administrative tasks using the Security Configuration and Analysis tool on Windows Server 2003 domain controller. What is the most common group membership required? (Select two.)

❏ A. Local Administrators group

❏ B. Domain Admin group

❏ C. System Operator

❏ D. Enterprise Admin group

❏ E. Power Users group

Question 8

You want to set up secure remote access and integrated dial-up and VPN connections for remote client access. Which of the following Microsoft services makes the best use of these technologies?

○ A. RRAS

○ B. IIS

○ C. Terminal Services

○ D. SUS

Question 9

Dorothy needs to change certain settings for a user's GPO. Which privileges can be restricted to filter the application of a GPO's settings?

- ❑ A. Apply Group Policy
- ❑ B. Change
- ❑ C. Modify
- ❑ D. Read
- ❑ E. Full Control

Question 10

AdepTek operates a Windows Server 2003 Active Directory domain that has 3,500 Windows 2000 Professional computers and users. AdepTek uses Microsoft Systems Management Server (SMS) 2.0 for centralized management and software deployment. AdepTek's management learns that Microsoft manages a Software Update Services (SUS) Web site for automated deployment of security fixes and patches. According to Microsoft's recommendations, what should AdepTek use for software deployment?

- ○ A. Use Software Update Services instead
- ○ B. Use SMS 2.0
- ○ C. Use SMS 2.0 and wait for an SMS-compatible integrated version release of SUS to be released
- ○ D. Wait for SMS 3.0

Question 11

You've been tasked with the creation of a new script that will create an **.ldf** file listing all user accounts on a server named SomeServer. Which of the following parameters would be used to specify the type of account to include?

- ○ A. **-b**
- ○ B. **-f**
- ○ C. **-s**
- ○ D. **-r**
- ○ E. **/?**

Question 12

Max, a local administrator, manages seven DNS servers in three domains for AdepTek. All seven DNS servers are Active Directory–integrated DNS servers. Max needs to change the zone type on one of the DNS servers to a stub zone. Max right-clicks the forward lookup zone and chooses Properties. He clicks the Change button on the General tab. What is the next selection Max must make to change the zone type to stub?

- ○ A. Target DNS server IP address
- ○ B. Source DNS server computer name
- ○ C. Source DNS server IP address
- ○ D. Target DNS server computer name

Question 13

Upper management has tasked Madelaine with using ASR to implement a disaster recovery solution. What is the first step she needs to take?

- ○ A. Create a full backup
- ○ B. Back up the users company data files and folders
- ○ C. Back up the server's system files
- ○ D. Create an ASR floppy disk

Question 14

You're the network administrator responsible for backing up a large number of GPOs monthly to have the ability to roll back to previous policy settings, as needed. Which of the following methods can be used to accomplish this with the least administrative effort using the Group Policy Management Console?

- ○ A. You should perform monthly backups of each GPO to a separate location for each GPO.
- ○ B. You should perform monthly backups of all GPOs to a standard location.
- ○ C. You should perform monthly backups of all GPOs to a location for each month.
- ○ D. You should perform monthly backups of all GPOs to a separate location for each GPO each month.

Question 15

Your boss has tasked you with explaining the uses for the command-line utilities **Csvde** and **Ldifde**. How would you best describe the uses for each command-line tool? (Choose two.)

- ❑ A. The **Csvde** command-line utility can be used to modify the Active Directory schema.
- ❑ B. The **Csvde** command-line utility cannot be used to modify the Active Directory schema.
- ❑ C. The **Ldifde** command-line utility can be used to modify the Active Directory schema.
- ❑ D. The **Ldifde** command-line utility cannot be used to modify the Active Directory schema.
- ❑ E. The **Csvde** command-line utility is used for editing comma-delimited text reports.

Question 16

You're in charge of a disaster recovery solution and have been told to use the ASR tool. What information is stored on the ASR floppy disk?

- ○ A. System State
- ○ B. Storage file information
- ○ C. User-mapped drives
- ○ D. Registry
- ○ E. User's profile settings

Question 17

AdepTek operates a Windows Server 2003 Active Directory domain. The domain has 200 Windows 2000 Professional computers, 50 Windows XP Professional computers, 50 Windows 98 (SP1), and two other Windows 2000 Servers. All the Windows 2000 Professional computers have Service Pack 1 (SP1) applied. The Windows XP Professional computers do not have any Service Packs applied; the Windows 2000 Servers have SP2 applied. What computers presently support the Automatic Update client software? (Select two.)

- ❑ A. Windows 2000 Professional (SP1)
- ❑ B. Windows XP Professional
- ❑ C. Windows 2000 Servers (SP2)
- ❑ D. Windows 98 (SP1)

Question 18

You've been assigned the task of setting up Web sites and Web-based applications. Which of the following Microsoft products should you use?

○ A.　RRAS

○ B.　IIS 6.0

○ C.　Terminal Services

○ D.　SUS

Question 19

Sara, a local administrator, manages five Windows 2003 DNS servers in two domains for InnoTek. All five DNS servers are Active Directory–integrated DNS servers. Sara needs to check and possibly reconfigure DNS replication. Sara's administrator tells her that Windows 2003 DNS servers have a new replication feature added to the DNS server's Zone Properties dialog box. Which tab does Sara need to click in the Zone Properties dialog box to view and or modify zone replication?

○ A.　Start of Authority (SOA)

○ B.　General

○ C.　Name Servers

○ D.　Zone Transfers

Question 20

AdepTek operates a Windows Server 2003 Active Directory Domain. The domain has 200 Windows 2000 Professional computers, 50 Windows XP Professional computers, 50 Windows 98, and two other Windows 2000 Servers. All the Windows 2000 Professional computers have Service Pack 2 (SP2) applied. The Windows XP Professional computers do not have any Service Packs applied, and the Windows 2000 Servers have SP3 applied. The Windows 2000 Servers have a Pentium III 500MHz CPU, 768MB of RAM, 10GB of free hard disk space, and Internet Explorer 5.0 installed. SUS needs to be installed on one of the Windows 2000 Servers. What components are missing or need to be upgraded on the Windows 2000 Servers? (Select three.)

❏ A.　IIS needs to be installed

❏ B.　The RAM needs upgrading

❏ C.　The CPU needs upgrading

❏ D.　The hard drive needs upgrading

❏ E.　Internet Explorer needs upgrading

❏ F.　Service Pack 4 needs to be applied

Question 21

A user account has four types of associated names: the user logon name, the pre–Windows 2000 logon name, the principal logon name, and the LDAP relative distinguished name. Which of the following is an example of the principal logon name of a user account?

- ○ A. **myuser**
- ○ B. **MYCORP\myuser**
- ○ C. **myuser@mycorp.com**
- ○ D. **CN=myuser,CN=Users,DC=mycorp,DC=com**

Question 22

Amy has Windows XP Professional on her computer. She accidentally deletes her PowerPoint file and wants to recover it. She right-clicks her shared data folder and chooses Properties, but the Previous Version tab is missing. Why can't Amy recover her PowerPoint file? (Select two.)

- ❑ A. Shadow Copies service is not activated on the Windows Server 2003.
- ❑ B. Amy should right-click the deleted PowerPoint file.
- ❑ C. Amy right-clicked the wrong folder.
- ❑ D. Amy does not have the Shadow Copies for Shared Folders software installed on her computer.
- ❑ E. Amy does not have permission to recover the file.

Question 23

John administers and manages two Windows 2003 DNS servers and a Unix DNS server, which uses an early version of BIND, in one domain for AdepTek. One Windows 2003 DNS server is the primary DNS server; the other is the secondary DNS server. John needs the Unix server to work with the Windows 2003 DNS servers. The Unix DNS server runs a mission-critical application that works only with its early version of BIND. John realizes that the Unix server cannot communicate with the Windows DNS servers until he changes the default security on the two Windows 2003 DNS servers. What is the *best* security setting for John to select for the Unix DNS server and the Windows 2003 primary and secondary DNS servers to work together?

- ○ A. Dynamic Updates
- ○ B. Non-secure
- ○ C. Secure and Non-secure
- ○ D. Secure

Question 24

Susan needs to create a Group Policy to manage Windows Updates on her Windows 2000 Server, but forgot the name of the administrative template used to set up Windows Updates. What administrative template is used to manage Windows Updates?

- ○ A. **inetres.adm**
- ○ B. **conf.adm**
- ○ C. **wuau.adm**
- ○ D. **system.adm**

Question 25

Jim needs to migrate an existing GPO to a new forest. Which action in GPMC should he take? (Select three.)

- ❑ A. Backup
- ❑ B. Copy
- ❑ C. Import
- ❑ D. Restore
- ❑ E. Export
- ❑ F. Transfer

Question 26

Chris noticed that there are duplicate names on the network. Which of the following associated names must be unique only within its container? (Select two.)

- ❑ A. User logon name
- ❑ B. Pre–Windows 2000 logon name
- ❑ C. Principal logon name
- ❑ D. LDAP relative distinguished name
- ❑ E. Unified logon name

Question 27

Susan later decides to unapprove a Windows update that was previously deployed to client computers. What actions must she take on the client computers to remove an unapproved update?

- ○ A. The unapproved update automatically uninstalls itself from client computers.
- ○ B. The unapproved update needs to be scheduled on the SUS server and later deployed to client computers.
- ○ C. The unapproved update must be manually removed from client computers.
- ○ D. The unapproved update automatically installs itself again on the client computers and then automatically removes itself.

Question 28

InnoTek operates a Windows Server 2003 Active Directory domain. The domain has 100 Windows 2000 Professional computers and 50 Windows XP Professional computers. SUS is installed on the Windows Server 2003. Amy, a user using Windows XP Professional, tries to open the SUS Administration Web page using Internet Explorer but receives an error. Why can't Amy open the SUS Administration Web page?

- ○ A. Amy must be a member of the Domain Admins group.
- ○ B. Windows XP IIS component needs to be installed.
- ○ C. Internet Explorer needs upgrading.
- ○ D. Amy must be a member of the local Administrators group.

Question 29

You've been tasked with explaining the latest technologies in Windows 2003 to upper management. How would you best describe the Resultant Set of Policy?

- ○ A. A listing of all settings from all GPOs, organized in order of evaluation
- ○ B. A listing of all settings from a selected GPO, organized by type (computer and user)
- ○ C. A listing of winning settings from all GPOs, detailing the source of each
- ○ D. A listing of winning settings from a target GPO, detailing the source of each

Question 30

Susan administers and manages four Windows 2003 DNS servers and a Unix DNS server in one domain containing two subnets for AdepTek. Two Windows 2003 DNS servers are primary DNS servers; two are secondary DNS severs. Primary DNS Server1 has an IP address of 192.168.1.4, and secondary DNS Server1 has an IP address of 192.168.1.8. Primary DNS Server2 has an IP address of 192.168.2.4, and secondary DNS Server2 has an IP address of 192.168.2.8. Susan needs the secondary DNS servers to obtain their zone information from their respective primary DNS servers. She is updating secondary DNS Server2. What IP address should Susan put in the Zone Transfers tab for secondary DNS Server2?

- ○ A. 192.168.1.4
- ○ B. 192.168.1.8
- ○ C. 192.168.2.4
- ○ D. 192.168.2.8

Question 31

Amy has Windows XP Professional with Service Pack 1 applied on her computer. Shadow Copies for Shared Folders is activated on the Windows Server 2003 and Shadow Copies client is installed on Amy's PC. Amy accidentally overwrites her PowerPoint file and needs to recover it. How does Amy recover her overwritten PowerPoint file?

- ○ A. Amy should right-click the overwritten PowerPoint file and choose Properties. Then she should select the Previous Version tab and click the Restore button.
- ○ B. Amy should right-click the overwritten PowerPoint file and choose Properties. Then she should select the Previous Version tab and click the View button.
- ○ C. Amy should right-click her shared data folder, choose Properties, click the Previous Version tab, and click the View button.
- ○ D. Amy should right-click the overwritten PowerPoint file and choose Properties. Then she should select the Previous Version tab and click the Copy button.

Question 32

You're the network administrator for SomeCorp and have been tasked with correcting a permissions error that is preventing the Alerter service from starting. Which account's permissions are the most likely source of this conflict?

- ○ A. **IUSR_myserver**
- ○ B. **LocalSystem**
- ○ C. **LocalService**
- ○ D. **NetworkService**

Question 33

Max has Windows Server 2003 installed on his computer. When he finishes installing updated drivers for his SCSI controller card, the computer stops responding. Max needs to get back to work. What action enables Max to resume working?

- ○ A. Max should use Device Manager and disable the SCSI controller device.
- ○ B. Max should use Device Manager and roll back the SCSI controller device.
- ○ C. Max should use Device Manager and uninstall the SCSI controller device.
- ○ D. Max should use obtain updated drivers and reinstall them using Device Manager.

Question 34

AdepTek operates a site containing two Windows Server 2003 Active Directory domains. Each domain has 100 Windows 2000 Professional computers, 125 Windows XP Professional computers, 25 Windows 98 computers, and 2 Windows 2000 Servers. Domain 1 has an OU called Sales. Domain 2 has an OU called Marketing. The Sales OU has an account policy established for creating complex passwords. The Marketing OU has an account policy for creating passwords with a minimum of six characters. Domain 1 has an account password policy for creating passwords with a minimum of eight characters. Which account policies are applied?

- ○ A. All three account policies are applied.
- ○ B. The account password policy for creating passwords with a minimum of eight characters is applied.
- ○ C. The account policy for creating complex passwords is applied.
- ○ D. The account policy for creating passwords with a minimum of six characters is applied.

Question 35

You're the network administrator responsible for rolling out a security policy intended to return the current settings to their default installation configuration on all domain controllers within a large forest structure. Which default security templates could be used to accomplish this most easily? (Select two.)

- ❏ A. CompatDC
- ❏ B. DC Security
- ❏ C. HisecDC
- ❏ D. SecureDC
- ❏ E. Setup Security

Question 36

Tom administers and manages 11 Windows 2003 DNS servers and two Unix DNS servers in 5 domains and 1 child domain for InnoTech Solutions. All the DNS servers, except the two Unix DNS servers, are Active Directory–integrated DNS servers. Two Active Directory–integrated DNS servers in each domain are configured as primary zones. Tom needs to set up the child domain DNS server. He would like to improve name resolution efficiency and keep delegated zone information current by providing the DNS server in the parent zone with its resource records list of name servers for its child zone. What zone type should Tom select for the child DNS server?

- ○ A. Active Directory–integrated zone
- ○ B. Secondary zone
- ○ C. Primary zone
- ○ D. Stub zone

Question 37

Tom is a domain administrator and is currently performing a task on a user's computer. He cannot finish the task until he adjusts a configuration setting on his server. He decides to use the **Runas** command to create a desktop shortcut and connect to his server's Active Directory Users and Computers module. Which **Runas** command is the correct one for Tom to use?

○ A. **Runas /user:ComputerName\administrator cmd**

○ B. **Runas /user:ComputerName\administrator "mmc%windir%\sys-tem32\ compmgmt.msc"**

○ C. **Runas /user:ComputerName\administrator "mmc%windir%\sys-tem32\ dsa.msc"**

○ D. **Runas /netonly /user:DomainName\UserName "mmc%windir%\system32\dsa.msc"**

Question 38

Susan has Windows Server 2003 installed on her server and tries to install an updated NIC driver but the installation fails. What can Susan do to get her server working normally again?

○ A. Susan should use Device Manager and uninstall the NIC device driver.

○ B. Susan should use Device Manager and disable the NIC device driver.

○ C. Susan should obtain updated NIC drivers and reinstall them, using Device Manager.

○ D. Susan should use Device Manager and roll back the NIC device driver.

Question 39

You're the network administrator tasked with the deployment of a kiosk system that will be used by visitors to the Museum of Fine Arts. In planning your deployment, you must decide the security settings that will be applied to the MyGuestLogon account. Which of the following settings is most appropriate to the solution presented?

○ A. User must change password at next logon

○ B. User cannot change password

○ C. Password never expires

○ D. Account is disabled

Question 40

Tom is the administrator for a network with 100 clients. He has been tasked with updating an application on all client systems. What component should Tom use to manage a software update infrastructure?

○ A. Group Policy

○ B. IIS

○ C. Terminal Services

○ D. SUS

Question 41

InnoTek operates a Windows Server 2003 Active Directory domain. The domain has 100 Windows 2000 Professional computers, 125 Windows XP Professional computers, 25 Windows 98 computers, and 2 Windows 2000 Servers. A GPO is created to audit logon success and failures and applied to the domain object. John, an assistant administrator, wants to view the auditing events. Where does John view the results of the logon success and failures?

○ A. Event Viewer, Security log

○ B. Security Templates Console

○ C. Security Configuration and Analysis Console

○ D. Active Directory Users and Computers Console

Question 42

Which of the following Security Policy MMC snap-ins are available, by default, within the Administrative Tools container of a Microsoft Windows Server 2003 standalone server?

○ A. Domain Controllers Security Policy

○ B. Domain Security Policy

○ C. Local Security Policy

○ D. Security Configuration and Analysis

○ E. Security Templates

Question 43

Tom administers and manages 11 Windows 2003 DNS servers and two Unix DNS servers in 5 domains and 1 child domain for InnoTech Solutions. All the DNS servers except the two Unix DNS servers are Active Directory-integrated DNS servers. Two Active Directory-integrated DNS servers in each domain are configured as primary zones. Tom configures the child domain DNS server for a stub zone. Tom wants to have a power user manage the stub zone DNS server. He wants to give the power user only enough authority to manage the stub zone DNS server. How can Tom best accomplish this?

- ○ A. Add the power user to the local Administrators group.
- ○ B. Add the power user to the Domain Admin group.
- ○ C. Add the power user to the DNS Admin group.
- ○ D. Delegate control of the child domain to the power user.

Question 44

You've been tasked with the creation of a script that will create a user accounts for Bob Jones on a server named MyServer using the **Dsadd** command-line utility. Which of the following parameters would be used to specify the UNC path to the location of Bob's logon script?

- ○ A. **-fn**
- ○ B. **-hmdir**
- ○ C. **-hmdrv**
- ○ D. **-ln**
- ○ E. **-loscr**

Question 45

You have been tasked with setting up an IIS Web site authentication method that provides a single, unified logon, uses encrypted passwords, and provides a high level of security. Which of the following authentication methods should you choose?

- ○ A. Advanced Digest Authentication
- ○ B. Digest Authentication
- ○ C. Integrated Windows Authentication
- ○ D. .NET Passport Authentication

Question 46

Amy administers and manages three Windows 2003 DNS servers in two domains for InnoTech Solutions. All the DNS servers are Active Directory–integrated DNS servers. Two Active Directory–integrated DNS servers for the domain are configured as primary zones. Amy configures the child domain DNS server for a stub zone. Amy does some research on stub zones and what they contain. She finds out stub zones contain an SOA record, NS records, Glue A records, and the Master server IP address used to update the stub zone. Amy doesn't know what a Glue A record is used for. What type of record is a Glue A record?

○ A. A resource record

○ B. A delegation record used for finding authoritative DNS servers

○ C. A delegation record used for finding nonauthoritative DNS servers

○ D. A delegation record used for finding secondary DNS servers for the delegated zone

Question 47

You've been tasked with the evaluation of what the effective policy settings will be after the addition of a new GPO. Which utilities can you use to perform this evaluation? (Select two.)

❑ A. Group Policy Management Console

❑ B. Security Configuration and Analysis MMC snap-in

❑ C. Security Templates MMC snap-in

❑ D. Group Policy Object Editor MMC snap-in

❑ E. **Ldifde** command-line utility

Question 48

AdepTek operates a Windows Server 2003 Active Directory domain. The domain has 1000 Windows 2000 Professional computers, 450 Windows XP Professional computers, 125 Windows 98 computers, and 4 Windows 2000 Servers. A GPO is created to audit logon success and failures and applied to the domain object. Three hours later, Max, an assistant administrator, notices an error message on the Windows Server 2003 domain controller stating that the Security log is full. Why is the Security log full after only 3 hours?

○ A. Because auditing is enabled for logon failures

○ B. Because Max never deleted the Security log events in Event Viewer

○ C. Because auditing is enabled for logon successes and failures

○ D. Because auditing is enabled for logon successes

Question 49

John maintains a Windows Server 2003 and needs to back up the Registry, but cannot find a product to do this. What product does John need to use?

- ○ A. Regedit
- ○ B. System State
- ○ C. Regedt32
- ○ D. NT32backup

Question 50

Max administers and manages 12 Windows 2003 DNS servers in 6 domains on 3 sites for AdepTek. Each site contains 2 domains. All DNS servers are Active Directory–integrated DNS servers. Two Active Directory–integrated DNS servers for each domain are configured with a forward lookup zone and a reverse lookup zone. AdepTek's 3 sites and 6 domains are interconnected with T1 lines and routers. Max has noticed lately that DNS traffic across the routers is very heavy. Max would like to reduce the DNS traffic across the routers. How can Max accomplish this? (Select two.)

- ❑ A. Enable conditional forwarding for one DNS server in each site
- ❑ B. Create a stub zone for one DNS server in each site
- ❑ C. Create a secondary DNS server in each site
- ❑ D. Create a caching-only DNS server in each site
- ❑ E. Create a primary DNS server in each site

Question 51

You're the network administrator for OldCorp. When configuring the settings for user accounts, you want to map a drive to the location of the operating system's files. Which of the following environmental variables would be used for this purpose?

- ○ A. **%HomeDrive%**
- ○ B. **%HomePath%**
- ○ C. **%SystemDrive%**
- ○ D. **%SystemRoot%**

Question 52

Sara manages a Windows 2003 Active Directory domain containing two Windows 2003 domain controllers. One of her domain controllers fails and is taken down for repairs. After repairing the domain controller, Sara powers it up. What type of restore must Sara perform on the domain controller to bring it back online with the network?

- ○ A. Authoritative restore
- ○ B. System State restore
- ○ C. Nonauthoritative restore
- ○ D. Differential restore

Question 53

Two network administrators disagree about which user groups have permissions to use the **Runas** command. What user group accounts have permission to use the **Runas** command? (Select all that apply.)

- ❑ A. Local Administrative accounts
- ❑ B. Local User accounts
- ❑ C. Domain Administrative accounts
- ❑ D. Domain User accounts
- ❑ E. Anonymous
- ❑ F. SELF
- ❑ G. Everyone group

Question 54

InnoTek operates a Windows Server 2003 Active Directory domain. The domain has 200 Windows 2000 Professional computers and 50 Windows XP Professional computers. Sara needs to create a Group Policy Object (GPO) using a security template to audit changing user passwords. What auditing event group is used to change users password security policy?

- ○ A. Account events
- ○ B. Account management
- ○ C. Object access
- ○ D. Policy change

Question 55

You've just written a new script and need to ensure that new policy settings are immediately applied when the script has been completed. Which of the following command-line utilities should you use?

- ○ A. **secedit.exe**
- ○ B. **gpupdate.exe**
- ○ C. **gpapply.exe**
- ○ D. **gpresult.exe**

Question 56

You've been tasked with the creation of a new script that will remove a series of user accounts on a server named MyServer. Which of the following parameters would be used to specify the account to be removed? (Select three.)

- ☐ A. **-d**
- ☐ B. **-s**
- ☐ C. **-u**
- ☐ D. **/?**
- ☐ E. **-z**
- ☐ F. **-x**

Question 57

Susan uses a Windows XP Professional computer on her company's network and wants to use the Remote Desktop Connection utility to connect to her company's server. Susan cannot find the program. Where does Susan need to navigate to?

- ○ A. Start, All Programs, Administrative Tools, Remote Desktop Connection
- ○ B. Start, All Programs, Accessories, Remote Desktop Connection
- ○ C. Start, All Programs, Accessories, Communications, Remote Desktop Connection
- ○ D. Start, Control Panel, Remote Desktop Connection

Question 58

Susan administers and manages 12 Windows 2003 DNS servers in 6 domains on 3 sites for AdepTek. Each site contains two domains. All the DNS servers are Active Directory–integrated DNS servers. One Active Directory–integrated DNS server for each domain is configured as a forward lookup zone. The other Active Directory–integrated DNS servers for each domain are configured with both forward and reverse lookup zones. AdepTek's 3 sites are interconnected with T1 lines and routers. Susan needs to configure refresh intervals for resource records on a DNS server. How does Susan accomplish this?

- ○ A. Configure Scavenge Stale Resource Records
- ○ B. Configure Update Server Data Files
- ○ C. Launch **NSLookup**
- ○ D. Configure Set Aging/Scavenging

Question 59

You're the network administrator for BigCorp.com and have just made a change to the user settings of a GPO applied to user of MyWorkstation1. You want these settings to be applied immediately to close a critical security hole, regardless of whether the current user is logged in. What will be the result of a script that uses the following code?

```
gpupdate /target:user /boot
```

- ○ A. The process will meet all the stated requirements.
- ○ B. The process will meet one of the stated requirements.
- ○ C. The process will not meet any of the stated requirements.
- ○ D. The target system will reboot.
- ○ E. The current user will be logged off.

Question 60

Sara, an administrative assistant, assists in managing a Windows 2003 Active Directory domain. She needs to restore some corrupted accounting data but receives an access denied message. What group membership must Sara have to perform the restore? (Select two.)

❏ A. Local Administrator

❏ B. System Operator

❏ C. Backup Operator

❏ D. Power User

❏ E. Account Operator

Answers to Practice Exam 1

1. A, B, C, D	**21.** C	**41.** A
2. A	**22.** A, D	**42.** C
3. A	**23.** C	**43.** D
4. A	**24.** C	**44.** E
5. C	**25.** A, B, C	**45.** D
6. B, C	**26.** A, D	**46.** B
7. B, D	**27.** C	**47.** A, B
8. A	**28.** D	**48.** D
9. A, D	**29.** C	**49.** B
10. C	**30.** C	**50.** A, D
11. D	**31.** A	**51.** D
12. C	**32.** C	**52.** C
13. C	**33.** B	**53.** A, B, C, D
14. B	**34.** B	**54.** B
15. B, C	**35.** B, E	**55.** B
16. B	**36.** D	**56.** A, B, C
17. B, C	**37.** C	**57.** C
18. B	**38.** D	**58.** D
19. B	**39.** B	**59.** C
20. A, C, E	**40.** D	**60.** A, C

Question 1

Answers A, B, C, and D are correct. The Group Policy Management Console provides a single location in which all GPOs can be created, linked, manipulated, evaluated, disabled, and deleted throughout your forest. The GMPC can be used to manipulate all Group Policy settings, including security settings, configured for OU-, domain-, and site-level applications. User and computer settings are changed through the AD Users and Computers MMC, not the GMPC utility. There is no option for changing forest settings using the GMPC console. Therefore, answers E, F, and G are incorrect.

Question 2

Answer A is correct. To perform most administrative tasks on a DNS server, John needs to be a member of the local Administrators group on the DNS server computer or have the administrator delegate control to him. DomainAdmins can have authority to manage DNS servers, depending on how the domain is set up, but this is not the default setting; therefore, answer B is incorrect. Neither System Operators or Power Users have proper permissions; therefore, answers C and D are incorrect.

Question 3

Answer A is correct. The Csvde command-line utility is used to import and export the attributes of Active Directory objects using a comma-separated (.csv) file type. Answer B is incorrect because the Dsget utility is used to display selected attributes of a pre-existing object within the directory and is not used to import or export the attributes of Active Directory objects using .csv files. Answer C is incorrect because the Dsmod utility is used to modify the attributes of an existing object. Answer D is incorrect because the Dsquery utility is used to list Active Directory objects that meet a specified set of criteria. Answer E is incorrect because the Ldifde utility is not used in conjunction with .csv files, but rather with its own .ldf format.

Question 4

Answer A is correct. To perform most administrative tasks on a Windows Server 2003 using the Security Templates, you must be a member of the local

Administrators group on the local Windows Server. The Domain Admin group membership grants too much authority, making answer B incorrect. Neither System Operators or Power Users have permission to use Security Templates; therefore, answers C and D are also incorrect.

Question 5

Answer C is correct. Integrated Windows Authentication uses Kerberos as the authentication protocol and provides a high level of security. Advanced Digest Authentication requires a user account and password and has a medium level of security; therefore, answer A is incorrect. Digest Authentication requires a user account and password and has a medium level of security because user credentials are sent across the network in a hashed message digest; therefore, answer B is incorrect. .NET Passport Authentication provides a single, unified logon, passwords are encrypted, and the level of security is high, but it does not use Kerberos; therefore, answer D is incorrect.

Question 6

Answers B and C are correct. Driver Rollback and ASR are two new storage management features. Backup is very similar to Windows 2000; therefore, answer A is incorrect. Windows 2003 does not use the ERD feature; therefore, answer D is incorrect. The System State backup is a new feature added to Windows 2000, not Windows Server 2003; therefore, answer E is incorrect.

Question 7

Answers B and D are correct. To perform most administrative tasks on a Windows Server 2003 domain controller using the Security Templates, you must be a member of either the Domain Administrators group or the Enterprise Admin group on the Windows Server 2003 domain controller. Neither local Administrators, Power Users, nor System Operators have permission to use the Security Configuration and Analysis utility; therefore, answers A, C, and E are incorrect.

Question 8

Answer A is correct. The Routing and Remote Access service uses the latest remote access technologies, including integrated dial-up and VPN. IIS is a Web site and application server; therefore, answer B is incorrect. Terminal Services deliver applications to client desktops and can also operate in remote administration mode; therefore, answer C is incorrect. SUS is Microsoft's Software Update Service; therefore, answer D is incorrect.

Question 9

Answers A and D are correct. Denying the Read and Apply Group Policy privileges will prevent the GPO's settings from being applied to the designated account or group—a process referred to as *filtering*. Answers B and E are incorrect because the Modify and Full Control privileges are not needed to apply GPO settings. The Change privilege is a share-access right and is not involved in GPO management, making answer C incorrect as well.

Question 10

Answer C is correct. Microsoft's recommendation is to continue using SMS 2.0 and wait for an SMS-compatible integrated version of SUS to be released. SMS 2.0 cannot automatically deploy critical updates to clients. Using SUS service instead of SMS is not recommended. Microsoft does not recommend waiting for SMS 3.0.

Question 11

Answer D is correct. The -r parameter is used to specify the LDAP filter criteria for the selection. Answer A is incorrect because the -b parameter is used to specify the username, domain, and password to be used for authentication on the target server. Answer B is incorrect because the -f parameter is used to specify the target .ldf filename that will be created. Answer C is incorrect because the -s parameter is used to specify the name of the target server. Answer E is incorrect because the /? switch is used to query the command's help file for its available parameters.

Question 12

Answer C is correct. If Max changes the zone type to stub zone, he must specify the source DNS server IP address used for obtaining updated zone information. The target DNS server is the server Max is managing; therefore, answers A and D are incorrect. There is no source DNS server computer name option available; therefore, answer B is incorrect.

Question 13

Answer C is correct. Madelaine first needs to create a complete backup of the server system files. A full backup is not necessary; therefore, answer A is incorrect. ASR does not back up user data; therefore, answer B is incorrect. The second step is to create an ASR floppy disk; therefore, answer D is incorrect.

Question 14

Answer B is correct. You can use the Backup All option to back up all the GPOs to a standard location, where they're stored in a versioned manner so that you can select a particular GPO backup from those stored in the location. Answers A, C, and D are incorrect because they specify the separation of backup storage based on GPO or version, which adds unnecessary administrative effort.

Question 15

Answers B and C are correct. The Ldifde utility can be used to modify the Active Directory schema attributes, making answer D incorrect, whereas the Csvde utility cannot be used to modify the schema, making answer A incorrect as well. The Csvde command-line utility is not used for editing comma-delimited text reports, which makes answer E incorrect.

Question 16

Answer B is correct. Storage file information is stored on the ASR backup. The Registry, System State, user profiles and user-mapped drives are not stored on the ASR floppy disk and must be backed up separately; therefore, answers A, C, D, and E are incorrect.

Question 17

Answers B and C are correct. Windows XP Professional and Windows 2000 Servers (SP2) support the Automatic Update client software. The Windows Professional 2000 clients all need SP2 or higher; therefore, answer A is incorrect. Windows 98 clients are not supported; therefore, answer D is incorrect.

Question 18

Answer B is correct. IIS is a Web site and application server. The Routing and Remote Access Service uses the latest remote access technologies, including integrated dial-up and VPN; therefore, answer A is incorrect. Terminal Services deliver applications to client's desktop and can also operate in remote administration mode; therefore, answer C is incorrect. SUS is Microsoft's Software Update Service; therefore, answer D is incorrect.

Question 19

Answer B is correct. The Zone Properties General tab contains the view or change replication status. The SOA contains information on primary server, refresh and retry intervals, expire, and TTL settings; therefore, answer A is incorrect. The Name Server tab contains the FQDN of the name server, with options to add, edit, and remove name servers; therefore, answer C is incorrect. The Zone Transfers tab configures secondary servers to receive zone transfers to any server, only the servers listed in the Names tab, or specific servers; therefore, answer D is incorrect.

Question 20

Answers A, C, and E are correct. The minimum requirements for installing SUS on a Windows 2000 Server are a Pentium III 700MHz or higher, 512MB of RAM, 6GB of free hard disk space, Internet Explorer 5.5 or higher, and Internet Information Server 3.0 or higher. 768MB of RAM exceeds the 512MB requirement; therefore, answer B is incorrect. 10GB of free hard disk space is more than the 6GB of free space recommended; therefore, answer D is incorrect. Answer F is incorrect because Windows 2000 only needs SP3 to install SUS.

Question 21

Answer C is correct. The principal logon name is composed of the user logon name and the fully qualified domain name to which it belongs (myuser@mycorp.com). Answer A is incorrect because the user logon name alone is insufficient to fully designate the principal logon name, lacking a designation of the authenticating domain. Answer B is incorrect because it specifies a pre–Windows 2000 logon name using the NetBIOS version of the domain name (MYCORP). Answer D is incorrect because it defines an LDAP relative distinguished name.

Question 22

Answers A and D are correct. There are two possible reasons: the Shadow Copies service is not activated on the Windows Server 2003 and Amy does not have the Shadow Copies for Shared Folders software installed on her computer. Windows XP Professional does not install Shadow Copies for Shared Folders by default. Amy would need to download the client version of Shadow Copies for Shared Folders from the Internet. Amy is selecting the correct folder. Amy cannot right-click the deleted file here; therefore, answers B and C are incorrect. Amy has permission to recover her PowerPoint file; therefore, answer E is incorrect.

Question 23

Answer C is correct. John should select the medium level security setting, Secure and Non-secure, for the Unix DNS server and the Windows 2003 DNS servers to communicate and update resource records properly. Secure Dynamic Updates and Secure can be used only with Windows 2003 Active Directory–integrated DNS servers; therefore, answers A and D are incorrect. The Non-secure setting should be avoided because it lacks security; therefore, answer B is incorrect.

Question 24

Answer C is correct. Wuau.adm is used to manage Windows Updates. Inetres.adm is used for Internet Explorer policies; therefore, answer A is incorrect. Conf.adm is used to manage Windows 95 and Windows 98 clients; therefore, answer B is incorrect. System.adm is used for managing Windows clients; therefore, answer D is incorrect.

Question 25

Answers A, B, and C are correct. Jim can back up and then import a GPO's settings when interforest migration is not possible or not convenient, whereas the copy function can be used to migrate an existing GPO between well-connected trusted forests. Answer D is incorrect because the restore function is used to restore a previous GPO backup from its storage location, rather than for migration between forests. Answers E and F are incorrect because there are no export and transfer actions in the GPMC.

Question 26

Answers A and D are correct. Both the user logon name and the LDAP relative distinguished name must be unique only within their container. Answer B is incorrect because the pre–Windows 2000 logon name must only be unique within the domain. Answer C is incorrect because the principal logon name must be unique within a forest. Answer E is incorrect because there is no unified logon name.

Question 27

Answer C is correct. The unapproved update must be manually removed from the client computers. Answers A, B, and D are incorrect because there is no way to automatically uninstall a previously approved update from a client computer.

Question 28

Answer D is correct. Amy must be a member of the local Administrators group to view the Administrators Web page. The Domain Admin group membership would give user Amy too much authority; therefore, answer A is incorrect. Amy does not need IIS installed because Windows XP Professional installs Internet Explorer 6.0 by default; therefore, answer B is incorrect. Additionally, IE does not need upgrading; therefore, answer C is incorrect.

Question 29

Answer C is correct. The Resultant Set of Policy is the resulting list of policy settings after evaluation of all relevant GPOs, often displayed with the source of the winning setting's source GPO. Answer A is incorrect because the Resultant Set of Policy does not display all possible settings, only the final resultant set. Answers B and D are incorrect because the Resultant Set of Policy involves the evaluation of all relevant GPOs for a target object or container, rather than those of a target GPO.

Question 30

Answer C is correct. On the Zone Transfers tab of secondary DNS Server2, Susan should select Only to the Following Servers, and type the primary DNS Server2 IP address of 192.168.2.4. Primary Server1 and secondary DNS Server1 are on a different subset address of 192.168.1.x; therefore, answers A and B are incorrect. The IP address of secondary DNS Server2 is 192.168.2.4; therefore, answer D is incorrect.

Question 31

Answer A is correct. Amy should right-click the overwritten PowerPoint file and choose Properties. She should then select the Previous Version tab and click the Restore button to replace the current PowerPoint file with the previously overwritten shadow copy file. Amy cannot recover her overwritten file by selecting her shared folder; therefore, answer C is incorrect. Viewing or copying her overwritten file does not replace the old file; therefore, answers B and D are incorrect.

Question 32

Answer C is correct. The LocalService pseudo-account is used to run system services that generate system audit events, including the Alerter service. Answer A is incorrect because the IUSR_<servername> account is used only by Microsoft's IIS service, by default. Answers B and D are incorrect because the LocalSystem and NetworkService pseudo-accounts provide access to only local logon rights (LocalSystem) or to additional network access (NetworkService) as required for the DNS client.

Question 33

Answer B is correct. Max should use the Driver Rollback feature and roll back the SCSI driver to its original driver. Disabling the SCSI controller would result in loss of function; therefore, answer A is incorrect. Uninstalling or obtaining new SCSI driver updates would work, but would take too much time; therefore, answers C and D are incorrect.

Question 34

Answer B is correct. The domain account password policy for creating passwords with a minimum of eight characters is applied. Domain account policies always take precedence over other account policies. Thus, the Sales and Marketing OU account polices are not applied, making answers C and D incorrect. You cannot apply all three account polices, only the domain account policy is applied; therefore, answer A is incorrect.

Question 35

Answers B and E are correct. The Setup Security template is generated at installation, carrying all the default security settings for the system at that time, whereas the DC Security template specifies the default security template for domain controllers. Answer A is incorrect because there is no CompatDC template by default, only the Compatws.inf template, which relaxes some forms of security on workstations that need to run legacy or non–Windows Logo Program–certified software. Answers C and D are incorrect because the HisecDC and SecureDC templates are used to configure secure and highly secure settings for domain controllers and do not define the default configuration settings specified.

Question 36

Answer D is correct. Tom should select stub zone for the child DNS server. Stub zones can simplify DNS administration by distributing their resource lists to authoritative DNS servers for the zone without adding, maintaining, or using secondary zones. Companies with multiple domains can use stub zones to simplify DNS administration. Adding another Active Directory–integrated server to a child zone would result in increased DNS traffic and administration; therefore, answer A is incorrect. Adding a secondary zone would increase administration; therefore, answer B is incorrect. You can only have one primary zone per subnet; therefore, answer C is incorrect.

Question 37

Answer C is correct. `Runas /user:ComputerName\administrator "mmc%windir%\system32\dsa.msc"` connects to Active Directory Users and Computers with domain administrator credentials. Answer A is incorrect because it uses a command prompt with administrative credentials. Answer B is incorrect and is used to connect to Computer Management with administrative credentials. Answer D is incorrect because it connects to Active Directory Users and Computers in another forest.

Question 38

Answer D is correct. Susan should use the Driver Rollback feature and roll back the NIC driver to its original driver. Uninstalling or obtaining new NIC driver updates would work, but would take too much time; therefore, answers A and C are incorrect. Disabling the NIC card would result in loss of function; therefore, answer B is incorrect.

Question 39

Answer B is correct. When configuring the security settings for a public kiosk's automatic logon account, the setting to prevent users from changing the password is the most obvious setting required. Answer A is incorrect because the requirement to change the password might result in a later inability to log on to the kiosk by this account without a manual reset of the password to its proper version. Answer C is incorrect because even the passwords of public, unprivileged accounts should be reset on a regular basis to avoid providing a target for brute-force unauthorized access attempts. Answer D is incorrect because a disabled account cannot be used for logon purposes and would prevent the kiosk from proper automatic logon.

Question 40

Answer D is correct. SUS is Microsoft's Software Update Service and should be used for rollouts of applications to client computers. Group Policies are used to manage users and computer in domains; therefore, answer A is incorrect. IIS is a Web site and application server; therefore, answer B is incorrect. Terminal Services delivers applications to clients' desktops and can also operate in remote administration mode; therefore, answer C is incorrect.

Question 41

Answer A is correct. John needs to use Event Viewer, Security log on the Windows Server 2003 domain controller to view the results of the logon success and failures. The Security Template tool is used to create and modify templates; therefore, answer B is incorrect. The Security Configuration and Analysis tool applies the Security Template settings; therefore, answer C is incorrect. The Active Directory Users and Computers module is used to manage users and computers, not security settings; therefore, answer D is incorrect.

Question 42

Answer C is correct. The Local Security Policy MMC snap-in is the only item from those listed that is installed by default on a standalone or member server. Answers A and B are incorrect because the Domain Controllers Security Policy and Domain Security Policy MMC snap-ins are present only for servers participating in domain membership and having had the AdminPak.msi run to install these items, which is performed during a dcpromo event automatically. Answers D and E are incorrect because the Security Templates and Security Configuration and Analysis MMC snap-ins are available only through a custom-created Microsoft Management Console to which you have added them.

Question 43

Answer D is correct. Tom should right-click the child domain and choose New Delegation. Using the New Delegation Wizard, Tom then adds the power user. The Local Administrators, DNS Admins, and Domain Admin groups would each give the power user too much authority; therefore, answers A, B, and C are incorrect.

Question 44

Answer E is correct. The -loscr parameter is used to specify the path to the account's logon script. Answers A and D are incorrect because the -fn and -ln parameters are used to specify the values of the first name and last name attributes of the account. Answers B and C are incorrect because the -hmdir parameter is used to specify the path of the home drive for the user account, whereas the -hmdrv parameter is used to specify the drive letter to be assigned to the user's home directory.

Question 45

Answer D is correct. .NET Passport Authentication provides a single, unified logon, passwords are encrypted, and the level of security is high. Advanced Digest Authentication requires a user account and password and has a medium level of security; therefore, answer A is incorrect. Digest Authentication requires a user account and password and has a medium level of security because user credentials are sent across the network in a hashed message digest; therefore, answer B is incorrect. Integrated Windows Authentication uses Kerberos as the authentication protocol and provides a high level of security, but is not a unified logon, making answer C incorrect.

Question 46

Answer B is correct. A Glue A resource record is a delegation record used for finding authoritative DNS servers for the delegated zone. The Glue resource record provides the IP address of the DNS server that is authoritative for the domain. SOA (Start-Of-Authority) and NS (Name Server) are resource records. A delegation record used for finding secondary DNS servers for the delegated zone is incorrect. Secondary servers maintain read-only copies of records. Nonauthoritative DNS servers do not maintain a database.

Question 47

Answers A and B are correct. Both the Group Policy Management Console and the Security Configuration and Analysis MMC snap-in can be used to evaluate the effective permissions that would result from the addition of a new GPO. The Security Templates MMC snap-in is used to configure and apply security policy templates, and does not have the capability for evaluative modeling, making answer C incorrect. Answer D is also incorrect because the Group Policy Object Editor is used to configure the individual policy settings and does not carry the capability to perform an evaluation of the Resultant Set of Policy. Answer E is incorrect because the Ldifde command-line utility is used to modify the Active Directory schema.

Question 48

Answer D is correct. Enabling logon successes in large companies causes the Event Viewer security log to fill quickly. Logon failures, on the other hand, should result in only a few security events and is the preferred event to audit; therefore, answer A is incorrect. The security log is empty by default until auditing is enabled; therefore, answer B is incorrect.

Question 49

Answer B is correct. John needs to perform a System State backup. Regedit edits the Registry; therefore, answer A is incorrect. Regedt32 also is used to edit the Registry, including security permissions; therefore, answer C is incorrect. NT32backup does not exist; therefore, answer D is incorrect.

Question 50

Answer A and D are correct. Max should enable conditional forwarding for one DNS server in each site to a master server in each of the other two sites. A conditional forwarder configures the DNS server to forward the query it receives to a DNS server listed in the header of the query. Conditional forwarding provides the ability to control routing of your DNS traffic on a network. Adding a caching-only server to each site could reduce DNS traffic across routers. A stub zone keeps the DNS server hosting the parent zone aware of all authoritative servers for the child zone; therefore, answer B is incorrect. Secondary servers are used for fault tolerance and contain a read-only copy of the database. Adding another primary or secondary server would not reduce inter-site DNS network traffic; therefore, answers C and E are incorrect.

Question 51

Answer D is correct. The `%SystemRoot%` variable specifies the directory for the operating system installation. Answer A is incorrect because the `%HomeDrive%` variable stores the drive letter assigned to the user's home directory. Answer B is incorrect because the `%HomePath%` variable is used to store the full UNC path to the user's home directory. Answer C is incorrect because there is not a `%SystemDrive%` environmental variable by default.

Question 52

Answer C is correct. Sara must perform a nonauthoritative restore on the domain controller. All data restored nonauthoritatively appears in Active Directory as old data and is never replicated to other domain controllers. It is not necessary to perform an authoritative restore; therefore, answer A is incorrect. Restoring just the System State or the last differential backup would not work; therefore, answers B and D are incorrect.

Question 53

Answers A, B, C, D are correct. The `runas` command is not limited to just administrator accounts. Use this command when you are logged on as a member on another group or need permissions other than what is currently assigned to the account with which you are currently logged in. Answers E, F, and G are incorrect. Anonymous is used for access over the Internet; SELF and the Everyone group are built-in accounts and not selectable.

Question 54

Answer B is correct. Sara needs to audit account management events that include creating, modifying, deleting, and changing user accounts and passwords. Account logon events audit user logon and logoff success and failures; therefore, answer A is incorrect. Object access is used to audit user or group access to files and folders; therefore, answer C is incorrect. Policy change audits access to modified policies; therefore, answer D is incorrect.

Question 55

Answer B is correct. The `gpupdate.exe` command-line utility can be used to force a reboot or logoff to ensure that new policy settings are applied, replacing the `/refreshpolicy` option of the `secedit.exe` utility within the Windows Server 2000 environment, which also makes answer A incorrect. There is no `gpapply.exe` utility provided, making answer C incorrect, as well. Answer D is incorrect because the `gpresult.exe` utility is used to review the Resultant Set of Policy (RSoP) rather than to force the immediate application of a new GPO's settings.

Question 56

Answers A, B, and C are correct. The `-d` parameter specifies the account's home domain, the `-s` parameter specifies the target server for this operation, and the `-u` parameter specifies the target user account. Answer D is incorrect because the /? switch is used to query the command's help file for its available parameters. Answers E and F are incorrect because the -x and -z parameters are not for removing user accounts.

Question 57

Answer C is correct. Start, All Programs, Accessories, Communications, Remote Desktop Connection is the only way to access the program; therefore, answers A, B, and D are incorrect.

Question 58

Answer D is correct. Susan should configure the DNS server option Set Aging/Scavenging for all zones to adjust the refresh intervals. Configure Scavenge Stale Resource Records is used to manually remove old outdated resource records; therefore, answer A is incorrect. Configure Update Server Data Files writes all zone file changes in Active Directory; therefore, answer B is incorrect. NSLookup is used for troubleshooting DNS problems; therefore, answer C is incorrect.

Question 59

Answer C is correct. By selecting the /boot option, you're specifying that the system should reboot if computer settings have been changed. Because you did not include the /force option, the settings will not be applied until the next logon, making Answers A and B incorrect because none of the stated requirements will be met. Without the /logoff option specified for a target user, the user of the computer will not be logged off automatically, making answers D and E incorrect.

Question 60

Answers A and C are correct. Sara must be a member of either the Local Administrators or Backup Operators group. Power Users, Account Operators, and System Operators do not have permission to perform restores; therefore, answers B, D, and E are incorrect.

Practice Exam 2

Question 1

You're the network administrator responsible for GPO documentation within the somecorp.com namespace. You are creating command-line scripting that will make use of the GPO scripts provided with the GPMC Software Development Kit. Which of these scripts would you use to find all GPOs within the namespace and then access the settings of the resulting list? (Select two.)

- ❑ A. **ListAllGPOs.wsf**
- ❑ B. **DumpGPOInfo.wsf**
- ❑ C. **QueryBackupLocation.wsf**
- ❑ D. **FindUnlinkedGPOs.wsf**
- ❑ E. **FindDisabledGPOs.wsf**

Question 2

Sara, a local administrator, assists in managing a Windows 2003 Active Directory domain. She needs to restore some corrupted accounting data from the latest tape backup on a new tape, but receives an access denied message. Why can't Sara use the tape backup?

- ○ A. Sara is not a Local Administrator.
- ○ B. Restrict Access was enabled on the new tape.
- ○ C. Sara is not a Backup Operator.
- ○ D. The new tape is defective.

Question 3

You've been tasked with using the **Dsmod** command-line utility for administration. Which of the following object types can you modify using **Dsmod**? (Select all that apply.)

❑ A. Computer accounts

❑ B. Contacts

❑ C. Groups

❑ D. Servers

❑ E. User accounts

Question 4

AdepTek operates a Windows Server 2003 Active Directory domain. The domain has 200 Windows 2000 Professional computers, 50 Windows XP Professional computers, and one Windows 2000 Server. Various security policy settings are applied throughout the domain. The Windows 2000 Server has a local policy defined. Other security policies are applied to AdepTek's site, domain, and OU. What is the order of precedence, from lowest to highest, of the security policies?

○ A. Local, domain, site, OU

○ B. Site, domain, OU, local

○ C. Local, site, domain, OU

○ D. OU, site, domain, local

Question 5

Susan uses a Windows XP Professional computer at her home office and wants to use the Remote Desktop Connection utility to connect to her company's server. Because Susan uses a modem, she needs to adjust her bandwidth connection speed. How does Susan accomplish this?

○ A. In the Remote Desktop Connection dialog box, click the Options button to display the client configuration options. Click on the Experience tab and select the appropriate connection speed.

○ B. In the Remote Desktop Connection dialog box, click the Options button to display the client configuration options. Click on the Local Resources tab and select the appropriate connection speed.

○ C. Choose Start, All Programs, Accessories, Communications. Then right-click Remote Desktop Connection, and choose Properties.

○ D. In the Remote Desktop Connection dialog box, click the Options button to display client configuration options. Click on the General tab and select the appropriate connection speed.

Question 6

John administers and manages four Windows 2003 DNS servers in two domains on one site for InnoTeck Solutions. All the DNS servers are Active Directory–integrated DNS servers. One Active Directory–integrated DNS server for each domain is configured as a forward lookup zone. The other Active Directory-integrated DNS servers for each domain are configured with both a forward and reverse lookup zone. Users have lately been complaining that Internet access and response times are slow. InnoTeck Solutions has an ISP that maintains the Web site. John needs to improve Internet access and response time. How does John accomplish this?

○ A. On each DNS server, configure the Forwarders tab with the ISP's primary and secondary DNS server's addresses

○ B. On each DNS server, configure Update Server Data Files

○ C. On each DNS server, clear each DNS server's cache

○ D. On each DNS server, configure the Interfaces tab with the ISP's primary and secondary DNS servers' addresses

Question 7

Max, a local administrator, assists in managing a Windows 2003 Active Directory domain. Max needs to restore some corrupted data from the latest tape backup. Max wants to make sure that all security permissions are restored. What restore option does Max check to ensure that all security permissions are restored?

○ A. Max needs to check the Restore Junction Points option in the Advanced Restore options.

○ B. Max needs to check the Security option in the Tape Properties dialog box.

○ C. Max needs to check the Preserve Existing Mount Points option in the Advanced Restore options.

○ D. Max needs to check the Restore Security option in the Advanced Restore options.

Question 8

You're the network administrator for MyCorp. A user had trouble remembering his password and tried several things. Now, he says his account is telling him he is locked out. You need to restore his ability to log on as quickly as possible with the least amount of administrative effort. How should you accomplish this?

- ○ A. You should use the command-line utility **Dsmod** to change the user's password.
- ○ B. You should use the Active Directory Users and Computers MMC snap-in to change the user's password.
- ○ C. You should use the Active Directory Users and Computers MMC snap-in to unlock the user's account.
- ○ D. You should use the Active Directory Users and Computers MMC snap-in to copy the user's account and create a new unlocked copy.

Question 9

You're trying to explain the principles of Remote Desktop and Terminal Services to a user. Which of the following statements are true regarding Remote Desktop connections to a Terminal Services host server running Microsoft Windows Server 2003? (Select two.)

- ❑ A. Input is directed to the client system.
- ❑ B. Input is directed to the host system.
- ❑ C. Application processing occurs on the host system.
- ❑ D. Application processing occurs on the client system.
- ❑ E. Printer processing occurs on the client system.

Question 10

Ralph works for AdepTek Solutions, which operates a Windows Server 2003 Active Directory domain in a site containing 2 Windows Server 2003 Active Directory–integrated domain controllers and an organizational unit. AdepTek Solutions also has 450 Windows XP Professional clients, 40 Windows 2000 Professional clients, 25 Windows 98 clients, and 1 Windows 2000 member server. Ralph needs to define a security policy that will lock out all user accounts after three unsuccessful logon attempts. What object or computer should Ralph use to create the security policy?

○ A.   The Windows 2000 Server

○ B.   The domain object containing a domain controller

○ C.   The Site object

○ D.   The OU object

Question 11

John administers and manages 11 Windows 2003 DNS servers and 2 Unix DNS servers in five domains and one child domain for InnoTeck Solutions. All the DNS servers, except for the two Unix DNS servers, are Active Directory–integrated DNS servers. The two Unix DNS servers use the latest version of BIND. John wants to make sure that the Windows 2003 DNS servers can communicate with the Unix DNS servers running BIND. What option should John check on each of the Windows 2003 DNS servers to ensure Unix compatibility?

○ A.   On each DNS server, configure the Forwarders tab with the Unix DNS servers' IP addresses.

○ B.   On each DNS server, configure the Advanced configuration options and enable BIND secondaries.

○ C.   On each DNS server, configure the Advanced configuration options and disable recursion.

○ D.   On each DNS server, configure the Interfaces tab with the Unix DNS servers' IP addresses.

Question 12

You've just installed Terminal Services on your classroom network and need to make sure that all students have access. What is the best method to allow everyone access to Terminal Services?

○ A.   Add the Domain Users group to the Remote Desktop Users group to allow everyone access to Terminal Services.

○ B.   Add the Everyone group to the Remote Desktop Users group to allow everyone access to Terminal Services.

○ C.   Add the Users group to the Remote Desktop Users group to allow everyone access to Terminal Services.

○ D.   Add the Domain Users and Domain Administrators groups to the Remote Desktop Users group to allow everyone access to Terminal Services.

Question 13

Which of the following can be redirected using RDP 5.2–compliant Remote Desktop clients connecting to a Microsoft Windows Server 2003 running Terminal Services? (Select all that apply.)

- ❑ A. Server audio
- ❑ B. Local drives
- ❑ C. Local printers
- ❑ D. Local serial interface devices
- ❑ E. Host drive
- ❑ F. Host audio
- ❑ G. Host printers

Question 14

You're creating a saved query within the Active Directory Users and Computers MMC snap-in. Which of the following query types are directly available for query selection by default? (Select three.)

- ❑ A. Users, contacts, and groups
- ❑ B. Computers
- ❑ C. Printers
- ❑ D. Servers
- ❑ E. Exchange recipients

Question 15

Christi, a local administrator, assists in managing a Windows 2003 Active Directory domain. She needs to restore some data on a mount point and wants to make sure that the mount point is properly restored. What two backup options should Christi check to ensure that the mount point will be properly restored? (Select two.)

- ❑ A. Christi needs to check the Restore Junction Points option in the Advanced Restore option.
- ❑ B. Christi needs to check the Security option in the Tape Properties dialog box.

❑ C. Christi needs to check the Preserve Existing Mount Points option in the Advanced Restore options.

❑ D. Christi needs to check the Restore Mount Points option in the Advanced Restore options.

❑ E. Christi needs to uncheck the Preserve Existing Mount Points option in the Advanced Restore options.

Question 16

Amy works for InnoTeck Solutions, which operates a Windows Server 2003 Active Directory domain in a site containing two Windows Server 2003 Active Directory–integrated domain controllers and an organizational unit. The Accounting group has a shared folder called Accounting on a Windows 2003 Active Directory–integrated server. Accounting users are complaining that someone has accessed their shared Accounting folder and deleted files. All the Accounting users say they did not delete any files. Using the Security Templates console, what security audit event must Amy enable to find who the intruder is?

○ A. Account Management

○ B. Directory Service Access

○ C. Object Access

○ D. Policy Change

Question 17

Michael completes installing Windows Server 2003 and cannot find the Internet Information Server (IIS) 6.0 program. What does Michael need to do in order to install IIS? (Select two.)

❑ A. Click Start, All Programs, Administrative Tools, IIS Manager

❑ B. Use the Add or Remove Programs applet in the Control Panel to install IIS 6.0

❑ C. Click Start, All Programs, Internet Services Manager

❑ D. Use the Configure Your Server Wizard to install IIS 6.0

Question 18

Mary administers six domains for AdepTek. She is in the process of designing a DNS strategy for AdepTek. AdepTek wants its DNS zones to be secure, have fault tolerance, and be easy to deploy. What type of DNS zones should Mary choose?

- ○ A. Primary zones
- ○ B. Active Directory–integrated zones
- ○ C. Stub zones
- ○ D. Secondary zones

Question 19

You've been tasked with setting up groups and organizational units for your network. After you complete that task, you must present an explanation to upper management of how the system is set up. Which of the following statements are true regarding groups and organizational units? (Select all that apply.)

- ❑ A. A group can be a member of other groups.
- ❑ B. A group can be located within an organizational unit.
- ❑ C. An organizational unit can be a member of a group.
- ❑ D. An organizational unit can be located within another organizational unit.

Question 20

Michael has just completed installing Internet Information Server (IIS) 6.0 program and can't find the ASP.NET Web server extensions. What does Michael need to do to use the ASP.NET Web server extensions?

- ○ A. Use the Add or Remove Programs applet in the Control Panel to install ASP.NET Web server extensions.
- ○ B. Use the Add or Remove Programs applet in the Control Panel and reinstall IIS 6.0 to add the ASP.NET Web server extensions.
- ○ C. Click Start, All Programs, Internet Services Manager. Select the Web Extension folder and then click Add.
- ○ D. Use the Configure Your Server Wizard to install ASP.NET Web server extensions.

Question 21

John administers and manages six Windows 2003 DNS servers in two domains on one site for AdepTek Solutions. All the DNS servers are Active Directory–integrated DNS servers. One Active Directory–integrated DNS server for each domain is configured as a forward lookup zone. The other Active Directory–integrated DNS servers for each domain are configured with a stub zone. AdepTek Solutions has an ISP that maintains its Web site. John points all the DNS servers, which are also domain controllers, to the ISP's DNS servers to improve Internet access and response time for the users. Now some users cannot log on to AdepTek Solutions' network. Other users are complaining that logon times are slow. What does John need to do to fix this? (Select two answers.)

❑ A. Reconfigure each DNS server to point to itself for DNS resolution

❑ B. Add the ISP DNS servers to the Forwarders tab

❑ C. Create stub zones

❑ D. Add a caching-only DNS server to each domain

❑ E. Tell the ISP to add AdepTek's DNS servers IP addresses to its zone.

Question 22

Which service is responsible for ensuring that lost connections to a Terminal Services server farm are reconnected to the previous terminal connection?

○ A. Remote Desktop for Administration

○ B. Terminal Server

○ C. Terminal Server Licensing

○ D. Terminal Server Session Directory

Question 23

Susan, a local administrator, assists in managing a Windows 2003 Active Directory domain. Susan creates an ASR file and floppy disk. A Windows Server 2003 has a hard disk drive failure. Susan purchases and installs a new hard drive in the server. She begins an ASR recovery, but receives an error stating that the hard drive capacity is insufficient. How does Susan fix this problem?

○ A. Susan needs to purchase a new hard drive that is larger in size than the old one.

○ B. Susan needs to purchase a new hard drive that is the same size as the old one.

○ C. Susan needs to purchase a new hard drive, from the same hard drive manufacturer, which is the same make, model, and size as the old one.

○ D. Susan needs to purchase a new SCSI hard drive controller card.

Question 24

Max works for AdepTek, which operates a Windows Server 2003 Active Directory domain. Max needs to create a security baseline template for AdepTek. AdepTek's security policy includes strong encryption using a secure channel. All software applications on AdepTek's network are Windows Logo approved. Max needs to modify the built-in security template that comes closest to meeting his company's requirements. Which security template should Max choose?

○ A. **setup security.inf**

○ B. **Securedc.inf**

○ C. **domain controller security.inf**

○ D. **hisecdc.inf**

Question 25

You want to establish a Remote Desktop Protocol (RDP) connection to a Microsoft Windows Server 2003 member server running the Remote Desktop for Administration service in a default configuration. Which port must be opened through the firewall?

○ A. 80

○ B. 389

○ C. 3268

○ D. 3389

Question 26

Kelly, a local administrator, assists in managing a Windows 2003 Active Directory domain. A Windows Server 2003 has startup problems and Kelly needs to find out what startup programs are running on the server. How does she accomplish this?

○ A. Kelly needs to use Event Viewer.

○ B. Kelly needs to the System Information utility.

○ C. Kelly needs to use Device Manager.

○ D. Kelly needs to use Last Known Good Configuration.

Question 27

James is the network manager for a Windows 2003 Server network with Windows XP clients. James wants the ability to deliver applications to client desktops. Which application should James choose?

○ A. RRAS

○ B. IIS

○ C. Terminal Services Server

○ D. SUS

Question 28

You're trying to troubleshoot a user's account. Which of the following statements are true regarding user account membership? (Select all that apply.)

❑ A. A user account can be a member of only a single group.

❑ B. A user account can be a member of multiple groups at the same time.

❑ C. A user account can be a member of only a single organizational unit.

❑ D. A user account can be a member of multiple organizational units at the same time.

❑ E. A user account can be a member of only a single domain.

Question 29

Susan works for InnoTeck, which operates a Windows Server 2003 Active Directory domain. Susan needs to create a security baseline template. She begins by importing a custom security template that she created and saved using Security Templates into the Security Configuration and Analysis console. What is next step that Susan needs to execute?

- ○ A. Choose Analyze Now
- ○ B. Save the imported template in a new database file
- ○ C. Choose Configure Now
- ○ D. Choose View Log File

Question 30

Mary administers and manages two Windows 2003 DNS servers in one domain using one subnet for AdepTek. The DNS servers are Active Directory–integrated DNS servers. The master Active Directory–integrated DNS server's IP address is 192.168.1.6. Mary needs to add an additional Active Directory–integrated DNS server to AdepTek's domain. She opens the new DNS server's TCP/IP properties dialog box and enters a static IP address of 192.168.1.12. What IP address should Mary use for the preferred DNS server and alternate DNS server? (Select two.)

- ❑ A. Preferred DNS server: 192.168.1.12
- ❑ B. Alternate DNS server: 192.168.1.6
- ❑ C. Preferred DNS server: 192.168.1.6
- ❑ D. Alternate DNS server: 192.168.1.12
- ❑ E. Preferred DNS server: 192.168.1.1

Question 31

You're the administrator of a large network with multiple domains in a single forest and need to assign access for users to resources in the various domains. Which of the following group types can be used to assign permissions over resources located in many domains throughout a forest?

- ○ A. Domain local
- ○ B. Local
- ○ C. Trusted
- ○ D. Universal

Question 32

You've been tasked with selecting an IIS Web site authentication method that is similar to Digest Authentication, requires a user account and password, and has a medium level of security. Which of the following authentication methods should you use?

- ○ A. Advanced Digest Authentication
- ○ B. Digest Authentication
- ○ C. Integrated Windows Authentication
- ○ D. .NET Passport Authentication

Question 33

Laura installs Windows Server 2003 for a small company called ACDC Solutions. ACDC Solutions does not have a registered domain name. ACDC Solutions has obtained the services of an ISP for Internet access. Four employees use computers with Windows XP Professional installed. Laura runs **dcpromo** to install the Active Directory service, chooses ACDC.local for the new small company's domain name, and finishes installing Active Directory. She configures the Windows 2003 Active Directory–integrated server's Forwarders tab with the ISP's DNS server addresses. Afterward, four users complain that they cannot access the Internet. How does Laura fix the users' Internet access problem?

- ○ A. Using the DNS console, Laura should create a reverse lookup zone.
- ○ B. Using the DNS console, Laura should disable recursion.
- ○ C. Using the DNS console, Laura should delete the "." zone.
- ○ D. Using the DNS console, Laura should delete the ISP DNS servers' addresses on the Forwarders tab.

Question 34

Max, a local administrator, assists in managing a Windows 2003 Active Directory domain. A Windows Server 2003 has startup problems. A message displays stating that at least one service has failed during startup. How does Max determine which service failed?

- ○ A. Max needs to use Event Viewer to investigate system events.
- ○ B. Max needs to use the System Information utility.
- ○ C. Max needs to use Device Manager.
- ○ D. Max needs to use Event Viewer to investigate application events.

Question 35

You are preparing to install Windows Server 2003 and need to decide which remote access services to install in addition to the default configuration. Which of the following Remote Desktop utilities are installed by default on Windows Server 2003?

❑ A. Remote Desktop Connection

❑ B. Remote Desktops MMC snap-in

❑ C. Remote Desktop Web Connection

❑ D. Remote Control within the Active Directory Users and Computers MMC snap-in

❑ E. Remote Control client

Question 36

AdepTek operates a Windows Server 2003 Active Directory domain. Amy creates a security baseline template, imports it, and analyzes the results using the Security Configuration and Analysis console. Amy compares the imported template's settings with the local Windows Server 2003, and notices several question mark icons next to the policies. What is the meaning of the question mark icon?

○ A. Security values in the analysis database do not match the computer system settings.

○ B. Security values in the analysis database match the computer system settings.

○ C. Security values in the analysis database are not defined and were not analyzed.

○ D. Security values in analysis database are defined but do not exist in computer system settings.

Question 37

You've been tasked with using a command-line script to create, delete, and display virtual directories under an IIS root. Which utility should you use?

○ A. **IISweb.vbs**

○ B. **IISftp.vbs**

○ C. **IISvdir.vbs**

○ D. **IISftpdr.vbs**

Question 38

You need to delegate authority to a group of junior administrators. Which of the following groups can log on to domain controllers within the appropriate domain? (Select all that apply.)

- ❏ A. Administrators
- ❏ B. Backup Operators
- ❏ C. Pre–Windows 2000 Compatible Access
- ❏ D. Print Operators
- ❏ E. Remote Desktop Users
- ❏ F. Server Operators

Question 39

Sara installs Windows Server 2003 for a small company called InnoTeck. InnoTeck has a registered domain name of Innoteck.com. Four employees use computers with Windows XP Professional installed. Sara installs the Active Directory service, chooses Innoteck.com for the internal domain name, and finishes installing Active Directory. InnoTeck has obtained the services of an ISP for Internet access and managing its Web site. Users are complaining that they can access the InnoTeck Web site only by typing in InnoTeck's IP address. When they type **http://www.InnoTeck.com**, they receive a Page Not Found error. What can Sara do to fix this problem?

- ○ A. Using the DNS console, Sara should create a reverse lookup zone.
- ○ B. Using the DNS console, Sara should add an SOA record.
- ○ C. Using the DNS console, Sara should add an MX record.
- ○ D. Using the DNS console, Sara should add an A record.

Question 40

Sam, a local administrator, assists in managing a Windows 2003 Active Directory domain. Sam needs to determine whether the NIC drivers are digitally signed. Where does Sam find this information?

- ○ A. Event Viewer
- ○ B. System Information
- ○ C. Device Manager
- ○ D. Driver signing options in the System applet

Question 41

InnoTeck operates a Windows Server 2003 Active Directory domain. Sara creates a security baseline template, imports it, and analyzes the results using the Security Configuration and Analysis console. Sara compares the imported templates settings with the local Windows Server 2003 and makes several changes. Sara needs to save the changes. What two methods can Sara use to save changes? (Select two.)

- ❑ A. Using the Security Configuration and Analysis console, choose Configure Computer Now
- ❑ B. Use the Security Templates console to save the file
- ❑ C. Using the Security Configuration and Analysis console, choose Save
- ❑ D. Using the Security Templates console, choose Apply Now
- ○ E. Use the Security Templates console and choose Save as to save the file

Question 42

To allow an administrative Remote Desktop connection for the local Administrator account to be made to a Windows Server 2003 member server in its default configuration, which of the following steps must be performed?

- ○ A. Install Terminal Services using the Add or Remove Programs applet
- ○ B. Authorize the server using the Terminal Services Licensing MMC snap-in
- ○ C. Enable Remote Assistance using the System Properties dialog box
- ○ D. Add the Administrator account to the Remote Desktop Users group
- ○ E. Enable Remote Desktop using the System Properties dialog box

Question 43

You've been tasked with creating a network map that outlines group and user access throughout your domain. Which of the following groups will be present only in the root domain of a forest? (Select all that apply.)

- ❑ A. DnsAdmins
- ❑ B. Domain Admins
- ❑ C. Enterprise Admins
- ❑ D. Group Policy Creator Owner
- ❑ E. Schema Admins

Question 44

David is a member of the Power Users group and needs to create a new Web site application using IIS 6.0. He opens IIS Manager, expands his local computer, and tries to right-click the Web site to create a new Web site application, but receives an Access Denied message. What is David doing wrong? Select the minimum group membership or authentication method necessary to enable David to create the application.

- ○ A. David needs to be a member of the Domain Administrators group.
- ○ B. David needs to be a member of the Local Administrators group.
- ○ C. David needs to log on using Integrated Windows Authentication.
- ○ D. David needs to log on using .NET Passport Authentication.

Question 45

AdepTek operates a site containing two Windows Server 2003 Active Directory domains. Each domain has 200 Windows 2000 Professional computers, 40 Windows XP Professional computers, 5 Windows 98 computers, and 2 Windows 2000 Servers. The Windows Server 2003 has a security template Audit Account policy applied. Domain 1 has an organizational unit (OU) called Sales. Domain 2 has an OU called Marketing. The Sales OU has a GPO audit policy enabled for object access failures. The Marketing OU has a GPO policy for folder redirection applied. Which policies are applied?

- ○ A. The Account policy and the Object Access Failure policy
- ○ B. The Account policy, Object Access Failure policy, and the Folder Redirection policy
- ○ C. Object Access Failure policy and the Folder Redirection policy
- ○ D. The Account policy and the Folder Redirection policy

Question 46

You find that you must adjust the Terminal Services settings that affect three of your users. Which of the following will not allow you to find and adjust related settings?

- ○ A. Active Directory Users and Computers MMC snap-in
- ○ B. Local Policy Management Console
- ○ C. Remote Desktop connection
- ○ D. Terminal Server Configuration MMC snap-in

Question 47

Susan administers and manages 12 Windows 2003 DNS servers in six domains on three sites for AdepTek. Each site contains two domains and a firewall. All the DNS servers are Active Directory–integrated DNS servers. One Active Directory–integrated DNS server for each domain is configured as a forward lookup zone. The other Active Directory–integrated DNS servers for each domain are configured with both forward and reverse lookup zones. AdepTek's three sites are interconnected with T1 lines and routers. Susan needs to configure the firewall for DNS conditional forwarding. How does Susan accomplish this?

- ○ A. Susan should open UDP and TCP port 80 on the firewall.
- ○ B. Susan should open UDP and TCP port 25 on the firewall.
- ○ C. Susan should open UDP and TCP port 53 on the firewall.
- ○ D. Susan should open UDP and TCP port 443 on the firewall.

Question 48

Amy, a local administrator, assists in managing a Windows 2003 Active Directory domain. Amy installs a new FireWire adapter card and the server immediately stops responding. Amy needs the server up on the network as soon as possible. How does Amy fix this problem?

- ○ A. Amy needs to use Safe Mode.
- ○ B. Amy needs to the ASR utility.
- ○ C. Amy needs to restore the System State.
- ○ D. Amy needs to use Last Known Good Configuration.

Question 49

You've installed IIS 6.0 and need to administer the server remotely. After selecting Add/Remove Windows Components, how do you install the Remote Administration Tool?

- ○ A. Select Application Server and click the Details button. Select Internet Information Server (IIS) and click Details. Select the Remote Administration check box.
- ○ B. Select Add New Programs. Select Internet Information Server (IIS) and click Details. Select Application Server and click Details. Select the Remote Administration check box.

○ C. Select Application Server and click the Details button. Select Internet
      Information Server (IIS) and click Details. Select the World Wide Web
      Publishing Service and click Details. Select the Remote Administration
      check box.

○ D. Select Internet Information Server (IIS) and click Details. Select the
      World Wide Web Publishing Service and click Details. Select the
      Remote Administration check box.

Question 50

You're in the process of evaluating which users should be members of the
Power Users group, but first want to make sure that they require the rights that
accompany that group assignment. Which of the following rights are granted to
the local Power Users group by default? (Select three.)

❑ A. Log on locally

❑ B. Back up files

❑ C. Reset local account passwords

❑ D. Create local file shares

❑ E. Take ownership of local files

Question 51

AdepTek operates a site containing four Windows Server 2003 Active Directory
domains spanning two sites. Each domain has 2,500 Windows 2000
Professional computers, 480 Windows XP Professional computers, and 4
Windows 2000 Servers. Max needs a tool to analyze all the computers security
settings. Which tool is the best one for Max to use?

○ A. Security Templates

○ B. Security Configuration and Analysis

○ C. **secedit**

○ D. **wuau.adm**

Question 52

You've been tasked with configuring your Terminal Services connection to allow for 25 concurrent connections using the TCP/IP connection type, and need to ensure that your governmental clients must connect to the Terminal Services system with the proper level of security mandated by federal standards. Which setting for connection encryption would be the best selection to meet this requirement?

○ A. Client Compatible

○ B. FIPS Compliant

○ C. High

○ D. Low

Question 53

John administers and manages 10 Windows 2003 DNS servers in four domains on two sites for AdepTek. All DNS servers are Active Directory–integrated DNS servers. Two Active Directory–integrated DNS servers for each domain are configured with forward lookup zones. The other two Active Directory–integrated DNS servers are configured for stub zones. John wants to delegate control for the stub zone DNS servers to two employees and needs to add their email address MX records to the other DNS servers. He tries to add an MX record, but cannot do so. How does John fix this problem?

○ A. Adding the MX record, John needs to replace the @ sign with a period.

○ B. Adding the MX record, John needs to replace the @ sign with a under-score.

○ C. John does not have the proper permissions to add MX records to other DNS servers.

○ D. Adding the MX record, John needs to replace the @ sign with a ~.

Question 54

Everet, a local administrator, assists in managing a Windows 2003 Active Directory domain. His Windows Server 2003 is acting strange. Everet restarts the Windows Server 2003 and receives a missing ntldr message. How does Everet fix this problem?

○ A. Everet needs to boot into Safe Mode.

○ B. Everet needs to use the Recovery console.

○ C. Everet needs to restore the System State.

○ D. Everet needs to use the Last Known Good Configuration.

Question 55

You're the network administrator for a corporate server implementation that provides access to applications for clients using Terminal Services connections to a central server. You've discovered that through some type of group membership, accounts are denied access to a needed resource. You have not created any new groups, although automatic group membership is believed to be at fault. Which of the following groups could be the source of this problem? (Select all that apply.)

- ❏ A. Authenticated Users
- ❏ B. Everyone
- ❏ C. Interactive
- ❏ D. Restricted
- ❏ E. System
- ❏ F. Terminal Server Users

Question 56

You're an administrator of a distributed Windows Server 2003 network and have been tasked with implementing the WMI tool to gain access to important data and statistics for reports to upper management. What actions can you perform with WMI? (Select two.)

- ❏ A. Manage query support
- ❏ B. Manage associations between objects
- ❏ C. Manage scripts
- ❏ D. Manage Web applications
- ❏ E. Manage permissions

Question 57

Amy administers and manages 20 Windows 2003 DNS servers in eight domains on three sites for Tek Solutions. Tek Solutions has 5000 client computers with Windows XP Professional. All DNS servers are Active Directory–integrated DNS servers. Two Active Directory–integrated DNS servers for each domain are configured with forward lookup zones. Because DNS query traffic is heavy, Amy needs to consider load-balancing. What are two solutions that will help Amy reduce the heavy DNS traffic? (Select two.)

- ❏ A. Configure secondary zones for four DNS servers
- ❏ B. Configure stub zones for four DNS servers

❑ C. Configure primary zones for four DNS servers

❑ D. Configure reverse lookup zones for four DNS servers

❑ E. Configure caching-only servers in each domain

Question 58

You've set up and configured a Terminal Services Licensing server, but clients complain that they cannot connect to sessions on the server. After some investigation, you determine that the Licensing server has not yet been activated and set about performing this task. Which of the following methods can be used for activation? (Select two answers.)

❑ A. Automatic connection

❑ B. Fax

❑ C. Telephone

❑ D. Email

Question 59

InnoTeck operates a site containing one Windows Server 2003 Active Directory domain. The domain has 200 Windows 2000 Professional computers, 125 Windows XP Professional computers, and 2 Windows 2000 Servers. Amy needs to create a group policy on a Windows Server 2003 for scheduling automatic updates of critical patches deployment. Amy opens Active Directory Users and Computers, right-clicks the Innoteck.com domain object, chooses Properties, and clicks the Group Policy tab. She creates a new policy called SUS Updates and clicks the Edit button to open the Group Policy editor. What are the next two steps that Amy must perform? (Select two.)

❑ A. Under User Configuration, expand the Administrative Templates folder, expand the Windows Components folder, and then select the Windows Update folder.

❑ B. Under Computer Configuration, expand the Administrative Templates folder, expand the Windows Components folder, and then select the Windows Update folder.

❑ C. Double-click Configure Automatic Updates and select the Enabled radio button.

❑ D. Double-click Reschedule Automatic Updates scheduled installations and select the Enabled radio button.

❑ E. Double-click Reschedule Automatic Updates scheduled installations and select the Disabled radio button.

Question 60

John, a local administrator, assists in managing a Windows 2003 Active Directory domain. His Windows Server 2003 is acting strange. John has rebooted the server more than once with the result of a Blue Screen error. How does John fix this problem?

- ○ A. John needs to boot into Safe Mode.
- ○ B. John needs to use the Recovery console.
- ○ C. John needs to use the Repair option feature.
- ○ D. John needs to use Last Known Good Configuration.

Answers to Practice Exam 2

1. A, B

2. B

3. A, B, C, D, E

4. C

5. A

6. A

7. D

8. C

9. B, C

10. B

11. B

12. B

13. A, B, C, D

14. A, B, C

15. A, C

16. C

17. B, D

18. B

19. A, B, D

20. A

21. A, B

22. D

23. C

24. D

25. D

26. B

27. C

28. B, C

29. B

30. C, D

31. D

32. A

33. C

34. A

35. A, B

36. C

37. C

38. A, B, D, F

39. D

40. C

41. A, C

42. E

43. C, E

44. B

45. B

46. B

47. C

48. D

49. C

50. A, C, D

51. C

52. B

53. A

54. B

55. A, B, D, F

56. A, B

57. A, B

58. A, C

59. B, C

60. C

Question 1

Answers A and B are correct. The ListAllGPOs script can be used to enumerate all GPOs within a domain, and the output can then be directed to the DumpGPOInfo script to display the settings for each. Answer C is incorrect because the QueryBackupLocation script is used only to list the versioned GPO backups stored within a particular backup location. Answer D is incorrect because the FindUnlinkedGPOs script returns only the subset of domain GPOs that are not linked to a particular container, which does not meet the stated requirements. FindDisabledGPOs.wsf is used to list any GPOs that are currently disabled; therefore, answer E is incorrect.

Question 2

Answer B is correct. It appears that a local Administrator or Backup Operator has checked the Restrict Access check box on the new tape. Sara is a local Administrator; therefore, answer A is incorrect. Sara's local Administrator account gives her the proper permissions for access, so Backup Operator permissions are not necessary; therefore, answer C is incorrect. A defective tape would not cause the access denied message; therefore, answer D is incorrect.

Question 3

Answers A, B, C, D, and E are correct. The Dsmod command-line utility can be used to modify the attribute values of computer and user accounts, contacts, groups, and servers, as well as other object types, such as organizational units.

Question 4

Answer C is correct. The policies will be processed in the following order: local, site, domain, OU, child OU. If settings conflict, the settings for the policy that was processed last will take precedence and will be the resulting setting. The main exceptions to this rule are account policies and loopback processing; therefore, answers A, B, and D are incorrect

Question 5

Answer A is correct. Susan should select the Experience tab and select the appropriate connection speed by clicking on the drop-down list box. The Local Resource tab is used to configure sound, keyboard, and local devices; therefore, answer B is incorrect. Right-clicking the Remote Desktop Connection program displays only the program's shortcut properties; therefore, answer C is incorrect. The General tab is used to configure logon and connection settings; therefore, answer D is incorrect.

Question 6

Answer A is correct. John should configure the Forwarders tab on each DNS server with the ISP's primary and secondary DNS servers' IP addresses. When clients perform recursive queries, the ISP's DNS servers' IP addresses on the Forwarders tab are used to forward the recursive queries to the ISP's primary or secondary DNS server. Update Server Data Files writes zone changes in Active Directory; therefore, answer B is incorrect. Clear Cache flushes the name server cache and would result in users complaining even more; therefore, answer C is incorrect. The Interfaces tab is used to configure IP addresses for DNS requests; therefore, answer D is incorrect.

Question 7

Answer D is correct. Max needs to check the Restore Security option in the Advanced Restore option. Restore Junction Points restores junction points and their data on your hard drive; therefore, answer A is incorrect. There is no security option in the Tape Properties dialog box; therefore, answer B is incorrect. Preserve Existing Mount Points prevents restored data from over-writing mount points; therefore, answer C is incorrect.

Question 8

Answer C is correct. You can simply right-click on the user's account within the Active Directory Users and Computers MMC snap-in and select Unlock to restore logon capability for the user's account. This is the simplest and fastest method for access recovery in this scenario. Answers A and B are incorrect because the scenario requires unlocking the account, rather than specifying a new password, which would require more keystrokes whether through the Active Directory Users and Computers MMC snap-in or the command-line Dsmod utility. Answer D is incorrect because copying and creating a new account would entail even more administrative effort.

Question 9

Answers B and C are correct. Input and application processing occur on the host system. Keyboard and mouse input are directed from the client system to the host, making answer A incorrect. Application processing occurs using the resources and processing capabilities of the host system, which makes answer D incorrect. Printer processing, likewise, would occur on the host system making answer E incorrect.

Question 10

Answer B is correct. Ralph should use the domain object containing a domain controller to create the account lockout security policy. Domain account policies cannot be created on Windows 2000 member servers; therefore, answer A is incorrect. Account policies created on the Site or OU objects would be overwritten by the default domain controller policy; therefore, answers C and D are incorrect.

Question 11

Answer B is correct. On each DNS server, John should configure the advanced configuration options and enable BIND secondaries to ensure compatibility and communication with the Unix BIND DNS servers. Configuring the Forwarders tab with the Unix DNS servers' IP addresses would result in the Unix servers resolving Internet recursive queries and would not work; therefore, answer A is incorrect. Configuring the advanced configuration options and disabling recursion would result in users not being able to browse the Internet; therefore, answer C is incorrect. Configuring the Interfaces tab with the Unix DNS servers' IP addresses would result in the Windows 2003 DNS servers listening to the Unix server for resource updates and this cannot be done on Unix servers, due to incompatibilities; therefore, answer D is incorrect.

Question 12

Answer B is correct. Add the Everyone group to the Remote Desktop Users group to allow everyone access to Terminal Server sessions. Adding any other groups, such as Domain Users, Users, or Domain Administrators, would not allow access for everyone; therefore, answers A, C, and D are incorrect.

Question 13

Answers A, B, C, and D are correct. Remote Desktop connections can be configured to redirect the audio and video output from the server to each client, as well as to make local resources such as drives, printers, and serial devices available within the virtual terminal session. Host drives, audio, and printers are not redirected, making answers E, F, and G incorrect.

Question 14

Answers A, B, and C are correct. The default query options include users, contacts, and groups, as well as options for computers and printers. Answer D is incorrect because the Computers option includes both workstations and servers, which are not provided with a unique separate query category. Answer E is incorrect because the option for Exchange recipients is present only if Microsoft Exchange Server 2000 or later has been installed, and would not be present by default, as specified.

Question 15

Answers A and C are correct. Christi needs to check Restore Junction Points for the mount points to be backed up. Christi also needs to check Preserve Existing Mount Points to prevent restored data from overwriting mount points. There is no mount point option in the Tape Properties dialog box; therefore, answer B is incorrect. The Restore Security option in the Advanced Restore option restores NTFS permissions; therefore, answer D is incorrect. The Preserve Existing Mount Points is unchecked by default, making answer E incorrect.

Question 16

Answer C is correct. Amy should enable Object Access, success and failure, to determine who the intruder is. Object Access includes access to files and folders. Account Management audits changes in users' accounts; therefore, answer A is incorrect. Directory Service Access is used to audit Active Directory service; therefore, answer B is incorrect. Policy Change audits changes in Group Policies; therefore, answer D is incorrect.

Question 17

Answers B and D are correct. Use either the Configure Your Server Wizard or the Add or Remove Programs applet in the Control Panel. Installing any of the Windows Server 2003 family of products, except Windows 2003 Web Server Edition, does not install IIS 6.0 by default. Administrators must explicitly select and install IIS 6.0 on all but the Web Server Edition; therefore, answers A and C are incorrect.

Question 18

Answer B is correct. Mary should use Active Directory–integrated zones for increased security, fault tolerance, and easier management and deployment. Primary and secondary zones increase administration. Furthermore, primary, stub, and secondary zones all lack fault tolerance and do not have high security settings; therefore, answers A, C, and D are incorrect.

Question 19

Answers A, B, and D are correct. A group can be located within a particular organizational unit and can itself be a member of one or more other groups. An organizational unit can also be located within another OU, which is called *nesting* of OUs. An organizational unit cannot be made a member of a group, making answer C incorrect.

Question 20

Answer A is correct. Use the Add or Remove Programs applet in the Control Panel to install ASP.NET Web server extensions. In the Windows Components dialog box, check the Application Server check box and then click the Details button. Check the ASP.NET check box. Reinstalling IIS will not add ASP.NET Web server extensions; therefore, answer B is incorrect. There is no Web Extension folder in IIS and the Configure Your Server Wizard will not add ASP.NET Web server extensions; therefore, answers C and D are incorrect.

Question 21

Answers A and B are correct. Users are using the ISP DNS server for registering their records at logon. To fix the netlogon problem, John needs to reconfigure each Windows 2003 DNS server to point to itself for DNS resolution instead of pointing to the ISP DNS server. John should then add the ISP DNS server to the Forwarders tab on each Windows 2003 DNS server. Creating a stub zone has nothing to do with logon problems; therefore, answer C is incorrect. Adding a caching-only server will not fix the logon problem; therefore, answer D is incorrect. Answer E is incorrect; asking the ISP to add AdepTek's DNS servers' IP addresses to its zone would not correct the problem.

Question 22

Answer D is correct. The Terminal Server Session Directory is used to ensure that reconnected sessions are re-established to their original session within distributed server farms supporting Terminal Services Remote Desktop connections. Answer A is incorrect because the Remote Desktop for Administration service provides access for up to two administrative control logons and is not used within a Terminal Services server farm for multiple client access. Answers B and C are incorrect because the Terminal Server service manages only remote logons to virtual sessions, without attempting to rebalance or reconnect lost connections to their origin, whereas the Licensing service is used to ensure that a Terminal Server running in Application mode is properly licensed for each allowed connection.

Question 23

Answer C is correct. Susan needs to purchase a new hard drive, from the same hard drive manufacturer, which is the same make, model, and size as the old one. For ASR to work properly, the hard drive's geometry must be identical. Just purchasing a hard drive of the same size or larger would not work; therefore, answers A and B are incorrect. Susan does not need to purchase a new SCSI hard drive controller card; therefore, answer D is incorrect.

Question 24

Answer D is correct. Max needs to use the Highly Secure template (hisecdc.inf) to provide strong encryption using a secure channel. setup security.inf contains the default security settings and cannot be used on domain controllers; therefore, answer A is incorrect. Securedc.inf is used for medium-level security; therefore, answer B is incorrect. domain controller security.inf contains security settings applied during the installation of Active Directory; therefore, answer C is incorrect.

Question 25

Answer D is correct. The Remote Desktop Protocol (RDP) operates on port 3389. Answer A is incorrect because port 80 is used as the standard port used for the Hypertext Transfer Protocol (HTTP). Answer B is incorrect because port 389 is used as the standard port for Lightweight Directory Access Protocol (LDAP) connections, whereas port 3268 is used to connect to the Global Catalog within an Active Directory structure, making answer C incorrect as well.

Question 26

Answer B is correct. Kelly needs to use the System Information utility and select Startup Programs. No startup programs are found using Event Viewer, Device Manager, or Last Known Good Configuration; therefore, answers A, C, and D are incorrect.

Question 27

Answer C is correct. Terminal Services Server delivers applications to client desktops. The Routing and Remote Access Service would not deliver this functionality; therefore, answer A is incorrect. IIS is a Web site and application server, but would not meet the stated requirements; therefore, answer B is incorrect. SUS is Microsoft's Software Update Service, which can be used to deliver applications to client desktops through installation and doesn't operate in Remote Administration mode; therefore, answer D is incorrect.

Question 28

Answers B and C are correct. A user account can be a member of multiple groups, but only a single OU. A user account can be a member of many groups, which makes answer A incorrect. A user account can be located only within a particular organizational unit, although that OU can itself be located within another, making answer D incorrect as well. A user account can be a member of many domains, not just a single domain; therefore, answer E is incorrect.

Question 29

Answer B is correct. Susan next needs to save the imported template as a new database file. After that, Susan should choose Analyze Now from the menu to compare the imported security template policy settings with the local Windows Server 2003; therefore, answer A is incorrect. Susan should make the necessary changes, choose Configure Computer Now from the menu, and view any errors in the log file, which makes answers C and D incorrect.

Question 30

Answer C and D are correct. For each additional domain controller that Mary adds to the domain, the preferred DNS IP address is the parent DNS IP address, or 192.168.1.6. The added domain controller DNS server's IP address of 192.168.1.12 is placed in the Alternate IP Address text box. Answer E is incorrect because although not specified in the question, IP address 192.168.1.1 is the gateway address.

Question 31

Answer D is correct. Both global and universal groups can be used to assign permissions over resources located within any domain in a forest. Answer A is incorrect because a domain local group can be used only to assign permissions over resources located within the same domain as the domain local group. Likewise, a local group would give access only to local resources; therefore, answer B is incorrect. Answer C is incorrect because there is no trusted group scope. Trusts are established between domains, rather than as a group's scope.

Question 32

Answer A is correct. Advanced Digest Authentication, similar to Digest Authentication in that it requires a user account and password, and has a medium level of security, stores user credentials in the Active Directory on the domain controller, as an MD5 message digest. Digest Authentication requires a user account and password and has a medium level of security because user credentials are sent across the network in a hashed message digest. .NET Passport Authentication provides a single unified logon, passwords are encrypted, and the level of security is high. Integrated Windows Authentication uses Kerberos as the authentication protocol and provides a high level of security.

Question 33

Answer C is correct. Using the DNS console, Laura should delete the "." zone created during the Active Directory installation. Because Laura created a domain name ACDC.local, she needs to delete the "." zone listed under Forward Lookup Zones; otherwise, clients can have external name resolution problems on the Internet. Creating a reverse lookup zone would not help users gain Internet access; therefore, answer A is incorrect. Recursion is enabled by default and should not be disabled; therefore, answer B is incorrect. Laura should not delete the ISP's DNS server addresses because doing so would cause more Internet access problems; therefore, answer D is incorrect as well.

Question 34

Answer A is correct. Max needs to use Event Viewer to investigate system events and discover the service that failed to start automatically. No startup services are found using the Event Viewer application log, Device Manager, or the Last Known Good configuration; therefore, answers B, C, and D are incorrect.

Question 35

Answers A and B are correct. A default installation of Microsoft Windows Server 2003 includes the single-session Remote Desktop Connection (mstsc.exe) utility, as well as the Remote Desktop's MMC snap-in. The Remote Desktop Web Connection ActiveX component, which replaces the Windows 2000 Terminal Services Advanced Client (TSAC), must be installed as a subcomponent of IIS using the Add/Remove Programs utility, making answer C incorrect. Answers D and E are also incorrect because the Remote Control add-in capability must be downloaded from Microsoft's download site and installed to be present within the Active Directory Users and Computers MMC snap-in.

Question 36

Answer C is correct. The question mark icon indicates that the security values in the analysis database are not defined and were not analyzed. The red X icon indicates that security values in the analysis database do not match the local computer system settings. The green check mark indicates that security values in analysis database match the local computer settings; therefore, answer B is incorrect. The exclamation point icon indicates that security values in analysis database are defined but do not exist in local computer system settings; therefore, answer D is incorrect.

Question 37

Answer C is correct. IISvdir.vbs is used to create, delete, or display virtual directories. IISweb.vbs is used to start, stop, create, delete, and list Web sites; therefore, answer A is incorrect. IISftp.vbs is used to start, stop, create, delete, and list file sites; therefore, answer B is incorrect. Answer D is incorrect because IISftpdr.vbs is used to create, delete, and display virtual FTP directories under a root.

Question 38

Answers A, B, D, and F are correct. Members of the Administrators, Backup Operators, Print Operators, and Server Operators groups have the ability to log on to domain controllers and so their membership must be carefully managed and monitored to minimize security risks. The Pre–Windows 2000 Compatible Access group is not granted the right to log on to domain controllers by default; therefore, answer C is incorrect. Remote Desktop users have the right to start a remote interactive session on the computer only if they have the Allow Logon Through Terminal Services right; therefore, answer E is incorrect.

Question 39

Answer D is correct. Because InnoTeck uses InnoTeck.com for both the internal and external domain name, Sara needs to add a Host (A) record to the DNS server. Otherwise, users will not be able to browse InnoTeck.com Web site home page and related links. Adding a reverse lookup zone would not solve the problem; therefore, answer A is incorrect. The Start of Authority record (SOA) is added by default; therefore, answer B is incorrect. An MX Exchange Mail resource record is used for email; therefore, answer C is incorrect.

Question 40

Answer C is correct. Sam needs to use Device Manager, right-click the NIC, choose Properties, click the Driver tab, and then click the Driver Details button. Event Viewer, the System Information utility, and the System applet would not help Sam; therefore, answers A, B, and D are incorrect.

Question 41

Answers A and C are correct. The Configure Computer Now and the Save options accessed by right-clicking Security Configuration and Analysis in the left pane perform the same actions: They both write changes to your database file. Changes you make to the analysis database are made to the stored template in the database, not to the security template file itself; therefore, answer B is incorrect. You need to use the Security Templates snap-in component to make changes to your templates. Applying changes and saving changes are done with the Security Configuration and Analysis tool, not the Security Templates utility; therefore, both answers D and E are incorrect.

Question 42

Answer E is correct. To enable a Remote Desktop connection for the local Administrator account, all you need do is to enable Remote Desktop access using the System Properties dialog box. The Remote Desktop for Administration service is installed by default, which makes answers A and B incorrect: No new services must be installed to meet the stated requirement. The Remote Assistance option is used to allow remote technical support of a user's session and is not necessary for remote server administration connections, which makes answer C incorrect. Answer D is also incorrect because the local Administrator account is a member of the Remote Desktop Users group by default.

Question 43

Answers C and E are correct. The Enterprise Admins and Schema Admins groups are present only in the root domain of a forest. Answers A, B, and D are incorrect because the DnsAdmins group is present in any domain in which the DNS service has been installed, whereas both the Domain Admins and Group Policy Creator Owner groups are present in all domains by default.

Question 44

Answer B is correct. David must be a member of the Local Administrators group to accomplish this task. Although David could accomplish this task by becoming a member of the Domain Administrators group, this would give David too much authority; therefore, answer A is incorrect. Using different authentication methods would not help David create a new Web site application; therefore, answers C and D are incorrect.

Question 45

Answer B is correct. The Account policy, Object Access policy and Folder Redirection policy are all applied. The Domain Account policy is applied first, and then the GPO policies in the OUs are next applied. Because the OUs contain policies that are not Account polices, they will not be applied; therefore, answers A, C, and D are incorrect.

Question 46

Answer B is correct. You cannot correct Terminal Services settings through Local Policy Management Console. Settings that relate to a client's Terminal Services settings can be configured within the Active Directory Users and Computers and the Terminal Server Configuration MMC snap-ins, as well as in the advanced options of the Remote Desktop Connection utility. Therefore, answers A, C, and D are incorrect.

Question 47

Answer C is correct. Susan should open UDP and TCP port 53 on the firewalls. UDP and TCP ports 80, 25, and 443 are open by default and provide Internet access, FTP, and secure sockets, respectively; therefore, answers A, B, and D are incorrect.

Question 48

Answer D is correct. Amy needs to reboot and select Last Known Good Configuration. Using Safe Mode, ASR, or restoring the System State would take too much time; therefore, answers A, B, and C are incorrect.

Question 49

Answer C is correct. Select Application Server and click the Details button. Select Internet Information Server (IIS) and click Details. Select the World Wide Web Publishing Service and click Details. Select the Remote Administration check box. Therefore, answers A, B, and D are incorrect.

Question 50

Answers A, C, and D are correct. The local Power Users group can fully administer local resources and accounts (except for members of the Administrators group). Power Users cannot back up or take ownership of files by default, which makes answers B and E incorrect.

Question 51

Answer C is correct. Max needs to use the secedit command-line tool to analyze large numbers of computers. The Security Template tool is used to create and modify templates for smaller organizations; therefore, answer A is incorrect. The Security Configuration and Analysis tool is used to view and apply security template settings; therefore, answer B is incorrect. The Wuau.adm template is used for Software Update Services; therefore, answer D is incorrect.

Question 52

Answer B is correct. To ensure that all connections occur using the Federal Information Processing Standard (FIPS) 140-1 validated encryption methods, you must select FIPS Compliant Encryption. Answer B is incorrect because client-compatible encryption adjusts to meet the maximum strength of encryption that the client system supports, making it possible to drop the encryption level at the client system. Answer C is incorrect because the High encryption setting requires clients to be able to connect at the highest encryption key strength present on the server, denying all lesser strength connections. Answer D is also incorrect because the Low encryption setting requires only a 56-bit encryption key.

Question 53

Answer A is correct. Adding the MX record, John needs to replace the @ sign with a period. For each person in charge of managing a zone, add that person's email address (MX) record to your DNS server database and replace the @ sign with a period. Underscores and ~ (tildes) will not work; therefore, answers B and D are incorrect. John is an administrator and does have proper permissions; therefore, answer C is incorrect.

Question 54

Answer B is correct. Everet needs to use the Recovery Console and copy the `ntldr` file from the Windows Server 2003 installation CD. Everet cannot use Last Known Good Configuration, Safe Mode, or Restore the System State until the `ntldr` file has been copied to the root directory; therefore, answers A, C, and D are incorrect.

Question 55

Answers A, B, D, and F are correct. Account logons through Terminal Services connections inherit membership in the Authenticated Users group through the logon authentication process required for a Terminal Services connection, which also grants membership in the Terminal Server Users group; all logon accounts are included in the Everyone group. Because no additional specifications are provided, the logon accounts will be members of the Restricted (non–Power Users) group. The Interactive group includes only users directly logging on to the local system console, which makes answer C incorrect. The System account refers to the server's operating system rather than a user account, making answer E incorrect as well.

Question 56

Answers A and B are correct. IIS 6.0 now includes WMI for managing query support and associations between objects. Managing scripts, permissions, and Web applications is performed using IIS Service Manager; therefore, answers C, D, and E are incorrect.

Question 57

Answer A and B are correct. Amy should configure secondary zones or stub zones to reduce DNS traffic. Secondary servers reduce network traffic by using incremental updates. Primary zones are already configured and adding more of them will increase DNS traffic; therefore, answer C is incorrect. Adding reverse lookup zones will help reduce DNS traffic a little but is not the best solution; therefore, answer D is incorrect. Configuring caching-only DNS servers for each domain will speed up user requests for Web pages, but will do little to reduce network traffic; therefore, answer E is incorrect.

Question 58

Answers A, and C are correct. When authorizing a Terminal Services Licensing server for operation, you can allow the licensing server to automatically connect to the Microsoft Clearinghouse over the Internet, use a separate computer's web browser, or obtain the licensing authorization through a toll-free (in most places) call. Neither fax-in nor mail-in authorization mechanisms are provided by default, which makes answers B and D incorrect.

Question 59

Answers B and C are correct. Under Computer Configuration, Amy should expand the Administrative Templates folder, expand the Windows Components folder, and then select the Windows Update folder. In the right pane, Amy needs to double-click the Configure Automatic Updates and select the Enabled radio button to enable automatic updates. The third step is to double-click the Reschedule Automatic Updates scheduled installations and select the Enabled radio button; therefore, answers A, D, and E are incorrect.

Question 60

Answer C is correct. John needs to use the Repair Option feature by booting from his Windows Server 2003 installation CD-ROM. John cannot use Last Known Good Configuration, Safe Mode, or the Recovery Console until repairs have been completed; therefore, answers A, B, and D are incorrect.

Suggested Readings and Resources

Because *Exam Cram 2* books focus entirely on Microsoft certification exam objectives, you can greatly broaden your knowledge of Windows Server 2003 by taking advantage of the plethora of technical material that's available. Books, Web sites, and even Windows Server 2003's built-in help system all offer a wealth of technical insight for network and system administrators. In the following pages, we've compiled a list of valuable resources that you can check out at your leisure.

Microsoft Windows Server 2003 Help and Support

Your first source for help with any aspect of Microsoft Windows Server 2003 should be the user assistance resources that Microsoft ships with its server products:

➤ **Help and Support**—This option is available within the Manage Your Server interface, as well as through the Start menu. It provides access to the Help and Support Center where you can search through the online help files installed with your server.

➤ **List of Common Administrative Tasks**—This option is available within the Manage Your Server interface and provides access to a listing of the more common administrative tasks you might be expected to use, along with examples of each.

Books

The following are some useful books on Windows Server 2003:

➤ Boswell, William. *Inside Windows Server 2003*. Sams Publishing, 2003.

➤ *Introducing Microsoft Windows Server 2003*, ISBN 0-7356-1570-5, Microsoft Press, Redmond, Washington, 2003.

➤ *Microsoft Windows Server 2003 Administrator's Pocket Consultant*, ISBN 0-7356-1354-0, Microsoft Press, Redmond, Washington, 2003.

➤ Minasi, Mark and others, *Mastering Windows Server 2003*. Sybex, 2003, ISBN 0-7821-4130-7.

➤ Morimoto, Rand, et al. *Microsoft Windows Server 2003 Unleashed*. Sams Publishing, 2003.

➤ Stanek, William R., *Windows Server 2003*, Microsoft Press, 2003. ISBN 0-7356-1354-0.

Web Sites

The following are useful online resources for Windows Server 2003:

➤ The Microsoft Windows Server 2003 site provides access to many documents and technical references for this product line—
http://www.microsoft.com/windowsserver2003/

➤ The Microsoft Server 2003 MSDN site provides access to any technical references and downloads—http://msdn.microsoft.com/library/
default.asp?url=/nhp/default.asp?contentid=28001691

➤ The MSDN Windows Script site provides extensive information on scripting—http://msdn.microsoft.com/library/
default.asp?url=/nhp/Default.asp?contentid=28001169

➤ The Microsoft Download site for the Group Policy Management Console (GPMC), including additional details on this free download (gpmc.msi)—http://www.microsoft.com/downloads/
details.aspx?FamilyID=f39e9d60-7e41-4947-82f5-3330f37adfeb&DisplayLang=en

➤ The Microsoft Download site for the Remote Control add-in to the Windows Server 2003 Active Directory Users and Computers MMC—
http://www.microsoft.com/downloads/details.aspx?FamilyID=0a91d2e7-7594-
4abb-8239-7a7eca6a6cb1&DisplayLang=en

➤ The Windows Server 2003 Terminal Services Technology site—
`http://support.microsoft.com/default.aspx?scid=fh;EN-US;winsvr2003term`

➤ The Software Update Service home page—`http://www.microsoft.com/`
`downloads/details.aspx?FamilyId=A7AA96E4-6E41-4F54-972C-AE66A4E4BF6C&dis-`
`playlang=en`

➤ The Automatic Update Client for the SUS service can be obtained here, along with additional information on the Automatic Update process—
`http://www.microsoft.com/windows2000/downloads/recommended/susclient/`

➤ The Windows Update site, which allows an automated evaluation of needed hotfixes and services packs—`http://windowsupdate.microsoft.com`

➤ Microsoft Software Update Services, Flash demo site—`http://www.`
`microsoft.com/windows2000/windowsupdate/sus/flashpage.asp`

➤ Software Update Services Components and Features—`http://www.`
`microsoft.com/windows2000/windowsupdate/sus/suscomponents.asp`

➤ What's New in Internet Information Services 6.0—`http://www.microsoft.`
`com/windowsserver2003/evaluation/overview/technologies/iis.mspx`

➤ *MCP Magazine* - IIS 6.0 Mature at Last: Microsoft's Internet Information Server—`http://mcpmag.com/features/article.`
`asp?editorialsid=330`

➤ White Paper: Technical overview of management services—
`http://www.microsoft.com/windowsserver2003/docs/Manageover.doc`

➤ Microsoft TechNet Windows 2003 Resources— `http://www.microsoft.`
`com/technet/treeview/default.asp?url=/technet/prodtechnol/`
`windowsserver2003/Default.asp`

➤ Microsoft Training and Certification Web site—`http://www.microsoft.`
`com/traincert/`

➤ Microsoft Preparation Guide for Exam 70-292—`http://www.microsoft.`
`com/traincert/exams/70-292.asp`

➤ The Shadow Copies of Shared Folders client can be obtained here—
`http://www.microsoft.com/windowsserver2003/downloads/`
`shadowcopyclient.mspx`

➤ Technical Overview of Windows Server 2003—`http://www.microsoft.com/`
`windowsserver2003/techinfo/overview/`

➤ Introduction to Shadow Copies of Shared Folders—`http://www.`
`microsoft.com/windowsserver2003/techinfo/overview/scr.mspx`

➤ An overview of the new features for Windows Server 2003 DNS—
`http://www.microsoft.com/technet/treeview/default.asp?url=/technet/`
`prodtechnol/windowsserver2003/proddocs/standard/`
`sag_DNS_ovr_NewFeatures.asp`

➤ Microsoft TechNet security information for DNS—
`http://www.microsoft.com/technet/treeview/default.asp?url=/technet/`
`prodtechnol/windowsserver2003/proddocs/standard/sag_DNS_ovr_topnode.asp`

➤ Microsoft TechNet information on managing Windows Server 2003—
`http://www.microsoft.com/technet/treeview/default.asp?url=/technet/`
`prodtechnol/windowsserver2003/proddocs/standard/`
`sag_DNS_imp_ManagingServers.asp`

➤ Microsoft TechNet security administration tasks—`http://www.microsoft.`
`com/technet/treeview/default.asp?url=/technet/prodtechnol/`
`windowsserver2003/proddocs/entserver/comexp/adsecuretasks_6dkj.asp`

➤ Microsoft TechNet security overview—`http://www.microsoft.com/technet/`
`treeview/default.asp?url=/technet/prodtechnol/windowsserver2003/proddocs/`
`standard/sag_SEconceptsSecModel.asp`

➤ Microsoft TechNet site for information on the Security Configuration
Manager—`http://www.microsoft.com/technet/treeview/default.asp?url=/`
`technet/prodtechnol/windowsserver2003/proddocs/standard/`
`seconcepts_SCM.asp`

➤ White Paper: Windows Server 2003 Security Guide—`http://microsoft.`
`com/downloads/details.aspx?FamilyId=8A2643C1-0685-4D89-B655-`
`521EA6C7B4DB&displaylang=en`

What's on the CD-ROM?

This appendix provides a brief summary of what you'll find on the CD-ROM that accompanies this book. For a more detailed description of the PrepLogic Practice Exams, Preview Edition exam simulation software, see Appendix C, "Using the PrepLogic Practice Exams, Preview Edition Software." In addition to the PrepLogic Practice Exams, Preview Edition software, the CD-ROM includes an electronic version of the book in Portable Document Format (PDF).

The PrepLogic Practice Exams, Preview Edition Software

PrepLogic is a leading provider of certification training tools. Trusted by certification students worldwide, PrepLogic is the best practice exam software available. In addition to providing a means of evaluating your knowledge of this book's material, PrepLogic Practice Exams, Preview Edition features several innovations that help you improve your mastery of the subject matter.

For example, the practice tests enable you to check your score by exam area or domain to determine which topics you need to study further. Another feature enables you to obtain immediate feedback on your responses in the form of explanations for the correct and incorrect answers.

PrepLogic Practice Tests, Preview Edition exhibits all the full-test simulation functionality of the Premium Edition, but offers only a fraction of the total questions. To get the complete set of practice questions, visit www. preplogic.com and order the Premium Edition for this and other challenging exam training guides.

For a more detailed description of the features of the PrepLogic Practice Exams, Preview Edition software, see Appendix C.

An Exclusive Electronic Version of the Text

As mentioned previously, the CD-ROM that accompanies this book also contains an electronic PDF version of this book. This electronic version comes complete with all figures as they appear in the book. You can use Adobe Acrobat's handy search capability for study and review purposes.

Using the PrepLogic Practice Exams, Preview Edition Software

This book includes a special version of the PrepLogic Practice Exams software, a revolutionary test engine designed to give you the best in certification exam preparation. PrepLogic offers sample and practice exams for many of today's most in-demand and challenging technical certifications. A special Preview Edition of the PrepLogic Practice Exams software is included with this book as a tool to use in assessing your knowledge of the training guide material while also providing you with the experience of taking an electronic exam.

This appendix describes in detail what PrepLogic Practice Exams, Preview Edition is, how it works, and what it can do to help you prepare for the exam. Note that although the Preview Edition includes all the test simulation functions of the complete retail version, it contains only a single practice test. The Premium Edition, available at www.preplogic.com, contains a complete set of challenging practice exams designed to optimize your learning experience.

The Exam Simulation

One of the main functions of PrepLogic Practice Exams, Preview Edition is exam simulation. To prepare you to take the actual vendor certification exam, PrepLogic is designed to offer the most effective exam simulation available.

Question Quality

The questions provided in PrepLogic Practice Exams, Preview Edition are written to the highest standards of technical accuracy. The questions tap the content of this book's chapters and help you review and assess your knowledge before you take the actual exam.

The Interface Design

The PrepLogic Practice Exams, Preview Edition exam simulation interface provides you with the experience of taking an electronic exam. It enables you to effectively prepare to take the actual exam by making the test experience familiar. Using this test simulation can help eliminate the sense of surprise or anxiety you might experience in the testing center because you'll already be acquainted with computerized testing.

The Effective Learning Environment

The PrepLogic Practice Exams, Preview Edition interface provides a learning environment that not only tests you through the computer but also teaches the material you need to know to pass the certification exam. Each question includes a detailed explanation of the correct answer, and most of these explanations provide reasons as to why the other answers are incorrect. This information helps to reinforce the knowledge you already have and also provides practical information you can use on the job.

Software Requirements

PrepLogic Practice Exams requires a computer with the following:

➤ Microsoft Windows 98, Windows Me, Windows NT 4.0, Windows 2000, or Windows XP

➤ A 166MHz or faster processor

➤ A minimum of 32MB of RAM

➤ 10MB of hard drive space

Performance

As with any Windows application, the more available memory, the better the performance.

Installing PrepLogic Practice Exams, Preview Edition

You install PrepLogic Practice Exams, Preview Edition by following these steps:

1. Insert the CD-ROM that accompanies this book into your CD-ROM drive. The AutoRun feature of Windows should launch the software. If you have AutoRun disabled, select Start, Run. Go to the root directory of the CD-ROM and select setup.exe. Click Open and then click OK.

2. The Installation Wizard copies the PrepLogic Practice Exams, Preview Edition files to your hard drive. It then adds PrepLogic Practice Exams, Preview Edition to your desktop and the Program menu. Finally, it installs test engine components to the appropriate system folders.

Removing PrepLogic Practice Exams, Preview Edition from Your Computer

If you decide to remove the PrepLogic Practice Exams, Preview Edition, you can use the included uninstallation process to ensure that it is removed from your system safely and completely. Follow these instructions to remove PrepLogic Practice Exams, Preview Edition from your computer:

1. Select Start, Settings, Control Panel.

2. Double-click the Add/Remove Programs icon. You're presented with a list of software installed on your computer.

3. Select the PrepLogic Practice Exams, Preview Edition title you want to remove. Click the Add/Remove button. The software is removed from your computer.

How to Use the Software

PrepLogic is designed to be user friendly and intuitive. Because the software has a smooth learning curve, your time is maximized because you start practicing with it almost immediately. PrepLogic Practice Exams, Preview Edition has two major modes of study: Practice Exam and Flash Review.

Using Practice Exam mode, you can develop your test-taking abilities as well as your knowledge through the use of the Show Answer option. While you're taking the test, you can expose the answers along with detailed explanations of why answers are right or wrong. This process helps you better understand the material presented.

Flash Review mode is designed to reinforce exam topics rather than quiz you. In this mode, you are shown a series of questions but no answer choices. You can click a button that reveals the correct answer to each question and a full explanation for that answer.

Starting a Practice Exam Mode Session

Practice Exam mode enables you to control the exam experience in ways that actual certification exams do not allow. To begin studying in Practice Exam mode, click the Practice Exam radio button from the main exam customization screen. It displays the following options:

> **Enable Show Answer**—Clicking this button activates the Show Answer button, which makes it possible for you to view the correct answer(s) and full explanation for each question during the exam. When this option is not enabled, you must wait until after your exam has been graded to view the correct answer(s) and explanation for each question.

> **Enable Item Review**—Clicking this button activates the Item Review button, which enables you to view your answer choices. This option also facilitates navigation between questions.

> **Randomize Choices**—You can randomize answer choices from one exam session to the next. This makes memorizing question choices more difficult, thereby keeping questions fresh and challenging longer.

On the left side of the main exam customization screen, you're presented with the option of selecting the preconfigured practice test or creating your own custom test. The preconfigured test has a fixed time limit and number of questions. Custom tests enable you to configure the time limit and the number of questions in your exam.

The Preview Edition on this book's CD-ROM includes a single preconfigured practice test. You can get the complete set of challenging PrepLogic Practice Exams at www.preplogic.com to make certain that you're ready for the big exam.

Click the Begin Exam button to begin your exam.

Starting a Flash Review Mode Session

Flash Review mode provides an easy way to reinforce topics covered in the practice questions. To begin studying in Flash Review mode, click the Flash Review radio button from the main exam customization screen. Then select either the preconfigured practice test or create your own custom test.

Click the Begin Exam button to begin a Flash Review mode session.

Standard PrepLogic Practice Exams, Preview Edition Options

The following list describes the function of each of the buttons you see across the bottom of the screen:

Button Status

Depending on the options, some of the buttons will be grayed out and inaccessible—or they might be missing completely. Buttons that are appropriate are active.

➤ **Exhibit**—This button is visible if an exhibit is provided to support the question. An *exhibit* is an image that provides supplemental information that's necessary to answer a question.

➤ **Item Review**—This button leaves the question window and opens the Item Review screen, from which you can see all questions, your answers, and your marked items. You can also see correct answers listed here, when appropriate.

➤ **Show Answer**—This option displays the correct answer, with an explanation about why it is correct. If you select this option, the current question is not scored.

➤ **Mark Item**—You can check this box to flag a question that you need to review further. You can view and navigate your marked items by clicking the Item Review button (if it's enabled). When your exam is being graded, you're notified if you have any marked items remaining.

➤ **Previous Item**—You can use this option to view the previous question.

➤ **Next Item**—You can use this option to view the next question.

➤ **Grade Exam**—When you have completed your exam, you can click Grade Exam to end your exam and view your detailed score report. If you have unanswered or marked items remaining, you're asked if you would like to continue taking your exam or view the exam report.

Seeing Time Remaining

If your practice test is timed, the time remaining is displayed on the upper-right corner of the application screen. It counts down the minutes and seconds remaining to complete the test. If you run out of time, you are asked whether you want to continue taking the test or end your exam.

Getting Your Examination Score Report

The Examination Score Report screen appears when the Practice Exam mode ends—as a result of time expiration, completion of all questions, or your decision to terminate early.

This screen provides a graphical display of your test score, with a breakdown of scores by topic domain. The graphical display at the top of the screen compares your overall score with the PrepLogic Exam Competency Score. The PrepLogic Exam Competency Score reflects the level of subject competency required to pass the particular vendor's exam. Although this score does not directly translate to a passing score, consistently matching or exceeding this score suggests that you possess the knowledge needed to pass the actual vendor exam.

Reviewing Your Exam

From the Your Score Report screen, you can review the exam that you just completed by clicking the View Items button. You can navigate through the items, viewing the questions, your answers, the correct answers, and the explanations for those answers. You can return to your score report by clicking the View Items button.

Contacting PrepLogic

If you would like to contact PrepLogic for any reason, including getting information about its extensive line of certification practice tests, you can do so online at www.preplogic.com.

Customer Service

If you have a damaged product and need to contact customer service, please call 800-858-7674.

Product Suggestions and Comments

PrepLogic values your input! Please email your suggestions and comments to feedback@preplogic.com.

License Agreement

YOU MUST AGREE TO THE TERMS AND CONDITIONS OUTLINED IN THE END USER LICENSE AGREEMENT ("EULA") PRESENTED TO YOU DURING THE INSTALLATION PROCESS. IF YOU DO NOT AGREE TO THESE TERMS, DO NOT INSTALL THE SOFTWARE.

Glossary

%HomeDrive%
The drive letter assigned to a user account's home directory.

%HomePath%
The full UNC path to the user account's home directory.

%SystemRoot%
The directory for the local operating system installation, such as `C:\Windows\` or `C:\WinNT\`.

%UserName%
Used to create a home directory folder, named for the current user, within a common file store location.

.NET Passport Authentication
A method of IIS authentication that provides a single, unified logon through SSL, HTTP redirects, cookies, and JavaScript using encrypted passwords.

Account Operators
A group whose members can create, modify, and delete computer and user accounts, with the exception of administrators, domain admins, and domain controllers.

Active Directory
The directory services system for Windows 2000 and Windows Server 2003 contains and controls all objects such that every object is fully controllable as to what it can do to another object and what that object can do to it.

Active Directory Domains and Trusts
Microsoft MMC snap-in used to manage the domains and trusts of a forest.

Active Directory Sites and Services
Microsoft MMC snap-in used to manage server replication.

Active Directory Users and Computers

Microsoft MMC snap-in used to manage computer and user accounts, groups, printers, and organizational units within a domain.

Active Directory–Integrated Zone

A securable zone whose data is transferred between domain controllers during the normal Active Directory replication.

Administrator

The predefined master administration account.

Administrators

A group whose members have full control over the domain.

Adprep

Command-line utility that can be used to prepare an existing Windows 2000 domain for upgrade to Windows Server 2003.

Advanced Digest Authentication

A method of IIS authentication that requires a user account and password, transferring user credentials using stored MD5 hash values.

Anonymous Authentication

A method of IIS authentication that requires no username or password.

Anonymous Logon

A Windows identity whose members automatically include anyone who accesses resources without using an authenticated logon and password.

Application Pool

A self-contained unit of resources allocated to Web sites and applications.

ASP.NET

Active Server Pages (.NET version) allow for the display and presentation of active Web content using the .NET Common Runtime Library.

ASPNET

The account used by the .NET Framework to run ASP.NET processes.

ASR (Automatic System Recovery)

A tool that enables the rapid recovery of a Windows Server 2003, including the server's System State, hardware configuration, and installed applications.

Authenticated Users

A Windows identity whose members automatically include anyone who accesses resources through a logon process.

Authoritative Restore

A restoration of the System State, overwriting more recent versions stored elsewhere in the directory during the next replication cycle. Used to restore objects that were mistakenly deleted.

Backup Operators

A group whose members can log in to, shut down, back up, and restore the files from any system in the domain, including domain controllers.

Basic Authentication

A method of IIS authentication that requires a user account and password, but the password is sent across the network in plain text.

Batch

A Windows identity whose members automatically include all processes and accounts that access resources through a batch job.

Biometric Authentication

A method of authentication that makes use of a quality (metric) of the user's physiology (bio), such as a fingerprint or retinal image.

Bootcfg

Command-line utility that can be used to configure, change, or review Boot.ini settings.

Caching-Only

A DNS server that does not host any zones and is not authoritative for a domain. Generally used in small, remote offices with relatively slow links to the main office.

Cert Publishers

A group whose members can publish security certificates for accounts.

Certificate Authentication

A method of IIS authentication that establishes a secure connection between client and server by using Secure Sockets Layer (SSL).

Change

A share-level permission that allows for the ability to create, modify, and delete resources within the share.

Choice

Command-line utility that can be used to prompt a user to select from a listing of choices.

Click Scripts and Executables

An IIS execute privilege that allows an authenticated user to run any application.

Client Automatic Updates

The SUS client component that is configured to connect to the SUS Server or the Windows Update Web site.

Clip

Command-line utility that can be used to send command-line output to the Windows Clipboard.

Cmd

Executable command that opens the command-line shell interface.

Cmdkey

Command-line utility that can be used to review, create, and delete stored usernames and passwords.

Compatws.inf

A security template used to relax security settings to allow users to make use of applications that do not conform to the requirements for the Windows Logo Program for Software.

Conditional Forwarding

A feature that allows DNS servers in one network to perform name resolution for another network's namespace.

Creator Group

A Windows identity whose members are inherited by sharing group membership with the account that created the resource.

Creator Owner

A Windows identity representing the account that created a particular resource.

Csvde

Command-line utility that can be used to import and export Active Directory data using a comma-separated file format (.csv).

Data Encryption Standard (DES)

A data encryption method that uses a private key selected at random from a large number of available keys.

DC Security.inf

A security template representing the default security template for domain controllers.

Device Manager

A graphical user interface utility that provides a graphical view of all the hardware installed on your computer.

DHCP (Dynamic Host Configuration Protocol)

A protocol that dynamically assigns Internet Protocol (IP) addresses to clients.

DHCP Administrators

A local group whose members can administer the DHCP service and its configuration.

DHCP Users

A local group whose members can view the DHCP service settings and its configuration.

Dial-Up

A Windows identity whose members automatically include anyone who accesses resources through a dial-up modem connection.

Differential Backup

A backup of all selected data that has changed since the last full backup.

Digest Authentication

A method of IIS authentication that requires a user account and password, with user credentials sent in a hashed message digest.

Digital Signature

An electronic signature that can be used to verify the originator of a file or email, and to verify also that its contents have not been modified since transmission.

Dispart

Command-line utility that can be used to manage disks, partitions, and volumes.

Distribution Group

A group used for email distribution lists when an integrated electronic mail service such as Exchange is present.

DNS (Domain Name System)

The Domain Name System is a service that provides a translation between a fully qualified domain name (FQDN) and its matching IP address (forward lookup), or between an IP address and its matching FQDN (reverse lookup).

DnsAdmins

A group whose members can administer the DNS service.

DnsUpdateProxy

A group whose members can perform dynamic DNS updates for other accounts.

Domain Admins

A group whose members have full rights over all resources in the domain and are members of the Administrators group on each computer in the domain.

Domain Controller

A Windows server that has been designated to provide authentication services within an Active Directory deployment.

Domain Controllers

A group whose members automatically include all domain controller computers joined to a domain.

Domain Guests

A group whose members have no rights assigned by default.

Domain Local Group

A group used to assign permissions over resources located only in their own domain.

Domain Users

A group whose members automatically include all user accounts in a domain.

Dsadd

Command-line utility that can be used to add a new object to the directory (user, computer, contact, group, or organizational unit).

Dsget

Command-line utility that can be used to display selected attributes of an object in the directory.

Dsmod

Command-line utility that can be used to modify an existing Active Directory object.

Dsmove

Command-line utility that can be used to rename an object or move an object to a new location within the same domain.

Dsquery

Command-line utility that can be used to display a list of objects within the directory that meet the specified search criteria.

Dsrm

Command-line utility that can be used to delete an object from the directory.

EFS (Encrypting File System)

Allows users to configure an NTFS-formatted folder so as to encrypt its contents, thereby preventing recovery by anyone other than the owner and the file recovery agent.

Enterprise Admins

A group whose members have full control over all domains in a forest and inherit membership in the Administrators group on all domain controllers. By default, the only member of this group is the administrator of the forest's root domain.

Enterprise Domain Controllers

A Windows identity whose members automatically include any domain controller computers with enterprisewide roles.

Event Viewer

A graphical user interface utility that allows review of the various event logs.

Eventcreate

Command-line utility that can be used to create an event in a specified event log.

Everyone

A Windows identity whose members automatically include all accounts logged on to the network, even if from another domain.

File Server Management MMC Snap-In

An MMC snap-in component that invokes the Share a Folder Wizard.

Forfiles

Command-line utility that can be used to specify files to use in batch processing.

Forward Lookup Zone

A DNS zone used to associate IP addresses to their hierarchical FQDN names, allowing the translation from FQDN to matching IP address.

Forwarding

The process of passing a DNS name-resolution query to the next-higher-order DNS server if the requested name is not present in the cache or zones of the requested DNS server.

FQDN (Fully Qualified Domain Name)

A portion of the uniform reference locator address that designates a system's hierarchical human-readable name. For example:
`myserver.mycorp.com`.

FTP (File Transfer Protocol)

A member of the TCP/IP suite of protocols utilized for rapid transfer of files between the host and a client using ports 20 and 21 by default.

Full Backup

A complete backup of all selected data.

Full Control

An NTFS- or share-level permission that encapsulates all the other permissions of the appropriate type, along with the capability to later change the assigned permissions.

Gettype

Command-line utility that can be used to identify the version of Windows being used.

Global Group

A group used to manage permissions over resources located in any domain within the forest.

GPMC (Group Policy Management Console)

A downloadable utility that brings together many standard management functions for the manipulation of GPOs and their links.

GPO (Group Policy Object)

A collection of settings that can be linked to one or more sites, domains, or organizational units within the Active Directory to be inherited by its members.

Gpresult

A command-line utility used to display Group Policy settings and the Resultant Set of Policy (RsoP) of a target user or computer account.

Gpupdate

A command-line utility used to refresh Group Policy settings.

Group

A unit of organization that can be used to allow or deny access over resources to its members through inheritance.

Group Policy

The functionality that allows assignment of complex rights and restrictions to users in a site, domain, or organizational unit.

Group Policy Creator Owner

A group whose members can create, delete, and modify Group Policy settings within a domain. Membership in this group does not give permissions to link a group policy to a container.

Groups

Administrative tool used to provide access rights and restrictions for member accounts and members of member groups. Through inheritance, member accounts can be granted additional privileges and access rights to distributed resources, and can also be restricted from accessing the same.

Guest

An unprivileged account created in a disabled condition. The guest account can be given minimal permissions so that a guest user can access a particular resource for a brief period of time without the need to create an actual user account.

Guests

A group whose members are not granted rights by default.

HelpServicesGroup

A local group whose members can be granted any desired standard rights and permissions granted to support staff accounts and the Remote Assistance group.

Hisecdc.inf

A security template used to implement the Highly Secure template for domain controllers.

Hisecws.inf

A security template used to implement the Highly Secure template for workstations.

Home Folder

The UNC path specifying the location in which a user's home file storage will be located.

HTTP (Hypertext Transfer Protocol)

A member of the TCP/IP suite of protocols utilized by Web servers to provide textual and graphical information to a client browser using port 80 by default.

Identity

A pseudo-group that can be used for assignment of access rights and restrictions based on automatic membership criteria.

IIS (Internet Information Services)

Provides support for Web (HTTP), FTP, and basic SMTP services. IIS is disabled by default on all Windows Server 2003 versions, with the exception of the Web Server Edition.

IIS_WPG

A memberless group used by the worker processes serving namespaces within IIS 6.0.

IISBack

Command-line utility that can be used to create and manage backups of the IIS configuration settings.

IISCnfg

Command-line utility that can be used to import and export IIS configuration details.

IISFtp

Command-line utility that can be used to start, stop, pause, resume, review, create, and delete FTP sites.

IISFtpdr

Command-line utility that may be used to create and delete FTP site virtual directories.

IISVdir

Command-line utility that can be used to create and delete Web site virtual directories.

IISWeb

Command-line utility that can be used to start, stop, pause, resume, review, create, and delete Web sites.

Incoming Forest Trust Builders

A group whose members can create a one-way, incoming-only trust to another forest to provide access to resources in the other forest.

Incremental Backup

A backup of all selected data that has changed since the last full or incremental backup.

InetOrgPerson

A new security principal type used in migrating from or interfacing with other non-Microsoft LDAP and X.500 directory services.

Integrated Windows Authentication

A method of IIS authentication that requires Kerberos as the authentication protocol.

Interactive

A Windows identity whose members automatically include any users logged in to a computer and accessing a particular local resource.

Inuse

Command-line utility that can be used to replace in-use operating system files.

Kerberos

An authentication method that makes use of an encrypted ticket to allow access to a protected resource.

LAN (Local Area Network)

A network utilizing network protocols to manage connectivity within a relatively centralized and well-connected site.

LDAP (Lightweight Directory Access Protocol)

A protocol that is used to identify the location of an object based on its location within the Active Directory.

Ldifde

A powerful command-line tool able to import and export Active Directory data and extend the schema, as well as to create, modify, and delete objects within the directory.

LKGC (Last Known Good Configuration)

An advanced startup mode that rolls back all drivers to their state at the last successful logon event.

LocalService

An account used to run system services that might need to generate system audit events in the security log.

LocalSystem

An account used to run many system services that require only local logon rights.

Logman

Command-line utility that can be used to schedule performance counter and trace log collection.

MAN (Metropolitan Area Network)

A network spanning multiple distributed network sites located within a particular geographic or politically designated zone, such as a city.

Metabase.xml

The IIS configuration file.

MMC (Microsoft Management Console)

A graphical user interface that provides a standard customizable container for many service and functionality snap-ins.

MMC Snap-in

A service or functionality-related module that may be imported into the Microsoft Management Console.

Modify

An NTFS-level permission that allows the creation, modification, and deletion of files and folders.

Net accounts

A command-line net service utility used to modify password and logon settings for all accounts.

Net config

A command-line net service utility used to display or modify the settings of available configurable services.

Net file

A command-line net service utility used to display a listing of shared files. It can also close open files.

Net help

A command-line net service utility used to display a listing of network commands.

Net send

A command-line net service utility used to send a message to other users or computers.

Net session

A command-line net service utility used to display a listing of current network sessions.

Net share

A command-line net service utility used to display, create, and modify file shares.

Net start

A command-line net service utility used to display a listing of running services and to start an individual service.

Net stop

A command-line net service utility used to stop a running service.

Net use

A command-line net service utility used to connect and disconnect from a shared resource.

Network

A Windows identity whose members automatically include any users accessing a particular resource over the network.

Network Configuration Operators

A group whose members can make changes to TCP/IP settings on any system in the domain, including domain controllers.

NetworkService

An account used to run services that also require network access.

Nonauthoritative Restore

The default restoration of the System State, allowing more recent versions stored elsewhere in the directory to update the settings during the next replication cycle.

None

An IIS execute privilege setting that prevents scripts from running.

notssid.inf

A security template used to remove Windows Terminal Server security identifiers (SIDs) from the Registry and file locations when the Terminal Server service is idle.

NTFS Permissions

Detailed access rights and restrictions that may be assigned directly to a particular file or folder, or inherited from its parent container, provided the files are stored on an NTFS-formatted partition.

Openfiles

Command-line utility that can be used to review or disconnect currently open files.

Organizational Unit (OU)

A mechanism used to group objects into a structured set of containers to which Group Policies may be applied; each object can be located in only a single OU.

Owner

The user who manages permissions on objects, and grants permissions for those objects to other users.

Performance Log Users

A group whose members can manage performance logs, counters, and alerts on any computer in the domain, including domain controllers.

Performance Monitor Users

A group whose members can monitor performance counters locally and remotely on any computer in the domain, including domain controllers.

Power Users

A local group whose members can fully administer local resources and accounts, except for accounts and resources owned by members of the Administrators group.

Pre–Windows 2000 Compatible Access

A group whose members have Read access over all accounts and groups in the domain.

Pre–Windows 2000 Logon Name

A user account designation that is used for NetBIOS account logons, as a single name or the single-word (NetBIOS) domain name followed by the logon name.

Primary Zone

A DNS zone configured to be authoritative for a domain. It replicates changes to secondary servers during a scheduled update cycle.

Principal Logon Name

A user account designation that is composed of the user logon name and the fully qualified domain name (FQDN) of the domain to which it belongs in the directory.

Print Operators

A group whose members can create, delete, share, and manage printers and print queues, as well as log on and shut down any computer in the domain, including domain controllers.

Prncnfg

Command-line utility that can be used to review and configure printer settings.

Prnjobs

Command-line utility that can be used to review, pause, resume, and cancel pending print jobs.

Profile Path

The UNC path specifying the location to be used to store a user account's profile.

Proxy

A Windows identity whose members automatically include any users accessing a particular resource through a proxy agent or delegate.

RAS and IAS Servers

A group whose member servers can access the dial-up and remote access properties on user account objects.

RDP (Remote Desktop Connection)

A protocol functioning on port 3389, allowing a remote client to display output data (such as audio and video) and accept input data (such as mouse and keyboard input) to a remote terminal session.

Read (NTFS)

An NTFS-level permission that allows the ability to read file and folder attributes, list folder contents, view files, and synchronize file access.

Read (Share)

A share-level permission that allows the ability to view file and folder names within the share, as well as the ability to view and execute files located within the shared folder.

Read & Execute

An NTFS-level permission that includes the rights of the Read permission in addition to the ability to traverse a folder and execute a file.

Recovery Console

A command-line tool used to troubleshoot and repair Windows startup problems, including master boot record (MBR) recovery attempts.

Regedit

A command-line utility that allows modification of Registry settings.

Relative Distinguished Name

A user account designation that is used to uniquely identify the account in terms of its LDAP location in the Active Directory.

Remote Desktop

A virtual connection used to allow a local client to connect to a remote terminal session using the Remote Desktop Protocol (RDP).

Remote Desktop for Administration

A service that allows up to two concurrent administrative RDP connections.

Remote Desktop Users

A group whose members can remotely log on to any computer in the domain, including domain controllers.

Replicator

A memberless group used by domain and file replication services.

Restricted

A Windows identity whose members automatically include users with restricted access rights.

Reverse Lookup Zone

A DNS zone database file that is sorted in numerical order by IP address and is used to associate FQDN names within a range of IP addresses, allowing the translation from IP address to matching FQDN.

Rootsec.inf

A security template used to implement the root directory permissions template.

Round Robin

A feature that allows a DNS server to offer a series of IP addresses in sequential order for successive requests for the same FQDN, allowing for distribution of access across a server farm, which is transparent to the user.

RSoP (Resultant Set of Policy)

A functionality used in troubleshooting the resulting settings that are produced through the application of GPO links across many levels of container inheritance.

RunAs

An option that can be used to specify the logon credentials that should be used in the execution of a command or utility operation by a secondary logon.

Safe Mode

An advanced startup mode that loads only basic device drives to facilitate the identification and removal of incompatible or corrupt device drivers.

Sc

Command-line utility that can be used to review or configure services.

Schema

A database consisting of classes and attributes, along with the rules for their use, that is used to create Active Directory objects.

Schema Admins

A group whose members can modify the Active Directory schema for a forest.

Schtasks

Command-line utility that can be used to review, add, and delete scheduled tasks.

Scripts Only

An IIS execute privilege that allows an authenticated user to run scripts.

Secedit

A command-line utility used to analyze and configure security settings based on templates.

Secondary Zone

A DNS zone configured to accept zone data from primary servers during a scheduled update cycle.

Secure Dynamic Updates

A feature that allows an authenticated client to register its current FQDN and IP Address within an authoritative DNS Server's zone. A DHCP server may perform this process on behalf of legacy clients that are unable to perform a secure dynamic update (Examples: Windows NT/98/Me).

Securedc.inf

A security template used to implement the secure template for domain controllers.

Securews.inf

A security template used to implement the secure template for workstations.

Security Configuration and Analysis MMC Snap-in

An MMC snap-in that can be used to model and apply security template settings.

Security Group

A group used to assign or deny user rights and permissions over resources located within the Active Directory.

Security Policy MMC Snap-in

An MMC snap-in that can be used to create and modify security template settings.

Security Principal

An object that may be granted or denied access rights over resources, such as user and computer accounts.

Security Template

A standard group of settings that can be applied rapidly through a GPO. Security templates are used to standardize security across multiple containers and prevent errors.

Self

A Windows identity representing an object referencing itself.

Server Management Wizard

A Windows Server 2003 utility that allows configuration of server roles for file server, application server, domain controller, and DNS server functionality.

Server Operators

A group whose members can log on to, shut down, and manage the local resources and services on any server computer in the domain, including domain controllers.

Service

A Windows identity that represents a service referencing itself.

Setup security.inf

A security template used to restore the default security settings for a system created during initial installation.

Setx

Command-line utility that can be used to set environment variable values.

Shadow Copies of Shared Folders

A functionality that allows point-in time recovery of files located in shared folders on computers running Windows Servers 2003. Users can view, copy, and restore previous versions of their shared files.

Share Permissions

Permissions assigned to a UNC share that define the level of access that is granted when accessing resources through the share.

Shared Folders

File storage locations that expose (share) contained resources through a UNC path share.

Shutdown

Command-line utility that can be used to restart or turn off a computer.

Smart Cards

An authentication token (physical object) containing a small microchip that provides part of a user's authentication; typically used in conjunction with a personal identification number (PIN).

SMB (Server Message Block)

The protocol used by Microsoft systems to share resources such as file and print services, and may be used in conjunction with the secure*.inf templates in order to negotiate signed packet data transmission.

SMTP (Simple File Transfer Protocol)

A member of the TCP/IP suite of protocols commonly utilized for transfer of electronic mail using TCP port 25 by default.

Software Update Services (SUS) Server

The SUS server service located on an intranet server that synchronizes with the Windows Update Web site whenever new critical updates are available.

Stub Zone

A zone used to redirect conditional forward lookups to the proper authoritative DNS server.

Support

An account used by the Help and Support service to run processes and batch jobs.

SUS (Software Update Services)

An automated-update system used to retrieve security patches and operating system fixes from a server on your corporate intranet and install on them on targeted computers.

System

A Windows identity representing the operating system referencing itself.

System Information Utility

A graphical user interface utility that displays a complete list of the hardware resources, system hardware components, and software environment.

System State

The components on a Windows Server 2003 necessary to recover Active Directory and boot up operating system files, the COM+ class registration database files, the system Registry, and the contents of the SYSVOL share, which contains domain GPOs and scripts.

Systeminfo

Command-line utility that can be used to review system configuration details.

Takeown

Command-line utility that can be used to take ownership of an existing file.

Taskkill

Command-line utility that can be used to stop one or more processes.

Tasklist

Command-line utility that can be used to review a listing of running processes.

TCO (Total Cost of Ownership)

The total cost of purchasing, supporting, and maintaining a resource.

Terminal Server

A service that provides licensed virtual terminal access for Windows and non-Windows based clients using the Remote Desktop Protocol (RDP).

Terminal Server Session Directory

A service that allows a client to reconnect to a disconnected session running within a Terminal Services server farm.

Terminal Server Users

A Windows identity whose members automatically include all users logging in through Terminal Services connections.

Terminal Services

A service that provides the capability to host multiple virtual terminal sessions, accessed by remote clients able to run on downlevel (earlier) versions of the Windows operating system.

UNC (Universal Naming Convention)

A naming convention that allows the specification of a resource's location based on server and share name, without requiring more detailed specification of the storage device and location.

UNC Authentication

A method of IIS authentication that is used to verify user credentials for access to shared folders and files on a remote computer.

Universal Group

A group used to manage permissions over resources that span multiple domains.

User

An account designation that represents an individual user logon.

User Logon Name

A user account designation that is up to 20 characters in length (characters beyond 20 are ignored) and can be made up of uppercase (A–Z), lowercase (a–z), numerical (0–9), and symbol characters (with some symbols disallowed).

Users

A group whose members can make use of domain resources.

Waitfor

Command-line utility that can be used to synchronize networked computers on a common signal.

WAN (Wide Area Network)

A network utilizing WAN protocols to span distributed network sites which may be globally deployed.

Web.config

The configuration file used by an ASP.NET application server to apply settings to the contents of a folder and its subfolders.

Where

Command-line utility that can be used to review files that match the specified criteria.

Whoami

Command-line utility that can be used to review user configuration information.

WINS (Windows Internet Naming Service)

A service that dynamically maps NetBIOS names to Internet Protocol (IP) addresses.

WINS Users

A local group whose members are able to view WINS database information.

WMI (Windows Management Instrumentation)

A framework of functionality that allows development of custom script solutions.

WMIC (Windows Management Instrumentation Command Line)

A command-line interface for Windows Management Instrumentation scripting.

Write

An NTFS-level permission that includes the rights of the Read permission in addition to the capability to create new files and folders, modify existing files, and write file and folder attributes.

wuau.adm

A template that may be used to import Automatic Updates–related options into the Group Policy options. This component is installed by default on Windows Server 2003 systems.

Zone Transfer

The transfer of data from one DNS server to another. Primary servers transfer zone data during scheduled replication, secondary servers can be configured to notify their primary upon a registration attempt, and AD-integrated zones are transferred during the normal process of AD replication.

Index

V-W-X-Y-Z